INDUSTRIALIZATION IN THE NON-WESTERN WORLD

INDUSTRIALIZATION IN THE NON-WESTERN WORLD

Second Edition

Tom Kemp

Longman
London and New York

Longman Group UK Limited,
Longman House, Burnt Mill, Harlow,
Essex CM20 2JE, England
and Associated Companies throughout the world.

Published in the United States of America
by Longman Inc., New York

© Longman Group Limited 1983
Second edition © Longman Group UK Limited 1989

First published 1983
Second edition 1989
Second impression 1990

British Library Cataloguing in Publication Data
Kemp, Tom
   Industrialization in the non-Western
   world.
   1. Industrialisation, to 1982 – Case
   studies
   I. Title
   338'.00722

ISBN 0-582-02182-0

Library of Congress Cataloging-in-Publication Data
Kemp, Tom.
   Industrialization in the non-Western world / Tom Kemp. — 2nd ed.
     p. cm.
   Bibliography: p.
   Includes index.
   ISBN 0–582–02182–0 (pbk.)
    1. Industrialization—History. 2. Economic development—History.
   I. Title.
   HD2321.K433 1989
   338.09—dc19
                              88–28581
                                 CIP

Set in 10/12pt Linotron Baskerville

Printed in Malaysia
by Sun U Book Co. Sdn. Bhd.,
Petaling Jaya, Selangor Darul Ehsan.

CONTENTS

Acknowledgements

We are indebted to the World Bank and Oxford University Press (New York) for permission to reproduce our table on pp. 214–17.

Preface to the first edition

Industrialization is increasingly being studied by economists and economic historians as a process in its own right which brought into being the modern world. It is widely seen as the major means through which those areas of the world which suffer from poverty and backwardness can move closer to the advanced nations. It is seen as the key to both 'growth', in the sense of an increase in per capita incomes and 'development', meaning a more rounded structural transformation.

In its approach to industrialization, this book follows two previous books. The first, *Industrialization in Nineteenth Century Europe* (Longman 1969) confined itself to those European countries which followed in Britain's tracks before the First World War. The second, *Historical Patterns of Industrialization* (Longman 1978), besides taking up some general themes such as technology, transport and banking and their relationship to industrialization, also included some brief case-studies of non-European countries. This volume carries on the story into the twentieth century, linking the case studies of the earlier books and concentrating on the 'non-Western World'.

The phrase, 'non-Western World', needs a word of explanation. It is used here in a mainly geographical sense, to indicate that the older industrial countries of Western Europe and North America have been excluded. The emphasis is thus on the late-comers or followers on the path of industrialization outside those areas. It is not denied that the Soviet Union shares many 'Western' traditions, or that they have made a deep imprint on some of the other countries discussed here. However, development in these 'non-Western' countries has to be seen, as far as possible in their own terms while avoiding a Euro-centred approach.

The choice of countries is not exactly arbitrary, though the earlier economic history of Russia, Japan and India has been dealt with in the previous books. First of all, the countries are large, if not in population and area alone, then in specific weight in the world economy, as in the case of Japan. That means, also, when the populations are added up, that they represent something like one-half of the total world population. It is difficult to be accurate though, as the population of China, India and other parts of the world is not known for certain. However, at the end of the 1970s the population of the selected countries was approximately as follows:

Soviet Union: 260 million
Japan: 112 million
Brazil: 110 million
India: 620 million
China: 850 million
Nigeria: 80 million.

The figures for China and India are the lowest estimates and the real totals may be very much larger. In any case their populations are increasing rapidly.

There seems to be more sense in taking countries of this scale rather than, say, dealing with the experience of small countries such as Taiwan, Cuba or Albania. On the other hand, large countries have distinct advantages: they may have a more varied raw material endowment, a larger labour force and a bigger potential home market, thus permitting greater scale economies. Because of this, their experience may bear little relation to that of smaller countries. However, even for large countries autarchic development is costly, if not impossible, as the Soviet policy of 'socialism in one country' shows. Even the largest countries are part of a world market and gain advantages from participating in the international division of labour.

This book deals with the recent economic experience of about half of humanity and considerably more than half of the 'non-Western world'. It will be shown that while industrialization has some common underlying features, it works itself out in distinctive ways in specific historical and national conditions. Moreover there are basic differences between industrialization in market economies, even where the state plays a positive role, and in those countries having nationalized property relations and a centrally-planned allocation of resources. The choice of countries enables variants of both types to be examined.

The approach adopted is an historical one, based upon the view that the path followed by each country is determined to a very large extent by its past. It is from a study of history that the differential receptivity of particular countries to industrialization can be understood.

Any discussion of industrialization in the twentieth century is bound to be concerned with the prospects of the 'developing' countries. Assessment of their achievement so far differs widely. Some of these countries have begun to industrialize with some success in purely quantitative terms (GNP per capita). On the other hand, it is claimed that their economies remain peripheral and dependent and that they have not been able to replicate successfully the experience of the older capitalist countries. A chapter illustrated by brief case studies is devoted to the problems of the developing countries.

This book is intended as an introductory text for students of economic history, political economy and development studies. It aims to open the way for further study by evoking interest, suggesting what the problems are and why they are important for the future of humanity and not just for academic reasons. The main authorities are indicated in the bibliography, which is also intended as a guide for more detailed study. One's approach and views are influenced by so much read, heard and experienced that it cannot be regarded as a full indication of sources. As with the previous books, I have avoided footnotes and long quotations from other texts; this is not because the authors to whom I am indebted may not have made the point at issue better or more clearly than I do, but because I feel that by reframing it in my own words, I can make the wider argument more comprehensible to the reader.

This book, like its predecessors, owes a great deal to discussions over many years with students and colleagues in the Department of Economic and Social History in the University of Hull and to the facilities offered by the Brynmor Jones Library. It was completed while enjoying the hospitality of the Department of History in the University of California, Irvine, in 1981–82. It is dedicated to the memory of the late Professor Herbert Kisch of Michigan State University, an admirable scholar and devoted friend.

Preface to the second edition

Written in the early 1980s when the world was in recession, oil prices were high and the dollar was strong, many parts of this book inevitably reflected the prevailing economic situation. The debt crisis had not yet struck with full force. Oil-producing countries seemed destined for prosperity, until reserves ran out, and consumers were adjusting themselves to what seemed to be permanently higher prices. Mikhail S. Gorbachev was an unknown provincial official and the Soviet Union seemed to be heading towards stagnation. The newly-industrializing countries of East Asia were at an earlier stage of their apparently relentless rise; the growing power of Japan was already palpable, but its consequences were not always clear, and perhaps are still not so today. It suffices to mention these factors for it to be obvious that certain assumptions and many statements made in the first edition have therefore dated. In this revision an effort has been made to eliminate the more dated parts of the text in the light of subsequent events and from the perspective of the end of the 1980s. It is hoped that these changes will prolong the usefulness of this short book, itself a modest introduction to vast and complex problems of great historical significance.

In carrying out this work of revision, I realized how ambitious the original volume had been in dealing with six countries as diverse as those which had been chosen as case studies. In the few years which had elapsed since the first writing, multiple, and sometimes dramatic, changes had taken place in each of these countries relevant to their industrialization. At the time of writing it is still too early to discern the future contours of the Soviet economy as they will emerge from the new departures in economic policy promoted by General Secretary Gorbachev; a review of the situation and his chances of success would require a study in itself. In fact, changes in prospect (rather than actually carried out) have generated a vast, specialized literature. No less dramatic have been the changes in China to which the first edition had already made some reference. An entirely new atmosphere seems to have been created in that vast country. So many changes have taken place, with more in the offing, that it can be seriously asked whether China will remain a 'socialist' country or whether it is already firmly on the capitalist road. Many of the reforms and policies adopted by Teng Hsiao-ping seem to be inspired more by the practice of Taiwan than by Mao-Tse-tung thought.

While the situation in the other four countries has been less dramatic, they have had their crises and problems. Japan continues to push forward, its continuing prosperity, like that of its East Asian emulators, dependent upon the continued ability, and willingness, of the other advanced capitalist countries to buy their manufactured goods. Their mounting trade surpluses threaten the stability of world markets. Within a few short years the United States has moved from creditor to debtor status. Japanese branch plants, banks and trading companies are operating worldwide.

Meanwhile it is clear that the industrialization of Nigeria and the further growth of Brazil (number eight in the industrial league table) are less favourable than they were at the beginning of the decade. Both are now burdened with heavy debts. Living standards have declined, or are declining, even for the more affluent classes in society. Under the pressure of the economic crisis the generals who had taken over in 1964 shifted into the background in Brazil, while in Nigeria civilian government collapsed under charges of corruption and squandermania. A full discussion of the reasons for these upheavals, and their possible outcomes, would go beyond the scope of this book. One obvious lesson is that the supply and demand conditions for vital commodities, such as oil, can have far-reaching effects on the world economy and its national components. The impact on particular countries can have a profound effect on their economies. So, indeed, can natural conditions. The state of the monsoon can be as important for India as the price of oil or the behaviour of the stock market.

It should not be overlooked that discussions of industrialization, and the policies proposed, are ideologically founded. At one time it was commonly accepted that the state had a positive role to play. Even countries as committed to capitalism as Japan, Taiwan or Nigeria drew up economic plans for four or five years ahead. The vogue for planning is under a cloud, even in India. The excesses of licences and controls have generated a counter-movement backed (not unnaturally) by business as well as by economists who have moved with the prevailing professional winds in the international community. The watchwords of 'privatization' and 'liberalization', favoured by the World Bank and the International Monetary Fund, are deeply influencing the strategy of industrialization in many countries. Again, it remains to be seen what effect the freer operation of market forces will have upon the less developed countries, and countries like India or Brazil in particular. Even in the East Asian countries, industrialization was not a product of unbridled capitalism and free market forces but owed a great deal to the (still) visible hand of the state. The Japanese had already shown the way. In any case, these countries constitute very special cases and they may not have many lessons for those countries which are still lagging seriously behind in their development, especially in Latin America and Black Africa.

This revision was completed while enjoying the hospitality of the Department of Economics, the University of North Carolina at Chapel Hill. I recall, particularly, discussions with Sandy Darrity. It also happened that an old friend, Ted Koditschek, was in Chapel Hill at the same time and was kind enough to read the book and make some suggestions.

Chapel Hill, 24 June 1988

CHAPTER 1

Industrialization: past and present

There is scarcely a country in the modern world where an improvement in the material level of living is not regarded as a desirable goal by rulers and ruled alike, and where industrialization is not seen as the necessary means to achieve it. History is clearly on the side of this view. The nations which are rich and powerful possess a technologically advanced industrial base, capable of turning out a large volume of manufactured goods. Nations which are poor and dependent have little or no industry and are primarily agricultural.

Industrialization has become a world process, no longer confined to a privileged group of leading countries. It embodies the technology and organization which have transformed production methods and ways of living at a staggering rate in the twentieth century. There are now scarcely any inhabitants of the globe unaffected, for good or ill, by its forward march. An understanding of its nature and consequences is indispensable if the major transformations taking place in social as well as economic life in our time are to make sense.

THE BEGINNINGS OF INDUSTRIALIZATION

The process began in a group of islands off the north-west coast of Europe some two centuries ago, with what is usually described as the British Industrial Revolution. More a technical term than an actual definition of what took place, it has been the subject of intensive research by innumerable scholars who have failed to come to any definitive conclusions about its origins. What seems clear is that it was the leading edge of a change of European dimensions

1

and that nothing else like it was taking place at that time anywhere else in the world. Whatever brought about industrialization in its original home, it can be said that other countries received it, along with much else of European origin, as an import. Such a statement poses many problems, not least how it was that countries which had developed civilizations many centuries ahead of Europe, were subsequently left behind because they failed to apply knowledge to raising the productivity of labour.

Consideration of European industrialization in a world perspective suggests that it was the outcome of a series of changes going back to the Middle Ages; cause and result of a dynamic lacking in other parts of the world. The landmarks in this dynamic process may be distinguished, though their precise contribution to industrialization may not be easy to explain. They include the Renaissance of learning (indicating the role of the Classical world and the ancient Mediterranean civilizations); the Reformation, which, though a religious movement, began the break up of existing modes of thought inimical to innovation and the pursuit of material success; and the voyages of discovery whereby, through their superiority in navigation, Europeans began to open up other continents for trade and domination. As some historians have observed, Europe, or rather its most advanced regions, became the core countries in a world economic system in which other areas made up the periphery. The starting point of change, however, is to be found, not in the expansion of trade and the opening up of new markets, but rather in the transformation of social relations in the leading European countries. This transformation, which had been going on for some time, had begun to assume a more decisive form in the course of the sixteenth century. The change, which can be briefly summed up as the rise of capitalism, provided the means and the impetus for overseas expansion and prepared the way for the transformation of production and the transition from an agrarian to an industrial society. It was, indeed, a long drawn-out process of which the Industrial Revolution was the first culmination.

It was characteristic of even the most advanced countries outside Europe that, having reached a certain equilibrium, they failed to generate further dynamic forces of change. European feudalism, on the contrary, gave freer rein to the individualist pursuit of acquisition both by the landowners and by the merchants and financiers whose strongholds were the towns. This may have been because it was a newer, less stable and less centralized system than, say, that which governed the tributary states of Asia. Within the framework of European feudalism, means of production were turned into capital, and a wage-earning class separated from the land came into existence. Agriculture turned over to producing for the market and, in some places, industrial production by the rural population made a greater contribution to income than did cultivation of the land. As the transition to the capitalist mode of production began to take place in the most advanced regions, so the surplus product, instead of going to the support of a largely parasitic ruling class, was, to an increasing extent, passing into the hands of dynamic entrepreneurs who used it to expand trade and production still further in a continuous process of capital accumulation. While merchant capital advanced in buying and selling was for a long time the predominant form, it was in Europe that capital, in the form of means of production, began to assume growing importance. Industrialization, properly speaking, only began as the merchant extended his control over production through his ownership of capital assets, or as the direct producer himself appeared in the role of employer and capitalist; the really revolutionary way, as Marx described it.

With the application of capital to industry, at first mainly in the form of circulating capital laid out on raw materials, wages and goods in process, profit provided a new and powerful incentive for increasing output and reducing costs. The rate of profit, the return on capital, became the governing motive of production and proved to be a most powerful instrument for bringing about a continuous improvement in the organization and technique of production and also of distribution and marketing. Industrialization, in its inception, issued from this drive for profits when it took hold of a sizeable part of production; it was the child of capitalism, though not a consciously desired or expected result. It came about through the spontaneous interaction of numerous 'entrepreneurs' obeying market indicators in their quest for maximum profits and, in doing so, engaging in a restless search for ways of producing and selling more goods, reducing costs of production and finding markets. Only with a certain combination of social and cultural conditions, however, could the industrial entrepreneurs emerge as a class capable of bringing about a far-reaching economic transformation. Such conditions appeared in Europe before they did in other parts of the world, if indeed they ever would have done. This favourable environment, as well as the existence of entrepreneurs who seized the opportunities for profit and accumulation which it presented, were the products of complex changes going back over centuries

3

which made particular areas of Europe, and nowhere else, the theatre for a transformation of dramatic historical significance. Whether there were in other continents signs of the beginning of such a change, or whether it can be assumed that it would eventually have taken place somewhere else, is a controversial point on which there can be no conclusive evidence. To stress the priority of Europe is merely to state an historical fact and not to succumb to 'Euro-centrism'. Once the capitalist mode of production had taken root, principally in parts of Britain and north-west Europe, during the sixteenth century and afterwards, competitive market forces compelled individual entrepreneurs to plough back part of their profits into expanding and improving plant and equipment, extracting more surplus from the dependent labour force of wage-earners. At the same time they were subject to market forces on the demand side: they had to follow changes in tastes and purchasing power, improve existing products, seek out new ones and continue the drive to reduce costs of production through more efficient organization and cost-reducing methods including new technologies. This was the dynamic of industrial capitalism which made it superior to all preceding and contemporary modes of production. It was this superiority in developing the productive forces of human labour which made possible revolutionary changes in one section of the economy after another, propelling it onto a path of ascending growth while giving a new shape to society as a whole. The view that the whole process was the happy result of a series of accidents does not seem plausible or, indeed, in accordance with the facts.

After taking shape in a few regions of Europe, industrialization spread not only to other parts but also to those 'non-Western' countries which are the subject of this book. It would be impossible to talk about the diffusion of industrialization if the process did not assume a broadly similar pattern whatever the period or the social and political environment in which it takes place. The underlying feature is the transfer of labour and resources from the agrarian (food-producing) to the manufacturing and associated sectors, with the corollary of a shift in consumption from food to non-food items as a proportion of total output/demand as income rises. It is, essentially, a dynamic process of change and growth which involves a continuous rise in production and productivity resulting from the application of machine technology and new ways of organizing the labour process. The non-agrarian population rises, while that part of the population engaged in food and primary production at some stage declines. This means an increase in the surplus available from agriculture, either as a result of rising productivity in the industrializing country, or of its ability to obtain the necessary food supplies by a lesser expenditure of resources through foreign trade. Further, as 'deagrarianization' takes place an increasing proportion of the population will be located in urban areas. With rising incomes and urbanization the demand for manufactured goods and then for services of all kinds from the tertiary sector will grow. The proportion of the occupied population in industry will peak at a more advanced stage; assuming continued income growth the primary sector will shrink still further while employment will continue to rise in the tertiary sector, especially in such fields as distribution, administration, health care, education and leisure activities. The end result of industrialization, therefore, is not a predominance of industrial workers, but a situation in which they remain fairly stable, amounting perhaps to one-third of the total labour force. It is, however, the highly productive and technologically advanced manufacturing sector upon which the resulting occupational distribution depends. In addition to this, to maintain its high per capita consumption the industrialized country makes insatiable demands upon raw material and energy supplies, some of which are non-reproducible and many of which have to be imported from dependent, primary-producing and low-income countries. 'Successful' industrialization thus depends upon many special conditions, including a particular balance of world forces favouring the advanced, or 'core' countries.

REASONS FOR INDUSTRIALIZATION

The specific examples of industrialization discussed in this book will suggest that some prior social, political and cultural arrangements are more conducive to the process than others. What exactly the prerequisites are is a matter for debate. Excluding resource endowment and factors relating to geographical position and climate, there has certainly to be receptivity to change, the acceptance of material values, a population adaptable to new forms of work, and a leadership of some kind, be it a class, or section of a class, or a party, able to take the initiative. Some societies have been particularly hospitable to industrialization, such as eighteenth-century Britain and Meiji Japan, whereas in India and China it has encountered serious obstacles. The examples suggest that colonial societies have generally not provided a favourable environment and that, for such countries, the ending of foreign rule has been necessary before industrialization could advance beyond an enclave type. Otherwise, the historical evidence is that industrialization can take place in very different geographical, social and political settings; that it can be adopted by people with every variety of ideological and religious conviction, but that the results are likely to be more successful where the conditions referred to above are most fully met. Deviations from the general pattern may reflect factors specific to a particular country or region and its relationship to the world market. An area which industrializes rapidly at one time may, at a later period, slow down or regress; 'deindustrialization' has afflicted many areas and is still doing so.

There are general characteristics common to every case and special features which can be attributed to national or regional conditions and timing. Without entering into a detailed typology, a broad classification may be made. The first group includes those countries, or regions, which began their industrialization at the same time as Britain or soon afterwards; the second group comprises the first 'late-comers' who began in the nineteenth century or early in the twentieth century; and the third group is made up of 'followers', who began in the 1930s or after the Second World War.

THE BRITISH MODEL

Britain was the pioneer and to a large extent the model for the regions following closely on her heels in Western Europe and North America, which were able to take over similar machines, methods of production and forms of organization. This was still more the case for the second group which would include the United States as a whole, Germany, Japan and Tsarist Russia. It is a valid claim that these countries enjoyed certain advantages over the pioneer, Britain, in that they were able to begin with a more advanced technology. They were also able to profit from an example, jump over stages, set up larger enterprises able to realize scale economies, and insert themselves into a growing world market under favourable conditions. As for the third group, which is largely made up of countries emerging from a primary exporting role as colonies and semicolonies, their late arrival on the scene has, in many ways, put them at a disadvantage. Some of these countries have, it is true, achieved rapid rates of growth, but the experience so far is incomplete and too mixed for easy generalization.

The British model of industrialization issued from an already well-developed market economy. The accumulation and concentration of capital as well as the creation of a wage-labour force were already well advanced; agrarian relations had already been substantially transformed on capitalist lines; and Britain held a strong position in world trade and shipping. The British Industrial Revolution was the product of the complex interaction of a multitude of private entrepreneurs seeking profit and following market indicators. It was a spontaneous, organic process and the end result was no part of the intention of those who brought it about. The industrial technology represented no great scientific break-through; it reflected the state of empirical knowledge at the time, and the needs of production. Industrial growth was, at first, confined to a few fields, chiefly textiles and not always based upon machinery. Of equal, if not more importance than machine-production, was the creation of a large, disciplined labour force, working partly in factories, and partly on labour-intensive processes in their own homes or small workplaces. Complementary expansion took place in the provision of fuel (coal-mining) and raw materials (the cotton-gin on the American plantations; iron smelted with coke), and in the creation of improved transport (canals and turnpikes) and financial facilities (country banking and the bill of exchange). Thus a more efficient (cost-effective) apparatus of production, exchange and distribution was built up, largely at first on the basis of an expanding internal market, and British manufacturers were able to preempt the main export markets for cheap manufactured goods (mainly textiles).

Once this process had begun, industrial profits provided the main source of continued capital accumulation: the ploughing back of profits. Agricultural efficiency improved before and during the industrialization process; labour was released from the land, food and raw materials were supplied to the growing industries and towns; the rural population provided a market for the manufacturing sector. The growth of consumer goods industries opened up a market for the capital goods industries (iron, coal, machine-making). Early industrialization generated a demand for a new source of power, and the response to this was the steam engine. Later, new machines and machine-tools, more accurate gauges and other instruments made it possible to turn out metal parts with greater precision and on a larger scale, thus enabling firms to make machines with machines. This story is well enough known. It could not be repeated elsewhere, nor was there any need to repeat it once the basic model existed in terms of practice and machines, as designs and skilled people could be imported.

The British model of industrialization was strongly marked by its timing; it was distinctly a product of the eighteenth century and it tended to be slow in adapting to changing conditions; this was evident even as early as the mid-nineteenth century when it was supposed to have reached its high noon. It was an individualistic, small scale and family type capitalism which prevailed in the first place. Not only did the state play no positive role, but capital still assumed a personalized rather than a corporate form and the banks took little part in financing long-term investment. The later industrializing countries (and Japan after 1868) while influenced by the British model in some particulars, modified it considerably in others and added new features of their own. They were able to take over an already developed technology and were poised to outdistance the pioneer, especially in the scale and integration of the production process, geared to expanding markets. The strong element of conscious imitation and borrowing visible in the later developing countries enabled the state to act more positively to assist private capital and speed up the accumulation process by providing infrastructure, educational and training facilities for the labour force, research and development, military contracts and protection for the home market. The late-comers also found that continued profitability depended upon extending the market beyond national limits and that they became increasingly dependent upon imported primary products: hence an interest in overseas expansion, the 'new imperialism' of the late nineteenth century. The agrarian population was drastically reduced in England, whereas a large peasantry survived in the European industrial countries until after the Second World War. Its presence helped to keep down per capita incomes, and at the same time provided a reservoir of labour for the rapid growth of the latter period. Thus, by the late nineteenth century, a more organized type of industrial capitalism had appeared in the newer industrial countries, notably in Germany and the United States. In the European countries, though not in the United States, the state tended to intervene more positively in the economy. Everywhere business began to be organized in a more corporate way, seeking control over unchecked market forces. Cartels, trusts and combinations of every kind reflected the increased demand for capital as the scale of production grew in line with the imperatives of more advanced technology able to obtain ever-larger scale economies. Instead of many competing firms there tended to be a small number of giant, integrated firms, each operating in many fields besides manufacturing. Oligopoly took the place of competition as the typical market situation of advanced industrial capitalism. The individual entrepreneur, investing his own capital and making the main decisions, was being superseded by a managerial hierarchy responsible to a board of directors, itself often representing interlocking interests with other concerns and with the banks. So-called 'managerial capitalism' was carried furthest in the United States but all countries followed the same course.

AMERICAN INFLUENCE

As industrialization moved into a higher gear the old British model became outdated, and it was in Germany and most of all in the United States that the new model took shape. At least from the time of the First World War there is no doubt that the United States had become the pace-setter for the older industrial countries as well as for the newcomers. As a new country of recent settlement, its economy formed in an environment richly endowed with natural resources where the restless search for material success and acquisition had uninhibited scope, this superpower of twentieth-century capitalism took industrialization to new heights. Making an increasingly powerful impression in Europe after the First World War, when Taylorism and Fordism became fashionable concepts, and even though its reputation was temporarily tarnished by the Depression of the 1930s, the massive capacity of its industrial machine in war as in peace impressed contemporaries, much as Britain had done in the early nineteenth century.

American industrialization was based first and foremost on the highly mechanized production of standardized articles for a large and expanding mass market. The ability of the giant American enterprises to develop the most advanced, science-based technology, to follow out the logic of the machine-process on a massive scale, made possible achievements in production and productivity which far out-stripped those of other countries. Certainly before the Second World War, the American worker had more power behind his elbow in the shape of a heavier investment in specialized and

9

complex machinery than his European counterpart. The large internal market based on high per capita income levels and a relatively standardized demand made it possible to realize enormous scale economies. American firms took the lead in the new industries of the late nineteenth and early twentieth centuries: domestic electric appliances, petro-chemicals, business machines, processed foods, motor vehicles and the equipment needed to manufacture them.

The American system of manufactures, already becoming distinctive in the mid-nineteenth century, was organized around assembly-lines requiring huge investments in fixed capital. Consequently, to maintain profitability, industrial firms were under compulsion to operate with the highest possible rate of through-put; they also had to have a correspondingly large market. As the market for one product reached saturation point, there was pressure to diversify into other fields so that capital should not lie idle. The US giants were thus driven to expand into contiguous fields of production and also to extend their operations into other countries, especially those having high tariffs. Well before 1914, branch plants had been set up in Canada and in some European countries, and the trend continued later into Asia and Latin America. United States capital export took the form primarily of direct investment. In the period after the Second World War the giant US enterprises, oddly described as 'multinational corporations' (MNCs), extended their operations worldwide to such an extent as to add a new dimension to industrialization. For some regions, the branch plants of MNCs were their first acquaintance with modern industry.

The powerful example of the United States, the high standards of living made possible by its enormous productive power, together with the role that it had played as a military arsenal during the Second World War, were potent factors in encouraging the drive to industrialization. This was true both of the incompletely industrialized European countries and Japan, which were still pursuing an earlier model, and of the newly independent 'developing' countries of the 1950s and 1960s. In the case of the former, new industries were set up and older ones modernized on American lines, often by American firms. This was especially true of the most advanced industries; in some of these US branch plants had existed since pre-war days, in others branch plants were newly founded or native firms bought up. Management went to school with the Americans and the renovation of European and Japanese industry took place on American lines. In time some local firms were so successful that they out-distanced their teachers. This was exemplified in the 1970s by the growing import into the United States of manufactured goods, including motor cars, from Japan and European countries. The successful new industrializing countries such as Brazil and South Korea also reflected the American model and the direct influence of American capital and the MNCs.

THE NEED FOR INDUSTRIALIZATION

Since the Second World War, industrialization has been generally sought by the newly-developing countries as the means to raise living standards and to ensure national independence. Widely publicized tables of income levels of the countries of the world leave no doubt that incomes are generally higher the greater is the contribution made by manufacturing industry. Countries which have little or no industry are almost invariably poor. The lesson is plain and simple: to overcome poverty and economic backwardness a country must industrialize. This is seen as the key to growth and the prerequisite for development. The chapters which follow provide some opportunity to test these propositions.

Until the Second World War industrialization had still only extended to a relatively small number of countries, mostly in the Northern hemisphere and, with the main exception of Japan, inhabited by Europeans or their descendants. Since then the process, backed by international bodies such as the United Nations and the World Bank, has spread to many parts of the world. It has become the declared policy of the governments of new states, large and small, formed from the old colonial empires. Conscious attempts have been made to follow models already in existence, as well as to develop new ones appropriate for particular areas or types of country. Industrialization has, without doubt, become a global process and, although it proceeds very unevenly, a new surge has been taking place. Even where it has scarcely begun it has been adopted as a goal, especially by the new governing elites hoping to consolidate their national independence, emulate the advanced countries and raise income levels (not least their own).

PLANNED INDUSTRIALIZATION

Until the Russian Revolution of 1917, industrialization had taken

11

place only on the basis of capitalist property relations: private ownership of industry with the allocation of resources and the distribution of goods determined by market forces. Socialists had, of course, projected the alternative of a planned economy in which the means of production would be nationalized or socially owned, though their view of how it would work was perhaps sketchy. Orthodox economists, or some of them, claimed that such an economy would not work. Socialists assumed that once capitalism had outlived its progressive role (which most of them granted it had) – that is, when it was no longer able to develop the productive forces – it would be superseded by a proletarian revolution (the Marxist interpretation) or would be gradually and by consent replaced by a nationalized economy (the Fabian or reformist interpretation). In any case, the new socialist order would inherit the assets of an advanced capitalist society; it would further develop this industrial base, substituting public for private ownership of the means of production and planning for the market as the allocative mechanism. It was assumed that production would then be determined by social needs rather than by the criterion of profit. Exactly how this would influence what was produced, and how consumer needs would be reflected in the plan, were questions very much left for decision when the time came. However, most socialists assumed that industrialization was desirable provided that it was subjected to planning embodying in some way the goal of satisfying social needs. Only a few romantics and utopians thought that the machine should be abandoned and that society should be reorganized into a commune system with a return to handicraft production.

Socialist planning, though conceivable in various forms, has to be distinguished from state intervention in the economy or the nationalization of some industries now general in the capitalist states. There are many examples of intervention of this kind going back, in some cases, to the seventeenth century. In the nineteenth century it was usual for the state to assist in the construction of the infrastructure or to set up and run certain industries. In this century, and especially since 1945, concerted intervention by the state in market economies has adopted the label of 'planning' while clearly not being socialist in the sense discussed above, since the main means of production remain in private hands.

The first opportunity to translate the planned alternative into practice came in Russia: a country which, although it had inherited some modern industry from the previous regime, remained backward in comparison with the advanced capitalist countries, and retained a huge peasant-dominated agrarian sector. Soviet planned industrialization, which began in the late 1920s, took place, therefore, in an unpromising environment. Instead of the planned economy taking over from the already high level established by industrial capitalism, it had to begin at a low level, in a society with many feudal remnants, where many of the basic tasks of capitalist development had still to be accomplished. Coupled with this was the fact that from 1914 onwards the economy had been battered by war, revolution and civil war, and income levels had fallen far behind those of the advanced countries of the West.

After Stalin had gained power in 1924, he had imposed the policy of 'socialism in one country' which meant a partially voluntary severance from the world market, on the assumption that the revolution would remain isolated in Russia for an indefinite period. While this isolation could not be complete it increased the burdens which were imposed upon the population once rapid industrialization was begun.

Stalin's imprint could be seen in the ruthless and barbarous methods used to break the resistance of the peasantry to enforced collectivization from 1928 onwards. What can properly be called the Stalinist model of industrialization contained features which conflicted with the aims of socialism. However, this model, with all its deformations, was subsequently imposed on the Russian satellite countries of Eastern Europe after the defeat of Nazi Germany and was also adopted by the new regime in China after the revolution of 1949.

The results of the Stalinist type of planned industrialization in its original home and elsewhere have been equivocal to say the least. While making possible the rapid industrialization of relatively backward areas, the costs have been extremely heavy in terms of human lives and sacrifices. It will be argued later that the methods used did not arise from the planned economy as such, but were the product of a political struggle waged by the dominant bureaucracy led by Stalin to preserve its power. In any case, the promise of Stalin and his successors to catch up and outstrip the leading capitalist countries in output per head is far from being fulfilled.

The attractive power of the Soviet model reached its peak when the capitalist world was plunged into the Depression of the 1930s, and retained it on the basis of the prestige gained by the victory over Germany. For a time, as new countries began to industrialize after 1950 it still held some interest or even fascination. Subsequently, however, interest in Soviet planning waned. This was partly because knowledge spread about the human consequences of the methods used during the 1930s, and the Soviet leaders themselves, after Stalin's death in 1953, added their own 'revelations'. It also became clear that its extension to the East European countries had created serious problems. Meanwhile, the 'economic miracles' enjoyed by a number of capitalist countries during the post-war boom, by increasing the quantity and variety of goods available to the mass of the population, considerably reduced interest in the tarnished 'Soviet experiment'. Even the Chinese developed serious criticisms of the Soviet model and adopted some new practices which gained them sympathy in the West. New industrializing countries were generally deterred from following Soviet methods by the need for foreign aid, unless they broke away from the capitalist world system, as did Vietnam and North Korea. In short, the Soviet model and its off-shoots or imitations have lost the power to attract. Rather than being models they are best regarded as experiments which should be studied for the lessons they might teach, often of how things should not be done. The validity of an alternative form of planned industrialization to the type preferred by capitalism cannot be based on these models with much conviction. On the other hand, their shortcomings do not prove that an alternative is not possible and preferable.

CONDITIONS OF INDUSTRIALIZATION

While it has been argued that industrialization as a process has certain characteristic and repeatable features wherever it has taken place or is going on, its specific form will depend upon conditions of time and place. On a national scale it will reflect numerous geographical, historical, cultural and social factors. The total environment, it has been suggested, may be more or less favourable. The same production lines may have different results, materially and socially, according to the country or region in which they are installed. The purpose of the studies in this book is to bring out the underlying similarities and the national peculiarities involved in specific national cases.

In any event, the economy of each country is also shaped to a greater or lesser extent by its relationship to the world market, to which the timing of its industrialization has made an important contribution; hence, for example, the difference between core and peripheral countries. Consequently, it is impossible to understand the economy of a particular country without reaching back into its history and recording the conditions under which it was drawn into the world market. Historical forces acquire a momentum which makes them important factors, both in the short term and in the long term. This is true whether we are dealing with the economic problems of an advanced country such as modern Britain or with those of a developing country.

Although the national state has been chosen as the framework for the studies which follow, it may not always be appropriate as industrialization is often a localized or regional phenomenon. Some degree of economic dualism is found in every country in which it takes place. In Brazil, for example, the São Paulo region was industrializing while much of the rest of the country remained underdeveloped. In India, under colonial rule, modern industry was largely isolated in a few enclaves; in China the treaty ports were the main setting for early industrialization. In the continents which experienced prolonged European colonial rule, the political division into nation-states follows no economic rationale. In Africa, for example, state frontiers existing today are largely the result of arbitrary decisions taken by foreign diplomats a century or more ago. The division of Latin America into twenty separate republics is no more logical from the economic point of view. In other words, in the world today there are many national units which are too small to support modern large-scale industry and are insufficiently related to their neighbours. Other states, especially the large countries of Asia, have limited resources in relation to population size and little chance of development without fundamental agrarian change and outside aid. On the other hand, there are countries fortunate enough to be endowed with valuable natural resources and which have small populations, like the oil-rich states of the Middle East. Other oil-producers, such as Algeria and Nigeria, have large and growing populations and have to face the problem of what condition their economies will be in when the oil runs out. Laying the basis for industrialization before that happens would seem to be an urgent need.

The prospects of successful industrialization thus appear very varied on a nation-by-nation basis. The most successful industrializers in recent decades can be regarded as special cases. There are the small Asian countries like South Korea and Taiwan without great natural resources but having abundant labour power. They have industrialized largely by supplying a certain range of manufactured goods to the world market with the help of foreign capital, and as hosts to the branch plants of the MNCs. They have produced profit-hungry local entrepreneurs backed by authoritarian governments encouraging the export drive and reassuring foreign investors. There are limited possibilities for other countries to follow their example. Most small and underdeveloped countries are locked into the world market in a dependent role as primary producers – a role which is unlikely to change in the short run.

The international environment for industrialization is a changing one and while it may provide opportunities for some countries to do what South Korea and Taiwan have done, it imposes almost insuperable obstacles for others. For example, the amount of capital and the level of technology necessary to establish modern, large-scale industry are increasing all the time. In many cases, therefore, without foreign assistance, and the economic dependence which that entails, industrialization may be difficult or impossible. The best that may be hoped for is that a country will fit into the so-called 'new international division of labour' as a producer of cheap manufactured exports for the world market. Nationalist regimes, such as that in Egypt, which have aimed at greater self-reliance and have built up industries with state aid, have found if difficult to continue without foreign capital. As will be seen, Brazil has made rapid strides on the road to industrialization, but only at the price of increased dependence on the MNCs. Even China, with its nationalized industry and commune agriculture, is resorting to the import of foreign technology and encouraging foreign investment on a limited scale.

The overall growth of industrialization on a world scale does not in fact mean that it has become less difficult than before. It is too early even to write success over examples where the industrialization drive has been most pronounced. These have generally been associated with the export of manufactured goods and thus must depend on continued growth of world demand. In the absence of an industrialization effort, however, there would seem to be little hope of promoting development and raising income levels in the developing countries. The gap between the industrializers and the non-industrializers is wide and may be growing. A solution may have to be found in new forms of industrialization: it may be possible, for example, to concentrate on small-scale industry, which would be more directly related to the needs of the mass of agricultural producers. Or an alternative to the exisiting inequitable international division of labour may have to be found which encourages specialization rather than the pursuit of greater national self-sufficiency. Such lines of approach would require revolutionary change, with a planned organization of the world's resources and productive capacity, which seems a long way off.

Meanwhile, where industrialization has been going on, its short-term effects have been contradictory. Much of it has been based on low wages and intensive work, even though wages may be higher than in the surrounding countryside. The major gains have been garnered by a minority of the population and been slow to percolate down to the lower strata. Class differences and regional disparities may have widened. Large masses of people may have found not only that economic development has passed them by, but that they are worse off than before. Masses of the rural poor have transferred to the urban slums and shanty-towns. In the more highly developed industries a better paid working class has appeared, constituting, it has been claimed, a labour aristocracy. In other cases industry has been built up on an abundant supply of low paid labour, women and even children, from a low income, rural background. This cheap labour supply has attracted export-oriented industry to the newly-industrialized countries of Asia and Latin America. Industrialization of this kind ought to be considered as 'peripheral'; it produces for foreign markets and is financed and controlled, very often, from abroad. It does not bring about the far-reaching structural transformation and social change which accompanied it in the advanced countries.

THE SOCIAL COST

It is true, of course, that every historical example shows that industrialization has a destructive as well as a positive side. It means the uprooting of masses of people from the land, the loss of traditional employments, the undermining and perhaps destruction of stable social structures. At the same time, it concentrates newcomers in cities which are ill-prepared to receive them, and the result is social disintegration, poverty and crime. While some of the new urban population rise to new-found heights of wealth and power others fall to depths below those of the old society. However, the problem of these social consequences of industrialization cannot

17

be gone into too deeply here. Such problems may suggest that industrialization has sometimes been of the wrong kind, or has been badly carried out, or that a coherent social policy is required to moderate or prevent them; but they do not invalidate the case for industrialization.

Meanwhile, in the advanced countries, increasing doubts have been expressed about the benefits of industrialization. What the critics usually complain of is its tendency to produce an unlovely and polluted environment, to impose uninteresting and monotonous work on the labour force (i.e. most adults) and to promote a competitive struggle for material success. There are certainly real and intractable problems arising from, or connected with, industrialization which cannot all be blamed onto the social system. Certainly where industrialization takes place in a capitalist market economy, its side-effects will require interventionist measures to prevent them doing irreparable damage. This was the significance of social reforms such as the Factory Acts in nineteenth-century Britain. Even where a comprehensive system of social legislation exists, however, basic problems remain. By all accounts it is no more pleasant to work in a Soviet or Chinese factory or mine, than it is in one in a capitalist country. The richest countries have such problems as urban decay and large numbers of people on or below the poverty line. Nevertheless it is mainly in these countries, where people are on the whole reasonably well off, that there is most criticism of modern technology.

That industrialization creates as many problems as it solves tends to be hidden when attention is concentrated on the indices of industrial production or of national income. This means that 'success' cannot easily be measured in quantitative terms; but it is even more difficult to measure it in any other way. In the case studies which follow, the aim will be to make some overall assessment which takes into account both the achievements and the social costs.

The countries chosen represent, in fact, varied paths to industrialization and different ways of dealing with its social consequences. Japan offers itself naturally as the best 'success story' of post-1950 industrialization. Its apparently irresistible rise represents a growing challenge to the older industrial countries. China, by contrast, took longer to embark on an independent course and when this did happen it was under a leadership dedicated to rapid industrialization on socialist lines. Influenced at first by the Soviet model, China under Mao introduced some variants of its own which his successors, in turn, have modified or abandoned. India, after a long period under foreign rule, emerged as an independent state under a leadership also committed to industrialization, but without the desire or the will to industrialize on the basis of a nationalized economy, or even to carry out far-reaching agrarian reforms. Despite its achievements, the Indian model cannot be counted a success, and the claim to abolish poverty rings as hollow today as it did in the past. The Soviet experience, though perhaps better known than other examples in this book, is also discussed. As the first planned industrialization it marked an epoch – however the results are to be judged. The very scale of Soviet industrialization taxes the imagination, while the enormous human suffering involved is a condemnation in the eyes of many. Brazil is probably the least known of the countries dealt with here. Latin America as a whole tends to be neglected and the rapid surge of industrialization in Brazil in recent years has not received the attention it deserves. As will be shown, in a sense Brazil is representative of a group of countries which have been hospitable towards the giant MNCs and has depended to a large extent upon them to bring about rapid economic growth, with results which will be summarized later.

Nigeria is the largest and economically most viable of the Black African countries. Although less industrialized than any of the other countries selected for study, it has at least made a start. Choosing a capitalist road, and still under the influence of foreign capital, its experience provides a test case for this course in an undeveloped, former colonial country.

Finally, an attempt will be made to examine the experience and prospects of the 'newly-industrializing' countries as a whole, including, particularly, South Korea, Taiwan and Egypt. Given the scope of the present book this can only be an invitation to further study along the lines suggested in the bibliography. The judgements and interpretations it presents must be regarded as provisional; on many issues there can be no definitive view.

CHAPTER TWO
Japan: a meteoric rise

The impressive, indeed meteoric, rise of the Japanese economy, since the Second World War, which has raised it to the position of the world's third largest industrial producer, has been one of the most significant and unexpected changes of recent history. Its ability, despite the destruction wrought by the Second World War, to overtake and outstrip the leading industrial countries, to build up powerful and technologically advanced industries almost from scratch, and to establish a leading position in the world market, has attracted wonder, admiration and foreboding.

At a time when older industrial countries were in a state of stagnation or decline, Japan continued to press forward vigorously in spite of enormous expenditure on imported oil. The rapid expansion of the motor car industry, for example, was not checked by the post-1974 energy crisis, and Japan established itself as the world's leading producer. World recession slowed Japan's advance, however, hitting hard some industries which had over-expanded during the boom. The economy also suffered high-level inflation. Nevertheless, Japanese business has taken such setbacks as a challenge, pushing all the harder to reduce costs of production, to develop new products and expand overseas markets. The appearance of continuous success and the ability to overcome problems with resolve conceals many weaknesses. There are internal contradictions, untoward side-effects of rapid expansion and increased vulnerability to external shocks which have to be examined before the picture can be complete. Nevertheless, the first task must be to discuss the reasons for Japan's success and to explore the peculiarities of the Japanese model of industrialization.

THE MEIJI PERIOD

The elite of the new regime which took power with the Meiji Restoration of 1868, while not wishing to break with the traditional way of life, deliberately set out to endow their still feudal agrarian country with the institutions and economic organization of a modern state. The closing of the gap with the advanced countries was seen as a question of national survival. If Japan did not learn from and emulate the foreigners who were battering at its door they might take over control and turn the country into a colony. What this would mean was clear enough from the experience of other Asian countries. The previous regime of the Tokugawas had met the threat of Western encroachment with the policy of seclusion: they simply reduced contact with the outside world to a minimum. Because of their geographical remoteness from the expanding frontiers of European domination, this policy worked well enough for a time. Japan developed in its own way but, at the same time, fell further behind the technologically advancing European countries and the United States. By the mid-nineteenth century the latter were intent on bringing the whole of Asia into their trading network and they rudely brought to an end Japan's self-imposed isolation. The Tokugawa regime had been obliged to accept unequal treaties which gave foreign nationals a privileged status in Japan. The succeeding regime, whilst being unable to repudiate these treaties, learned a lesson and made a cardinal principle of its policy opposition to foreign penetration, by adopting the foreigner's own methods and instruments.

The early decades of the Meiji period saw rapid modernization as Japan consciously incorporated into the traditional framework, much of which was preserved, the attributes of a modern society. A new administrative and legal apparatus was adopted to sanctify the position of the ruling class and give it more effective instruments of power. The armed forces were completely reorganized and reconstructed on modern lines, while retaining and even enhancing the prestigious role they held in society. A basic infrastructure of transport, communications and other facilities began to take shape; a development policy which ensured that the modern features were integrated with the society rather than remaining as enclaves. The state strenuously promoted industrial development and encouraged the importation of advanced technologies from the West, both in the shape of machinery and foreign technicians. A strong economy was seen as a necessity for national survival. The agrarian surplus extracted from the peasantry had previously gone, in the main, into the consumption of the old ruling class. It was now chanelled into productive outlets. Market forces were encouraged and a stimulus offered for investment by the merchant cliques and the *samurai*, once they had been compensated for their loss of stipends.

Thus, unlike any other Asian country, Japan entered the twentieth century under the guidance of a modernizing elite committed to building a strong national economy both to preserve the independence of the state and also to extend its power and influence on the Asiatic mainland and the Pacific area. Nevertheless, Japanese industrialization was clearly not a home-grown product. Although economic progress had been visible under the Tokugawa regime along capitalist lines, it can hardly be claimed that Japan would have embarked upon industrialization without borrowing the technology and organization of the West. What was significant was that the existing social and cultural framework proved particularly receptive to change and innovation. Even so, much of the impetus had to come from above, from a powerful reforming elite drawn from the old ruling class, highly nationalist in inspiration, which saw a modern economy as the basis for a strong state and also a firm basis for their own rule.

There was little in existing models in the last quarter of the nineteenth century which suggested that this sort of industrialization could be carried out through state planning. The market mechanism and the theories of economic liberalism found ready acceptance; they were among the factors which accounted for the economic strength of the Western countries. The role of the state was not to run the economy but to blaze the trail for ill-equipped or reluctant entrepreneurs, mostly from the old merchant class. In the early stages the state set up and financed industries but disposed of them, on very favourable terms for the new owners, as soon as it could. Only those industries directly related to armaments production remained under state control. Overall, the public sector in Japan has never been large. Instead, a close working relationship grew up between the bureaucrats of the administration and the representatives of the *zaibatsu*, the giant family concerns, which came to dominate the modern sectors of the economy. The Meiji reformers thus opened the way for capitalist relations of production and found a place in the new order for the privileged strata of the old order – landowners and *samurai* – together with the merchants. Agrarian change was carefully regulated from above, in the face of peasant discontent, in a way calculated to assist economic development rather than to improve the conditions of the rural population.

The form of guided industrialization which began after the Meiji reforms had specific features which cannot be explained from market forces alone or from Japan's comparative advantage in the world economy at that time. Given the predominantly rural character of Japan it was inevitable that the textile industries should play a leading role in the new industrialization. Silk was already an established industry and raw silk proved to be an important export staple. With abundant labour, a potential home market and possibilities for export, it was reasonable to encourage the setting up of a cotton industry. A complete range of technology was available from the West, including steam power. Modern factories could be established at an early stage of the industrialization process, but there was also traditional small-scale production. For the government, with its nationalist aims, it was also of primary importance to encourage heavy industry as a necessary basis for political as well as economic independence. Japan could enjoy the advantages of the late-comer in taking over the technology and organization already proved in the advanced countries. Besides retaining some control over strategic industries, the state was also instrumental in the setting up of modern infrastructure, especially transport facilities; thus the railway, the telegraph and the steamship were already available. The relatively high level of education and literacy, the maturity of the pre-industrial economy, the absence of any strong prejudices against change in the sphere of production – indeed, a bias in the other direction on the part of the military as well as the bureaucracy – made Japan remarkably receptive to Western models in every sphere. Not that these models were adopted mechanically; they were assimilated, developed and brought into conformity with national conditions.

One example of this was the often-noted persistence of industrial dualism: the combination of the old forms of small-scale, decentralized production, highly labour-intensive, with the new large-scale and more capital-intensive industries using, at first, imported technology. The former employed the old craft skills, worked on traditional materials and turned out products used in frugal Japanese households. The latter produced not only cheap textiles and other new products, for which a market might be found abroad as well as at home, but also the minerals, capital goods and armaments which were the bases of economic and political power. It was this modern sector, dependent upon imported technology, more capital-intensive and organized in larger units, which was to provide the thrust for continued industrialization. While part of the increased output could be absorbed in the home market, where there were new demands and government requirements, especially concerning the armed forces, markets abroad were to become of growing importance as expansion continued. The economic need for raw materials together with the need for new markets fitted in with the nationalist drive to expand overseas, in order to prevent Japan being hemmed in by hostile countries.

By the time of the First World War it could be said that the basis for a modern industry had been laid in Japan and that there was a built-in momentum towards further expansion, both economic and political. Japan assumed an imperialist posture in Asia, having proved its military strength in the wars against China and Russia. While being unique among Asian countries, and having gained a position of equality with those of the West, symbolized by the treaty with Britain of 1902, Japan was still a long way behind the leading industrial powers in aggregate output and in income per head. The mass of the population were still peasants and, although agricultural production had been growing steadily, once taxes, rents and other payments had been met, its purchasing power was low. At the same time, there was a low-wage labour surplus in the rural areas which could be tapped by industry. Despite rapid rates of growth in industrial production, in total output of steel, coal and consumer goods, Japan was still outclassed by the advanced countries. If Japan's military victories had impressed outsiders, they had been the result of the disproportionate claim made upon resources by armaments production and of the pursuit of political power as a priority. The living standards of the masses were still desperately low, though probably well above those of other Asian countries, and Japan's main asset seemed to be its abundant reserves of cheap labour power. State policy was concerned with measures to assist capital accumulation and the benefits went disproportionately to the rich and powerful. But the Japanese people were frugal and part of any additional income went into savings; the 'demonstration effect' (that is, the impact of seeing a larger variety and superior quality of goods than are customarily available at existing income levels, thus stimulating a demand for them) was hardly operative. War expenditure, although in one sense a burden, offered a market to heavy industry and may have helped to lay the foundations for subsequent industrial growth.

The close alliance between state and business which grew up in the Meiji era, marked a departure from liberal capitalism and resembled more the mercantilist policies which some European countries had employed in their own pre-industrial stages or the organized capitalism which was taking shape in Germany. An important result was that it enabled Japan to acquire and preserve its economic autonomy as well as its political independence. The home market was not flooded with imported goods and by the early years of the twentieth century cheap textile exports were highly successful in Asian markets, foreshadowing what was to follow. Although there was some recourse to foreign capital, industry was mainly financed through government borrowing. Policy from that time on was designed to ensure that foreign capital could not dominate industry. The nationalist goals of the rulers, with which business leaders concurred, ensured that the country not only maintained its political sovereignty, ridding itself of the unequal treaties by 1899, but also prevented it from falling victim to economic imperialism. To be sure, the economy became increasingly integrated into the world market, but this was on terms which, as far as possible, were determined by national interests as perceived by the state-business alliance.

The decades of Meiji (1868–1912) were undoubtedly of great formative importance for the economy of modern Japan. By the end of the period it was well launched on the road to industrialization, and it had already taken a form which was distinctively Japanese. While preserving many of the original social and cultural traits which had characterized traditional Japan, a modern sector had been built up under the aegis of a particular form of organized capitalism in which nationalism and militarism played a central role. Much of the old industrial structure had survived or even been extended. At the same time, there was large-scale production and giant firms and banks played a dominant role in the modern sector.

Traditional features, such as close-knit family ties, the dependence of women on fathers and husbands, the habit of obedience to social superiors and of disciplined cooperative labour, were turned to advantage in the creation of a labour force and the organization of industrial production. However, similar traits are to be found in societies which remained backward. The relatively high level of literacy before the Restoration and the attention paid to expanding educational facilities assisted the dissemination of the new technologies and the process of learning and assimilation which went on. The Japanese proved very willing to go to school with the foreigner, displayed enormous curiosity about foreign models, and employed foreign experts and technicians to help found new industries. All the same, they carefully avoided dependence and maintained their own culture. At an early stage of the borrowing process, improvements were made to borrowed technology and resourceful entrepreneurs were responsible for innovations and improvements which adapted forms of technology to their own national environment. A tradition was thus established which was not that of slavish imitation.

While Japanese society constituted a hierarchy, it did allow for some mobility through educational achievement and the acquisition of wealth. Moreover, once adaptability to new influences and a readiness to learn had developed, a habit was established which ensured that new developments abroad would be closely followed and quickly adopted if they promised to suit local needs. Since Japan owed so much to foreign models from the start of her industrialization, this was perhaps a natural response. Nevertheless, the foreigner was kept at arm's length while the maximum was extracted from foreign contacts. It was a direct reversal of the seclusion policy in appearance whilst conserving much of its motivation underneath.

ECONOMIC EFFECTS OF THE FIRST WORLD WAR

The First World War acted as a forcing house for the industrialization of Japan. Although formally a belligerent, her part in the war was a very minor one. Meanwhile, exports from the main belligerent countries were greatly reduced or cut off altogether, especially in the Far East, and Japanese goods were able to fill the gap. It was an excellent chance for manufacturers whose home market was still relatively small. Industrial production and foreign trade increased four-fold during the war. Home production had to be stepped up to take the place of imports into Japan. At the same time, a larger market opened up for the underdeveloped countries of the Pacific area, who were already among Japan's trading partners and with whom she was able to extend her economic ties still further. With booming trade, investment at a high level and profitability good, the war proved to be a prosperous affair for business. For the mass of the people, however, there were new hardships. Prices rose about two and a half times, outstripping the wage rises of factory workers, many of whom were new recruits from the countryside. Price rises hit all consumers including those in the rural areas. There were serious social strains and unrest, culminating in the rice riots of

1918. Meanwhile Japan made territorial acquisitions in the Pacific area at Germany's expense and consolidated her position on the mainland. With the interest of the great powers focused on Europe, Japan's external position improved. At the same time, the favourable balance of payments enabled foreign debts to be cleared, and Japan became a creditor country. In short, the war benefited Japan both directly and indirectly and when it was over she was apparently poised to make further gains.

As it happened, Japan was affected by the economic difficulties of the post-war period and she faced some unexpected problems. The war boom, after all, had been comparatively short-lived. It left behind a great weight of industrial capacity built up during a period of unlimited demand and rising prices. Much of Japan's increased foreign trade had been with primary producing countries now afflicted with falling prices and lower incomes. Overseas demand shrank at the same time as Japan's competitors were coming back into the field. Home market demand failed to rise to take up the slack. In short, Japan's economy suffered particularly severely from the slump in the capitalist world in the early 1920s and the situation was made worse by the devastating Tokyo earthquake of 1923. The main reaction of industry to these adverse changes was to pursue a policy of concentration and rationalization. The tendency for the modern sector to be dominated by a small number of giant firms was thus intensified, consolidating the position of the *zaibatsu*.

Industrialization was accelerated by war and, despite these setbacks, continued steadily through the inter-war years. The contribution of industry to national income overtook that of agriculture and a more diversified industrial structure took shape. In the modern sector were located the rapidly growing cotton textile and light manufacturing industries, which used machinery and steam or electric power. These industries were to make the major contribution to exports during the period, competing successfully with the British and other exporting countries with low-priced products. Meanwhile, the decline of the export of raw silk, a foreign exchange earner, especially in the depressed 1930s, emphasized Japan's need to expand the export of manufactures. The other major component of the modern sector consisted of heavy industries, notably mining, iron and steel, shipbuilding and engineering. Most of these industries used imported raw materials or energy sources. Although some foreign firms set up branch plants, the main industries were controlled by the *zaibatsu* and, in the case of some armaments production, by the state. Thus there was little direct foreign capital investment. The *zaibatsu* and the banks were able to raise capital for expansion and for the setting up of new branches of industry. They also provided a certain measure of integration between the diverse enterprises which made up each *zaibatsu*, or Japanese-style conglomerate.

When Japan entered upon a hectic course of imperialist expansion in China, after 1931, the war-related industries, which used advanced technology, began to grow rapidly. As in the earlier period, industrial dualism continued; much industrial production was carried on in small- and medium-sized units still organized in the old way and using much hand labour. The gap between enterprises of this sort and the organized large-scale industries tended to widen from the 1920s onwards, especially in productivity and wage levels. However, the two sectors were not altogether separate and distinct. Large firms often found it economical to have parts and components manufactured by small sub-contracting firms; this reduced their overheads and gave flexibility when market demand was variable. Some small firms were able to buy up second-hand machinery cast off by the larger ones. Many were, in any case, producers of traditional articles and specialities for the home market and only needed simple machines such as sewing machines or lathes. Some cheap, often shoddily made, goods found their way onto the export market, giving Japanese products a bad reputation.

CONDITIONS OF LABOUR

Generally speaking, the continued existence of industrial dualism was an indication of a lack of maturity in Japanese industrialization up to this time. The dualism was also reflected in the peculiarities of the Japanese labour market, some of which were to be held up almost as a model in the light of Japan's later industrial success. As had been the case since the very start of industrialization, many factory workers were women and girls recruited from the villages or from urban working class families. Their pay was low and conditions of work were poor, with adverse effects on their health. In any case, it was assumed that they would only work for five or six years before marriage, and there was thus a constant supply of fresh female workers. Male workers were required in more highly skilled or arduous manual jobs, as well as in a supervisory capacity where women were employed. As heavy industry grew and technology became more advanced, employers required a trained and stable labour force of adult males. Traditionally, much factory labour had been recruited by middlemen and worker loyalty was often to these labour bosses rather than to the factory owner. This system of recruitment proved unsatisfactory in the more highly-organized, large-scale industries which had become increasingly important since the earlier years of the century. Employers in these industries required a cadre of trained and skilled workers who would be loyal to the firm rather than to the labour boss or to a trade union, so far as wage bargaining was concerned.

What evolved in the modern advanced industry was a system of seniority which virtually guaranteed lifelong employment to the loyal male worker. He was recruited on leaving school, or at the apprentice stage, with the prospect of regular progression up the wage scale until he reached his maximum capacity; as he grew old he might be moved to less exacting work and then retired on a small pension. While employed, he received certain social and medical benefits and, ideally, became a 'company man'. Similar schemes were used for managerial personnel coming out of the institutions of higher learning. This kind of paternalism, which linked the employee to the enterprise in a corporate relationship lasting a lifetime, was not unknown in Europe and America, but in Japan it assumed a more systematic form and seems to have been preferred by more firms. While it had disadvantages from the employer's point of view – it might add to his overheads or make it difficult to get rid of dead wood – it ensured a stable, loyal and subservient labour force, too afraid of losing their accumulated benefits to be attracted to militant trade unionism. In any case, lifelong employment continued to be confined to the basic core of more highly trained and qualified male workers. It did not generally apply to women, who might make up over half of the work force in many enterprises, nor to the less skilled, temporary workers who might also form a considerable part of the labour employed and who would be the first to be laid off in time of slump.

It is possible that Japanese workers entered more readily into such lifetime contracts than their counterparts in other countries because the system fitted in with existing social customs: the rela-tionship between father and sons in a family or between superiors and dependents in the feudal order. All kinds of sociological and psychological explanations have been offered for the peculiarities of Japanese labour relations. It may simply have been that the development of trade unions lagged behind and was impeded by the law. In any case, the more skilled and better-paid Japanese worker often became a 'company man' and his proletarian status and class consciousness were overshadowed by the relative job security which he enjoyed, as compared with the majority of those competing for jobs.

ECONOMIC CRISIS

The Japanese economy underwent a series of troubles during the 1920s, which made for instability. Exports fell off in the face of intensive trade competition and protectionism abroad, and, with the yen over-valued, did not exceed their 1919 peak for another ten years. Prices tended to fall, profits were squeezed and there were many bankruptcies. Big business responded by further rationalization, by price maintenance and by increased interest in foreign markets and colonial expansion. In 1927 there was a financial crisis and many banks collapsed, thus enabling a smaller number of the larger and sounder banks to secure a dominant position. In 1930–31 Japan was hit by the onset of the world economic depression with a sharp fall in prices and in exports. The overseas market for raw silk – for long a useful foreign exchange earner – contracted disastrously. Higher tariffs in the United States and European countries hit the export trade. Surprisingly, Japan was able to overcome these setbacks within a few years, becoming the only capitalist country to experience rapid growth despite the depression. Two main reasons can be given for this. On the one hand, in a period of worldwide falling prices and contracting trade, cheap Japanese exports of textiles and light manufactures successfully penetrated markets previously held by the older industrial countries, notably Britain, which were now high cost producers. On the other hand, especially from 1936 onwards, government orders for war materials stimulated the expansion of the heavy industries. Japanese capital was meanwhile active in promoting development in the colonial empire, especially in industrializing the newly-acquired territory of Manchuria. This was facilitated by supplies of cheap labour, borrowed technology and a colonial expansionist policy which made it possible to carve out a protected market sphere in East Asia. This led to a demand for plant and equipment which encouraged further investment at home, while the colonies were also able to supply food and the raw materials of which the mother country was seriously short.

Economic crisis and war mobilization thus created abnormal conditions during the 1930s to which the government and big business responded by further measures of protectionism and concentration. Whether or not the *zaibatsu* and business generally promoted the aggressive expansionist policy of the 1930s and 1940s, or were forced reluctantly to acquiesce in decisions made by the military and imposed upon the government, there is no doubt that they prospered at a time when the rest of the capitalist world was plunged into its worst-ever depression. In addition, a number of new business groupings, the so-called new *zaibatsu*, were formed to take advantage of opportunities offered by overseas expansion and war demand. Increasingly, industry was dominated by a few, powerful giant firms, which enjoyed a privileged relationship with the government and worked closely with it and the armed forces to increase production for war purposes. From 1937, war mobilization moved into high gear; there was some contraction of output in light industries such as textiles, while the industrial effort was concentrated on iron and steel, armament production and naval shipbuilding. As Japan was fighting a modern war, where the standards were set by the most advanced economies, increasingly sophisticated material was required: aircraft, tanks, communications equipment, range-finders, bomb-sights and automatic weapons.

WAR AND THE GROWTH OF NATIONALISM

There is an obvious continuity between Japan's wartime experience and what had gone before; there had, after all, always been a close association between economic development and national-military aims. The question was that until the 1930s the latter had been pursued without an open clash of interests with the Western imperialist powers. As an empire was carved out of Chinese territory and her rulers dreamed of dominating the whole Pacific area, the other world powers could not remain unconcerned and a clash was probably inevitable. No doubt the more conservative elements in the ruling class in Tokyo were only reluctantly pushed into what was clearly a gamble by the militant nationalists and military adventurers. That they accepted expansion on the Asiatic mainland, knowing that this would meet with the disapproval of the Western powers, and embarked on the gamble, was not only a function of an internal power struggle; it also reflected the pressures on Japan of the world economic crisis and, indeed, of the pent-up contradictions of its development since the Meiji Restoration.

Industrialization from that time until the surrender in 1945 has to be seen in a context of resurgent nationalism, in which the preservation of sovereignty came to be equated with military strength and expansionism. This gave the military, with its base in the countryside and the traditional ruling classes, a central role in the state and in the nation as a whole. At the same time, the industrialization of Japan enabled the military to operate from a new basis of power. An important part of this process was bound up with government military spending intended to keep Japan strong and this policy was welcomed by the *zaibatsu*. Patriotism and profits were able to go hand-in-hand while the hold of the military was strengthened. Once the economy was hit by the world crisis of the 1930s, following the difficulties of the previous decade, it was tempting for influential sections of the ruling class to seek a way out in the pursuit of Japan's manifest destiny in Asia for which the way had long been open. Further imperialist expansion meant the risk of war with the United States and Britain; it was a war which, on sober calculation, Japan could hardly hope to win except by a speedy and successful first strike. Doubtless there were alternative courses, favoured by the more prudent, but opposition and dissent were stifled and suppressed under the authoritarian regime sanctioned by the emperor-system, itself a product of the Meiji Restoration.

Once the conflict had been begun by the attack on Pearl Harbour in December 1941, it was surprising that Japan did so well both on the battle fronts and in organizing her war effort. This was done by giving priority to the armed forces, both by increasing total output and drastically reducing civilian consumption. The main problem facing the planners, and in a sense this was what the war was all about, was dependence upon imported raw materials and fuel. The sea-lanes were Japan's vulnerable lifelines and once they were cut the economy could not survive. The initial successes, the over-running of much of the Pacific and the short-lived realization of the grandiose Greater East Asian Co-Prosperity Sphere encouraged the illusion that this could be averted.

When American industrial potential was turned to war production, Japan was revealed as a pygmy by comparison. At its peak, her armaments production was no more than one-tenth of that achieved in the United States. Once the military reverses cut off overseas sources of supply, industry was starved of raw materials and production slowed down. No plans had been made for a long war and arrangements for the allocation of scarce materials became increasingly chaotic. The war revealed the incomplete nature of Japan's industrialization. At least half the population was still employed in primary production. This limited the recruitment of labour to war industries and, despite this, calorific intake fell almost to subsistence level for a large part of the population. American bombing, and the final horror of the atomic bombs, further disrupted the economy and aggravated the hardships of the civilian population.

When the Allied occupation began, the economy was in a desperate state. Food and raw materials were running short and a surge of inflation began. There had been some destruction of industrial plant; more serious was the lack of raw materials and energy supplies and the fact that much industrial capacity had been turned towards war production so that a period of reconversion would be necessary before there could be a revival of the economy on a peace-time basis. Japanese business leaders were anxious to save what they could from the wreckage and saw their best course in cooperation with the Occupation authorities. American policy began with the assumption that there would have to be far-reaching reforms, including a major restructuring of the economy, to prevent further Japanese aggression. In the event, however, the defeat and Occupation represented a turning point in Japanese history almost on a par with the Meiji Restoration, clearing the way for the great surge in industrialization which was to elevate Japan into third rank among the economies of the world.

At first Occupation policy, determined as it was principally by the United States, conceived of a reduction in Japan's industrial power as a way of preventing further aggression, and some plant was dismantled for reparations purposes. At the same time, measures of democratization were proposed to undermine the power of those held responsible for past warlike policies: the military, big business and the land-owners in particular. Although democratization was aimed precisely at the old ruling class, there was no revolution and no general redistribution of property. In fact, the ruling class retained its overall position in the economic as well as the social and political fields. Symbolically, the Emperor Hirohito remained head of state, and continuity was preserved. However, the armed forces were abolished and Japan's military capacity was reduced to a small defence force. Some war plants were dismantled, while others built for military purposes were made available for other forms of production. Considerable effort went into the attempt to break up concentrations of economic power, notably the *zaibatsu*. Amercian policy-makers were deeply divided over this issue and as the international political situation changed during 1946–47, with growing tension between the United States and the Soviet Union and the threat of revolutionary movements in Asia, policy towards big business became more lenient. In effect, the attempt to impose a liberal, free-market capitalism through a form of anti-monopoly legislation was abandoned. *Zaibatsu* dissolution was not seriously pursued and, although some changes did take place in business organization, there was little change in control. It came to be accepted by the Occupation authorities that United States interests required an economically viable Japan and that this could only be brought about through cooperation with big business in sponsoring an industrial revival.

Since the American policy-makers were firmly opposed to a social revolution which would have unseated the existing ruling class, there was no real alternative but to cooperate with it. The idea of a de-industrialized Japan, put forward in some quarters, was unrealistic as it would have condemned the population to permanent poverty and increased the danger of revolution. In the early years of the Occupation, Japan was economically dependent upon the United States, particularly for food supplies and raw materials. There seemed little prospect that she would become a serious competitor, even when the Occupation came to an end in 1952. Recovery from the war took some years and it was not until the mid-1950s that industrial production recovered its pre-1941 level. War damage had wiped out perhaps a quarter of Japan's wealth; almost all the merchant fleet had been lost, and shipping was Japan's vital link with raw material supplies and markets. Repatriated citizens from the colonies and occupied territories, numbering about six million, competed for jobs and housing. The armed forces had been demobilized and there were all the problems of rehabilitation and reconversion. In a situation of general penury, the black market flourished. Instead of being self-sufficient in food, Japan became dependent upon American agricultural surpluses to meet basic needs. There could be no economic recovery, in any case, unless industry could once again obtain the imported raw materials upon which it depended and until exports had recovered in order to pay for them. Economic recovery meant reinstatement in the world market.

RECOVERY

Yet, although the prospect may have seemed very bleak in the early post-war years, and economically Japan had been driven down to rock-bottom, the very extent of the decline offered prospects for the future. The masses of impoverished unemployed and underemployed people, hoping to restore shattered lives, made up a large potential, mobile labour force. Industrial plant could be renovated and turned over to peace-time production. Contact with the United States brought immense changes and stimulated the desire for material improvement, encouraging the appearance of entrepreneurs. In the top levels of the administration and business, some of the old guard had been swept away in the turmoil. Their place was taken by new men, anxious to see Japan restored to its true place in the world, open to new ideas, and ready to learn from the occupant.

Meanwhile, in 1946, in accordance with Occupation policy, a major land reform was initiated aimed at abolishing the allegedly militaristic landlord class by transferring land ownership to the peasants, almost half of whom rented their land on some kind of tenancy. Absentee ownership was abolished and a ceiling was set upon the amount of land which could be held by a cultivator. As a result of the agrarian reform, about four million peasant households acquired new land and the proportion of cultivated land held under tenancy was reduced to 10 per cent. The big landowner disappeared from the rural scene with only a limited amount of compensation. The results of this land reform were far-reaching. Whilst consolidating a class of peasant proprietors, now able to retain a larger proportion of their product than before, it also loosened the ties of many villagers to the land. There was no longer much land available to rent and the peasant cultivators mainly depended upon family rather than hired labour. The fortunate peasants who now acquired land, or who no longer had to pay rent for it, could increase their purchases of consumer goods, as well as inputs for agriculture such as fertilizers and machinery.

Reform thus tended to have a two-fold action: it expanded the home market for industrial goods of the kind consumed by rural households, and it released labour for employment in the cities as it became available with economic recovery and expansion. The limited size of the home market, with its large low-income, rural component, had always been a factor shaping the development of Japanese capitalism, turning it towards external expansion. At the time of the reform, it is true, there was already a labour surplus rather than the reverse; over the longer period, however, it provided a reservoir of labour for continued industrialization in the 1950s and 1960s and without which industrialization would have been considerably impaired. It has to be remembered that at the end of the war the economy was still only partially industrialized. Approximately 50 per cent of the occupied population was still employed on the land. This was the main labour reserve of the industrialization process, when it began in earnest again in the 1950s. Between 1950 and 1970, the primary sector shed about ten million people, while employment in manufacturing industry rose from six million to almost fourteen million. Employment in electricity, gas, water, transport and communications rose from three million to over seven million. A considerable re-shaping of the contours of Japanese society took place in the course of this massive shift. There was further large-scale urbanization of a country which had hitherto been largely rural. The newcomers to industrial and urban employment had known only frugal living standards before; they were raw recruits with no tradition of organization and therefore excellent material for the industrial upsurge of the period.

Despite the effects of the war and the changes brought about by occupation policy, Japanese capitalism preserved many pre-war features which dated back to the Meiji era. Control of organized, large-scale industry continued to be highly concentrated and the attempt to dissolve the *zaibatsu* had been abandoned. The same firms and banks and, to a large extent, the same personnel, remained in charge. The reshuffling which did take place brought in younger and more pushing men, inspired by a vision of restoring Japan's position in the world by peaceful conquest, and who accepted that this had to be done in cooperation with the United States. Close relations between business and the administration had been maintained, and there was no question of establishing a laissez-faire economy. The question was where the line between the two should be drawn, the assumption being that the state should encourage, rather than hold back, the dynamism of the private sector. It had always been the role of the state to assist industry with the appropriate policy at home and abroad.

As we have seen, Japan entered the post-war period as a follower country, still only partially industrialized. As well as large labour reserves, available for transfer to more productive activities, it also had a large potential home market of some one hundred million people. Many of the techniques long incorporated into the industrial structure in the United States and other countries had hardly been applied as yet. There was, for example, no motor car industry to speak of and little production of modern consumer durables. Borrowing foreign technology had always been characteristic of Japanese development; with a war-shattered economy to be rebuilt, there was now more opportunity for it than ever. The field for potentially profitable investment seemed unlimited.

Meanwhile, the whole capitalist world, from the early 1950s, entered into an unprecedented long-term phase of expansion and prosperity which could only be favourable to a Japan aspiring to become the workshop of Asia and, indeed, the entire world. Economic aid in the form of capital and technology flowed in from the United States. Once expansion began, however, it tended to feed on itself with a very high rate of reinvestment of profits. Initial capital for new projects came from the already sophisticated banking and financial system. There was a high propensity to save, but significantly there was a wide gap between productivity gains and the rewards of labour. A politically conservative regime and the weak bargaining power of the trade unions in the early 1950s contributed to the creation of exceptionally favourable conditions for the accumulation of capital. Japan was poised to astonish the world; perhaps even those whose decisions had helped bring about the new surge of industrialization.

What was remarkable about the new phase which began in the 1950s was that growth took place at a rapid rate and was sustained for so long a period. Although at various times a slow-down or halt appeared likely, especially in the 1970s under the influence of the energy crisis and general world recession, the expansion continued. Expansion survived the Nixon shock of August 1971 and the oil shock of 1973–74, despite Japan's dependence on imported petroleum. When the growth of the other leading countries flagged in the late 1970s, Japan's industrial upsurge continued and further marked successes were scored with export products in the highly competitive world markets. By 1980, when the major American car manufacturers were all making losses, Japan had become the world's largest motor vehicle manufacturer, selling 1.8 million cars in the United States. Japanese products did not sell on cheapness but on quality, finish, reliability and high technology. This was true in the car market and also in such fields as consumer electronics and cameras. Japanese products held the leading position in many fields. The shipbuilding industry had grown to make good war-time losses and established itself as the largest in the world on the construction of super-tankers and bulk-carriers. Like some other sections of heavy industry, however, it did suffer from recession in the 1970s.

By the early 1960s, Japan's rapid resurgence had begun to attract the attention of outside observers who saw it as one of the most astonishing success stories of all time. Now, after a further two decades of sustained growth, in contrast with the slow-down or stagnation of other industrial countries, the seriousness of the Japanese challenge is apparent to all. The sheer weight of Japanese competition has caused the collapse of some foreign industries, such as the manufacture of motor cycles in Britain. The same thing seems to be happening with motor cars, colour television and audio-visual sets. Japanese branch plants have spread from Asia into the United States and Europe.

At one time, Japanese experience might have been seen principally as a useful model for the 'developing' countries. Now it is more a case of whether the older, advanced countries will not have to learn from Japan if they are to grapple successfully with their own problems. For many, Japanese successes have seemed to be little short of miraculous and every aspect of Japanese society and culture has been scrutinized in an effort to discover the secret. Journalists describe the atmosphere in Japanese factories where busy and contented workers cooperate eagerly with solicitous managers in a joint effort to promote the firm's success. Bureaucrats and businessmen are depicted as working harmoniously together to promote growth industries and wind down declining ones for the greater glory, and prosperity, of the nation. The *sogo shoshas* (the general trading companies unique to Japan) are shown as linked to the markets of the world, with intricate communications networks which the intelligence services of other countries might envy, commanding trade flows with the precision of a military operation. The frugal Japanese are praised for devoting such a high proportion of their income to savings, making it possible for industry to maintain a high investment rate in new plant and machinery. Trade unions cooperate with management, and workers in a trade dispute go on working with a label in their button-hole rather than walk out. According to some, the secret is to be found in a peculiar psychological make-up derived from past patterns of social living. It is said that the Japanese are happy to work as a group and accept their role, be it ever so humble. Best-selling books and frequent newspaper articles drive home the same message: Japan is seen as a challenge, but also as a model; perhaps the alternative face of capitalism if it is to survive into the twenty-first century. An attempt has to be made to distinguish fact from fable in what tends to become a stereotype.

REASONS FOR SUCCESS

It is first necessary to demystify the economic history of modern Japan. Its rapid, and in terms of material output, highly successful, industrialization, can be explained on strictly economic grounds. Japan was able to take advantage of being a late-comer, both in the early preparatory stages of industrialization under Meiji and, once more, in the period from 1950. Sustained high rates of investment in modern, imported technology, together with abundant supplies of labour under conditions where capital was able to appropriate a major proportion of the gains in productivity, ensured continuous growth as long as markets could be found for increasing production. The high rates of investment ensured a market for capital goods and in turn extended the market for consumer goods industries and services of every kind. Assisted by world conditions, such as the Korean War boom and then the general expansion of world demand in precisely the type of commodity Japan's industry was able to supply, the economy was locked into a virtuous circle. Such a growth pattern was by no means unique; it was a classic case of what Marxists call 'expanded reproduction', the interesting question is why it went on for so long. It has to be added that growth is an imperative. The consequences of a halt could be very severe and could have cumulative effects throughout the economy, causing serious financial problems to an industrial and commercial structure based upon a pyramid of credit. For that reason, as some observers have pointed out, the Japanese economy resembles a cyclist who must continue pedalling or risk falling off.

When all this has been said, however, there remains the question of the specifically Japanese elements which conditioned the way in which economic forces worked themselves out. The cultural and social environment, if not exactly designed to promote industrialization, posed no obstacles to it of the kind found, for example, in the Indian caste system. The reforms carried out in the Meiji era had deliberately cleared the ground of left-overs from the past which might have impeded modernization as carried through at that time. Institutions necessary for industrialization were adopted and an infrastructure built to promote economic development. Then, and later, it is true, resources were diverted into expansionism and war: but not without some spin-off which may have assisted industrialization. There were no religious or caste barriers to the pursuit of material success, though this was not so much openly avowed, as seen as the result of working for the national interest. The pursuit of nationalist goals harmonized with the successful operation of a capitalist market economy which strengthened and enriched the business class. The strong state (appealing to traditional elements) and the healthy economy (for the modernizers) were goals which could command a wide consensus of approval. Japan had to overcome its inferiority to the foreigner by adopting his technology and doing better; it was a simple but compelling ideology.

The Japanese economy developed highly capitalist forms, but government policy played a vital role from the start of industrialization and continues to do so today. There was no intention of establishing a state-run economy, but rather a mercantilist-style symbiosis of state and private enterprise. In practical terms this meant an alliance, and one which did not always run smoothly. Different and often conflicting interests had to be harmonized through the state. In the 1930s, for instance, the influence of the military and part of the old ruling class geared the economy to expansionist aims. Some sections of business may have had doubts, foreseeing the dangers, but they hardly dared to oppose what was a patriotic course. After the war, similar alliances and compromises had to be made; it was generally accepted that the state had a positive role to play in coordinating economic development, laying down national guidelines and assisting business expansion. It did not always play its role very well and, in fact, played it best when it had least to do.

Post-war Japan was not exactly a classic free market economy, but it was highly favourable to business enterprise and capital accumulation. The state, and more generally the political set-up, encouraged this state of affairs. The two economic ministries – the Ministry of Finance and the Ministry of International Trade and Industry – had (and have) a considerable influence upon overall policy. Other ministries – Agriculture, Construction and Transport and Communications – are influential in their own spheres. In addition, there are other government bodies, notably the Economic Planning Agency (from 1955 onwards), which draw up perspective plans for the medium and long term. American specialists on Japan, upon whom we depend a good deal for our knowledge of the working of the system, tend to play down the role of the state for ideological reasons. On the other hand, the popular impression of Japan Inc., functioning efficiently under the harmonious direction of an alliance between bureaucrats and businessmen is equally suspect. Depending on the point of view, Japan can be depicted either as an example of free-market capitalism or as an economy guided by a benevolent and omniscient state.

In fact the exact situation eludes a simple definition. Certainly economic policy has had, and continues to have, a profound effect on the development of Japanese trade and industry, and the role of the Ministry of International Trade and Industry, while it may be exaggerated in some accounts, has been decisive. The Ministry works closely with business, itself highly organized in several associations, as much in an informal way as through legal enactments. The top men in business and administration share a common social and educational background. Together they have, in a sense, inherited from the generals and admirals of the past a mission to make Japan great and prosperous, though now by peaceful conquest.

Relations between the different ministries, and those between the state and industry, are not always harmonious. Nor are the ministries at all infallible. Planners have not had real power to shape the course of economic development; the major economic decisions have mostly been taken by business. On the other hand, business has looked to government for support where necessary; it assumes its backing and expects that its own activities form part of a concerted economic policy for which the state is responsible. Leading ministers have been solicitous of business interests. Japanese still recall with bitterness General de Gaulle's description of Prime Minister Ikeda as 'a transistor salesman'. The state is expected to protect the home market, to support the export drive, to prevent foreign capital from getting too much of a foothold and to assist industries in difficulty. The total outcome has been a relationship specifically Japanese, elusive and ambiguous, pragmatic rather than doctrinaire. The state sector proper remains smaller than in most other capitalist countries, but the state's influence seems wholly pervasive. It is doubtful whether Japanese industrialization would have proved so successful had it not been for the constant support of the state bureaucracy.

When the early steps were being taken towards recovery and new industrial resurgence in the early 1950s, this support from the state was particularly necessary. The many crucial decisions made at this stage helped to shape the future course of development and, by accident or design, ensured rapid growth. For instance, decisions had to be made about which sectors of industry should be encouraged or promoted. Japan's pre-war industrial pattern and comparative advantage at that time would have suggested a concentration on textiles and light consumer goods industries. However, an analysis of trends in world trade, and observation of the industrial structure of more advanced industrial economies, showed that the market for these industries would be unlikely to expand rapidly. With rising incomes, world demand was changing, with such commodities as consumer durables coming to the fore. Industrial development was also creating a demand for machinery and Japan had, of course, to renew its shipping tonnage almost from scratch. Thus the decision was made to direct investment towards future demand, to adopt a dynamic view of comparative advantage and to promote highly capital-intensive, high-technology, 'heavy' industry (the Japanese classification including not only means of production industries but also the consumer goods' industries based upon advanced technologies). These were, then, the industries whose products were expected to be in future demand. This did not mean that the more traditional, or light, consumer goods industries were neglected; it was rather that they could not be counted upon for future sustained growth, especially export-led growth.

Decisions of this kind, which might not have been made had market forces been allowed to determine the allocation of resources, seem to have been crucial for future success. They assumed state support for new investments and especially for the development of new technologies imported from abroad. The way was also cleared for the entry of a new generation of entrepreneurs in fields such as electronics, cameras, motor cycles and other products which were soon to flood the markets of the world.

From the 1950s, therefore, a new heavy industrial complex began to take shape, changing the very landscape around Japan's great cities. Iron and steel, shipbuilding and heavy engineering, building on a pre-war basis, took a leading role. They could equip other industries in Japan and in a period of world boom there was a constantly growing market overseas. A petrochemical and oil-refining industry came into existence. A whole new range of more labour-intensive industries producing 'new' consumer goods came on the scene and made their products – cameras, optical instruments, transistor radios, TV sets, motor cycles and, more recently, motor vehicles – famous throughout the world.

As in many fields Japanese industry was a relative newcomer, its machinery embodied technology often in advance of that of its competitors. Where success in foreign markets enabled profits to be increased they were ploughed back into a continuation of the process. While the home market was growing, much of it could be supplied by the small- and medium-sized enterprises of a more traditional sort. The new large-scale modern plants needed foreign markets for continuous growth and new investment.

It was fortunate for some industries, and for the economy as a whole, that the Korean War and an intensification of the Cold War took place at about this time (the early 1950s) when the new industrial drive was beginning. American military spending and stock-piling meant orders for machinery, steel, chemical products and armaments. Japan became a forward military base and arsenal for operations in Korea. In April 1952, Occupation was formally ended, but Japan was still strategically linked to the United States through the US-Japan Security Treaty. Japan was now permitted, once again, to have its own armed forces.

Already, during the 1950s, some Japanese products had begun to establish a strong position in foreign markets. The subsequent growth of exports and foreign trade was, because Japan's growth depended absolutely upon the ability to import raw materials and energy supplies, backed up by the general trading companies, or *sogo soshas*, which have no real parallel in other countries. They established control over more than half the country's import-export trade. Hard selling abroad, bulk-buying, detailed and up-to-date market information supplied by their own communications networks, made them a key factor in Japan's industrial expansion. The *sogo soshas* represented a new concentration of economic power, parallel to the *zaibatsu* to which they were related. They acted as bankers, financing trade flows, insurers, warehousers and distributors. Today they have a strong position in relation to suppliers and their knowledge of foreign markets makes them indispensable for all but the largest firm.

In unravelling the sources of Japan's industrialization it is clear that they were multiple and complex. Partly the product of past development and peculiarities in the Japanese social structure, their working out also depended on favourable international conditions and the ability to exploit them. The relationship between government and business, already described, made possible an empirical adaptation to circumstances and created a climate favourable to continued growth. A virtuous spiral thus came into being, tending to perpetuate growth through high profits and high investment levels and generate the forces able to overcome adverse changes as for instance, the Nixon shock of 1971, the oil shock of 1973–74, and the world recession of the later 1970s.

As we have seen, the conditions under which industry recovered from the war and entered on a new stage of expansion endowed it with a high proportion of modern, technologically advanced plant. This established a bias favourable to continued technological change; scientific and technological developments were thus closely followed and bought or borrowed from abroad. The abundant labour supply which had characterised the 1950s and had figured as an important condition for growth largely disappeared as surplus labour was absorbed and fresh supplies from the countryside dwindled. Industry thus tended to move on to a more capital-intensive programme, with a higher level of technology, especially in electronic-related fields and motor vehicles. Indeed, Japanese firms began shunting the more labour-intensive processes off onto branch plants in other countries where labour was still cheap, while concentrating on capital-intensive processes at home. Difficulties arising from the oil crisis, notably a balance of trade deficit, were met by still more aggressive exporting. With the onset of world recession, some of the most successful industries of the 1960s, such as shipbuilding, had to contract. Adaptation continued with industry moving swiftly into more sophisticated branches of electronics, computers, robotization, industrial biology and other science-linked fields. It is difficult not to see here a concerted industrial strategy, absent in most other capitalist countries. Undoubtedly it involves great risks, assuming, in particular, that there will be a growing market at home and, as always, in the outside world as well. The keynote of Japanese response to the recession has therefore been: try harder and keep ahead of the competition. Other countries have responded with caution, contraction and protectionism, thus tending to worsen the situation rather than provide means for overcoming the problems. By keen entrepreneurial behaviour and continued investment in high technology – often financed by bank lending – productivity gains have been made which have kept Japanese products highly competitive, notably in the success of the car export drive in Europe and the United States. So far the gamble has paid off, but still it rests on a precarious basis, particularly on the highly-geared financial structure of many Japanese firms and the dependence for profitability upon continued market growth.

The period since the 1950s has seen further remarkable changes in Japanese society. There has been a massive growth of cities and a decline in the rural population, creating many new problems such as traffic congestion, pressure on public transport, atmospheric and environmental pollution. Incomes and consuming power have risen; Japan has ceased to be a low-wage economy. This has meant higher living standards, but the pressures of urban living have also increased. Basic to economic growth has been a shift of resources from less to more productive uses. Until the end of the 1970s there was still scope for this process to continue, but the possibilities may be narrowing. However, although it is clear enough that Japan is a much more affluent society than it was in the 1950s and that the masses have gained, the lion's share of productivity gains have gone to capital. The weakness of the independent labour movement, its willingness to accept compromise rather than confrontation, has contributed to this. Employers in other countries may look enviously at Japan's harmonious labour relations, but there is no guarantee that they will remain that way.

Business remains highly concentrated and has probably become more so over the past decade or so. The dualism which has long characterized Japanese industry remains deeply-rooted. Small- and medium-sized firms continue to produce a wide range of light manufactured goods, largely for the home market, but also partly for export. They are widely employed at first, or even second or third remove, as sub-contractors for the big firms. There has been a marked tendency for the small- and medium-sized firms to bear the brunt of the depression; paying higher prices for their inputs and accepting lower prices for their products. The smaller firms, in particular, have had to accept lower profit margins and their bankruptcy rate has been high. Moreover, as the large firms face difficulties in markets for existing products, there has been a tendency for them to diversify, sometimes into fields previously dominated by the smaller firms. On the other hand, the specialization made possible by the sub-contracting system has advantages which the big firms would not like to lose. Industrial dualism seems likely to continue, though its form will undoubtedly change, to the disadvantage of the small- and medium-sized firms.

Wages and working conditions in the smaller firms tend to be less favourable than in the big firms: workers cannot count upon lifetime employment or retirement pensions. Few of them belong to trade unions and wage levels tend to be forced down below price increases. The smallest firms depend upon the family and its relations for labour. Others have been facing recession by increasing part-time employment of retired workers and married women. Something like half of the industrial labour force is affected by these conditions – a fact often overlooked when praise is lavished upon Japanese labour relations and working arrangements. Of course, there are big differences between enterprises in this sector. Some smaller manufacturers have adopted new technologies, extended their product range and gained ground. Since the 1950s, productivity gains appear to have been larger in the small- and medium-sized sector than in large-scale industry. The former have also been able to obtain credit from the banks. Perhaps the gap between the more efficient smaller firms and large-scale organized industry was narrowing, giving scope for further increases in output and productivity. The recession from the late 1970s may have checked this process; the big firms have sought to maintain their profits at the expense of their smaller competitors and have driven harder bargains with their sub-contractors.

Japanese industrialization has maintained a momentum which has pushed it ahead of most of its rivals. Thrusting and aggressive sales policy, efficient organization and scientific management have all made their contribution. None of the elements of Japan's success have been trade secrets. Indeed, the Japanese firms often simply copied the best techniques of other countries, and adapted them to their own needs. Their models, in the main, were drawn from the United States; subsequently they were able to penetrate the American market, as well as competing successfully with American and other foreign firms in third markets. The general dynamism of the economy, the lack of any serious domestic social or political challenge to the dominant cliques in politics and business have no doubt facilitated the process of expansion, giving Japanese capitalism its distinctive identity in the post-war period.

In a sense this process could be described as production for production's sake, bearing in mind that high profits are necessary for the dominant firms to justify continued investment at a high rate. Dedicated company men, seconded by their counterparts in the economic ministries, have master-minded the industrial effort after the style of an operation of war. As in war, there are wastes and casualties and the environment bears the marks of battle. In the interest of continued profitable expansion, caution tends to have been thrown to the winds. The big corporations have taken risks, but their risks have also been spread and hedged by their own diversified structures. Resort to bank lending and inflationary finance has been used on a scale which would have been regarded as most imprudent in many other countries. Government spending has regularly exceeded tax revenues, making the Japanese economy one of the most highly indebted in the world. On the other hand, it is an internal debt. It has been a cardinal policy of Japan to avoid dependence upon foreign capital, whereas other economic 'miracles', such as those of South Korea and Brazil, have entailed enormous foreign debts. Apart from the oil companies, the foreign MNCs have generally failed to establish much of a position in Japan, and when they have done so, domestic finance or control has often been present. On the other hand, the growing financial strength of Japanese corporations has enabled them to open their own branch plants in many countries, including the United States and Western Europe.

Japanese firms displayed considerable resilience in the face of the sometimes violent economic changes of the period from 1974. Serious recession or stagnation were averted. Depressed industries were run down but new, high-tech industries continued to grow. Some labour-intensive processes were transferred to other, low-wage Asian countries. The main anti-crisis response was an intensified drive for markets, especially in the high-income countries of Western Europe and North America. These markets became indispensable for the continued growth of the Japanese economy; at the same time, building up current account surpluses available for investment in branch plants or the purchase of stocks and bonds and real estate. The home market grew slowly, though there was some shift to services, but formal or informal protective barriers restricted imports. The Japanese continued to manifest a high propensity to save, a tendency which was perhaps reinforced by the ageing of the population. The American government continued to exert pressure on Japan to lower trade barriers and to expand internal demand, with little success.

At the same time the economy was showing signs of 'maturity'. The phase of technological catching-up had come to an end. Wages and costs had risen while production had grown in countries like South Korea and Taiwan. Japan was no longer a high-growth country; a steady rate of around 4 per cent was the best that could be expected. The huge trade surpluses and the savings habits of the population had made Japan a capital-rich country seeking new investment fields. As a major creditor, increasingly integrated into the world market, with powerful multinational corporations operating on a world scale, Japan was thrust into a new and unaccustomed position for which neither government or business seemed to be fully prepared. The appreciation of the yen in 1987–88 was an omen of possible difficulties to come, notably by making exports more expensive. In the past, industry has faced up to such a challenge by cutting profit margins and cutting costs. While many countries, including the United States, are being urged to adopt austerity programmes to deal with their economic problems, the Japanese are being told to save less and consume more, for their own good as well as that of others. Because Japan has an inefficient and protected agriculture, food is more expensive than it might be. Even if food prices came down, for example by admitting more American farm products, it is not certain that this would open up a market for manufactured goods on a scale which might substitute for sales abroad. Because of lack of space and the small scale of houses and apartments, there is a limit to the number of consumer durables and cars that the home market can absorb. Rising incomes are likely to go into more savings and services. There is room for much more social spending on the part of the government: a prescription which runs contrary to the currently prevailing trend towards liberalization and less state intervention in the capitalist world and is not likely to find favour in Tokyo.

SOCIAL COSTS

The emphasis on production, the subtle propaganda effort to create and maintain a consensus built around the assumption that what is good for the big corporations is good for all Japanese, has meant that social goals have been given low priority. Consequently, industrialization has been attained at a social cost which is not taken into account in the overheads of firms or in the enthusiastic accounts of foreign journalists. Japan has one of the most serious problems of environmental disruption and atmospheric pollution of any country in the world. Industrial and urban sprawl have ravaged large areas of the countryside. The rapid pace and increasing strain of urban living have caused health hazards, psychological disorders and a high suicide rate. While industry has been capable of turning out a huge volume of consumer goods, housing standards have remained low for the wage-earners. The still poor working standards and inadequate wages, as well as the exploitation of women workers, especially in the smaller firms, has to be measured against the rise in real wages, and relatively good conditions found in the organized industrial sector. Thus rapid industrialization has had some profoundly disturbing social consequences in modern Japan.

The major question for the future is whether the phenomenal industrial upsurge will continue and, if so, what will be its effects for Japan and for the world. Will Japan become the number two, or even number one industrial power? Is it the super-state of the future, the alternative form of capitalism from which other countries in the capitalist world will have to learn if they are to survive? The study of history provides no answers to these questions, but the answers that are given will affect the destiny of the whole of mankind in the twenty-first century.

CHAPTER THREE
The Soviet model: a critical view

Soviet industrialization will remain enshrined in history as marking an epoch, by its scale, its rapidity, its unprecedented character and the heavy human costs involved. It was the first case of industrialization under centralized state direction in accordance with a predetermined plan. Since the outcome was the transformation of a relatively backward and predominantly agrarian country into an industrial giant, it became something of a model. Because a prerequisite for it had been a revolution which had dispossessed the landowners and capitalists and brought in its wake violence and repression, it stirred opposition and hostility abroad. Even those who were sympathetic to its declared aims followed its course with mixed feelings. Inevitably, therefore, Soviet industrialization has generated an enormous amount of interest and controversy which is still going on. Indeed, because of the nature of the regime established by Stalin in the 1930s, much of the history of the process is shrouded in secrecy and inextricably connected with the political struggles of the contemporary world.

EARLY INDUSTRIALIZATION

Until the Five Year Plans, the first of which began in 1928, the rate and character of economic development, and thus of industrialization, had been determined mainly by the laws of the market under conditions of private ownership of the means of production. Certainly, the state had never been entirely neutral and in some countries had played a positive role, assisting the accumulation of capital in various ways: protecting national industry, providing infrastructure, fostering technological change. Indeed, such had been the role of the state in pre-revolutionary Russia. Capitalist relations had not become established until the nineteenth century. The Industrial Revolution came to Russia as an import, not as an autonomous process. Industrialization, when it began, had been largely a product of state policy, rather than of the free working of market forces. To that extent there was a certain continuity between the Tsarist regime and revolutionary Russia after 1917. In the scales of history, however, this factor surely weighed little compared with the sharp break with the past represented by the Bolshevik Revolution of 1917.

It has been the fate of the territory of the Russian Empire and the Soviet Union to be a vast laboratory for the testing out of economic theories and programmes. By the time capitalist relations began to develop on an appreciable scale, in the second half of the nineteenth century, Russian intellectuals were able to make a more conscious appraisal of the implications than had been possible in countries which had developed earlier. There were those who wished to see an accelerated capitalist development; others feared the consequences for Russia and sought either to block its path or propose alternatives. In any case, with the industrialization of West European countries, the Tsarist regime itself found its previous position of power in Europe undermined by the backward economic base upon which Russian society rested.

Until after the Emancipation of 1861, the mass of the Russian peasantry, which comprised the great majority of the population, remained in one or other category of serfdom. The upper class of landowners, the governmental machinery, the army and the court depended upon the surplus extracted from these unfree peasants either from the labour performed on the large estates producing for the market, or from the payments in cash or kind exacted from the serfs tilling their own strips of land. Peasant agriculture was of low productivity and, once dues and taxes had been paid, the peasantry could buy little in the market.

The lack of a mass internal market had, as a counterpart, the low level of development of industry, the small size of the merchant class and the weakness of the urban bourgeoisie. These features of backwardness were reinforced by the large distances separating complementary raw materials and producers from potential markets. By the 1830s and 1840s, Russia was receiving the Industrial Revolution as an import, chiefly in the form of textile machinery and, later, other technology including the railway. Such imports continued throughout the century and until 1914, but, although they endowed Russia with a modern industrial sector, they could not bring about an all-round structural transformation in the society and economy as a whole. Such a transformation revolved around the massive agrarian sector and thus raised the question of serfdom and, after emancipation, of the fate of the peasantry.

The first sign of modern industry in Russia, the growth of a cotton textile industry, was a spontaneous response to market forces, but they were quite inadequate to initiate a reshaping of the economy as a whole on West European lines. Indeed continued industrialization in other European states exposed the relative economic backwardness of Russia, thus jeopardizing the political ambitions of the Tsarist regime. The Crimean War of 1854–56 demonstrated the growing disparity of forces in a dramatic way. This posed a new problem for the government which it never succeeded in resolving until its downfall. If Russia was to remain a great power, fundamental changes had to be made in the economy, and at the same time in the social structure. Industry had to be built up, which meant an increase in the social weight of the bourgeoisie and the creation of an urban proletariat. Agrarian relations had to be changed by abolishing serfdom and giving more scope to the development of capitalist relations in the agrarian sector. Modernization would have to take place in every field, thus opening the way for Western influences such as liberalism, democracy, and socialism. The changes necessary to enable Russia to remain a great power meant the intrusion of forces likely to challenge the social dominance of the landowning class and the autocratic rule of the Tsar, with which it was inextricably bound up.

After the Crimean War it became clear to the Tsar and his advisors that some reforms, however undesirable, were necessary for the survival of the regime. The most significant reform was the emancipation of the serfs, announced in the edict of 1861. As it turned out, the change disappointed the serfs as well as their owners; it was carried into effect by stages, left the traditional peasant village (the *mir*) intact, and effected no rural revolution. Most peasants were more or less tied to the soil; as a class they lost land; the landlord estates remained and former serfs had to purchase their freedom. The regime dared not emancipate the peasants without land, and it did not redistribute land in such a way as to create a viable land-owning peasantry. With some exceptions, the former serfowners were ill-prepared for the role of innovating landlords or entrepreneurs. Capitalist relations slowly penetrated the villages, leading to differentiation within the ranks of the peasantry. Some, later to be known as *kulaks*, turned towards production for the market, becoming employers of labour, moneylenders and grain dealers. Those with little or no land became a rural labour reserve for the estate farmers and kulaks. In between were the mass of the peasants, struggling to support themselves and their families on insufficient land and with backward methods. As village ties loosened and the *mir* lost some of its hold, more of the younger people moved off to find work in the city, though often retaining links with their native villages. In short, in many different ways, the peasant village was drawn into market relations. The hope that the village community could provide the foundation for some kind of agrarian socialism had waned by the end of the nineteenth century.

The peasant problem remained to haunt Tsarism. Meanwhile, under pressure of international competition, the state had taken a series of steps to modernize society. Railways began to open up Russia's natural resources and strengthen its ties with the world market via the export trade. Foreign capital was attracted both to finance the growing expenditure of the government, especially on armaments, and to establish new industries. During the period in which Sergei Witte was Finance Minister, the state played a decidedly forward role, through tariff protection, railway building and the granting of contracts on favourable terms to business firms. During the 1890s, Russia experienced its first big industrial spurt largely supported by government spending and promotion. It proved to be short-lived as there was insufficient impetus, in the shape of a growth of the home market, to encourage big investments of private capital. The boom faltered and the early years of the twentieth century were difficult. The economic slow-down encouraged an adventurous foreign policy in Manchuria and Korea, leading to the disastrous clash with Japan in 1904 and the failed Revolution of 1905.

The spurt of the 1890s had already begun to endow Russia with a modern industrial sector embodying the most advanced technology imported from the leading capitalist countries. In the years leading up to the outbreak of war in 1914, this industrial sector went through further rapid growth concentrated in a few main centres. Plants were built on a large scale and on the most up-to-date lines in such fields as iron and steel, engineering and armaments. Correspondingly there was a growth in the size of the industrial proletariat, particularly heavily concentrated in large plants and a few great industrial centres. There had also been a growth in the railway and transport system, though these were still very inadequate for Russia's needs, where large numbers of wage-earners were employed. Although new drafts of industrial workers were being recruited from the countryside as industry expanded, there was now a growing hereditary proletariat in the towns. While still greatly outnumbered by the huge peasant mass, this concentrated urban working class played a crucial role in the Revolutions of 1917 and was the main social force behind the Bolsheviks when they took power in November of that year.

Continued industrial growth was not sufficient to overcome Russia's backwardness and the gap with the leading capitalist countries widened in the quarter of a century before the First World War. Average income per capita and the growth of national income as a whole were held back by the poor performance of the agrarian sector, still dominated by the small-peasant economy. The peasant revolts in 1905 induced the regime to change its policy on the agrarian front in the series of measures, known after the Interior Minister Stolypin, which aimed to create a prosperous peasantry. The intention was to enable peasants to leave the *mir* and to pursue individual farming on their own plots separated from the village lands. These peasant proprietors, able to farm for the market, would, it was hoped, enjoy prosperity and be pillars of the regime in the countryside. There had already been some growth of peasant capitalism. The state now put its weight behind this development, abandoning the idea, current after 1861, that the commune was a factor of stability. In the nature of things, the Stolypin reforms were bound to take some time to work themselves out and were overtaken by the war. In any case, they could not solve the agrarian problem. Population was growing rapidly and land hunger was acute in many places. Besides, although the gentry had been selling off lands or leasing them to peasants, they still retained large amounts which were regarded with covetous peasant eyes.

Although capitalist relations had made substantial inroads into Russian agriculture, there had been no structural transformation and the fate of the peasantry remained to be determined. An advanced modern industry had been built up, with all that that entailed, but it was confined to a few areas. Russia was still dependent upon the more advanced countries for most kinds of machinery and for the more sophisticated manufactured products. The home market was still dominated by a mass of peasant households able to buy only the cheaper consumer goods and a few essentials for housekeeping and husbandry. Change in the agricultural sector was particularly slow and a healthy basis for industry was still missing. Industrialization as a process affecting the whole of society, capable of diminishing the weight of agriculture, had hardly begun. In one sense, though, pre-war Russia experienced pseudo-industrialization, as industry remained an imported product, an enclave development in a predominantly peasant agrarian society.

THE REVOLUTION AND ITS AFTERMATH

This was the social-economic system which broke down under the strain of the First World War, carrying away the political superstructure of Tsarism and creating the conditions for revolution. Russia experienced all the typical wartime problems, made worse by the weaknesses of some sectors of the economy. There were serious distribution problems and scarcities resulting from breakdowns in the transport system and the cutting off of trade connections. Government administration of the war machine was inefficient and broke down under stress. The Russian divisions were lightly armed and poorly supplied, reflecting the backwardness of the economy. Inflation, food shortages and unemployment inflamed working class feeling against the government. Badly-equipped troops suffered defeat and demoralization. Confronted by a growing wave of hostility and unable to cope with the organization of a modern war, the Tsarist regime was swept away by the spontaneous mass movement of March 1917. The Provisional Government which took its place, since it wanted to keep Russia in the war, was forced into unpopular measures and steadily lost the support of the urban workers to the energetic leaders of the Bolshevik Party led by Lenin and Trotsky. Meanwhile, the long-pent-up anger of the peasants burst out all over the country in a manner reminiscent of France in 1789. Taking matters into their own hands, they seized and divided up the landed estates of the gentry. It seemed that the agrarian problem would be solved along the lines of the Great French Revolution, by the creation of a class of peasant proprietors. Recognizing the need for an alliance with the peasantry, Lenin endorsed the peasant actions in line with a policy worked out some years before. It was, indeed, essential if the seizure of power by the Bolshevik-led workers in the towns in November 1917 was to succeed in establishing a viable government.

The taking of power by the Bolsheviks ended a period of 'dual power' in which the Provisional Government, looking towards a parliamentary system, was confronted by soviets (committees or councils) which had taken over much of the real power in the factory districts, the army and in the villages. After November, the central government was controlled by the Bolshevik leadership, but its ability to govern was determined by the soviets and other local institutions.

The leaders of the new regime, while taking advantage of Russian conditions in order to seize power, were internationalist in outlook and assumed optimistically that before long capitalism would collapse in the belligerent countries and that working-class governments would follow their example. They fully understood Russia's economic weaknesses as deriving from a predominantly peasant country, and they had no illusions about the attitude of the peasants towards socialism. They hoped that if they held out until the revolution spread to the more advanced countries, Russia would be able to obtain economic and technical aid to speed economic growth and raise living standards. They did not believe that a socialist society could be built unaided in a backward country such as Russia, though they did accept that the necessary first steps should be to take into state ownership the 'commanding heights' of economy: the banks, the mines, and the main industrial concerns. Even so, the Bolsheviks began cautiously; there were fears that capitalist owners and managers could not readily be replaced from the ranks of the working class and intelligentsia sympathetic to the new regime. However, as far as that goes, the workers tended to take matters into their own hands much as the peasants had done, taking over their places of work and arresting or chasing away their former bosses. The government was thus, in effect, obliged to endorse these moves by speedy blanket measures of nationalization, also extended to the land.

Although, under pressure, the new Bolshevik government rapidly laid the legal foundations for a socialist society their hopes for a spread of the revolution were to prove illusory. Instead, they soon found themselves fighting a civil war against those who wished to restore Tsarism and, in addition to this, they were surrounded by hostile capitalist states. In the struggle for survival, the economic measures taken were geared mainly to the needs of the situation. Although glorified under the title of War Communism these measures were basically those of a siege economy in which the demands of the front came first. However, they were also measures of a kind which could only have been taken by a government determined to carry through a revolution in property relations and thus to lay the basis for a socialist society. There could be no question of pursuing a policy of industrialization at this stage; indeed, it was impossible to prevent a further running down of the economy under conditions of civil war.

Food supply constituted a major problem. The peasant revolution meant that the cultivators were now able to retain a larger proportion of what they produced. The landlord estates no longer provided a marketable surplus because they had been divided up among the peasantry. In fact, free rein had been given to agrarian individualism and this heightened class differentiation. The Bolsheviks had little support or influence in the villages but they depended upon the peasants to provide food (and some industrial raw materials) for the towns and the armies engaged in the civil war. The *mir* generally retained its powers and tended to be dominated by the richer peasants. There was practically no interest in collective farming and only a few such farms were formed. Since industrial production had declined catastrophically and the civil war had priority claims, there were few goods available to supply the peasants and to induce them to part with surplus grain. Consequently, in 1919–20 'surplus' grain was requisitioned by force and peasants were ordered to carry out sowing plans to supply the government. This policy caused growing discontent and some peasant revolts in 1920. By this time, the White armies were being driven back and the Civil War was nearly over.

Industrial policy during the period of War Communism was determined by the priority needs of the army. Control over industry was centralized in a state organ, the Supreme Council of National Economy (VSNKh according to its Russian initials). The main nationalized industries were grouped into 'trusts' responsible to VSNKh. The shortage of raw materials became increasingly acute, forcing the closure of many factories, or the concentration of production in the most efficient. Many workers joined the newly-formed Red Army in the civil war, or were drawn off into the administration of the Party and the state. With food shortages acute and factories closing down, other workers drifted back to their villages of origin. Payment of wages sometimes took the form of products manufactured in the factory to be bartered and sold on the black market. There were even cases of workers dismantling their factories and selling the bits and pieces. Nothing could stop the industrial decay which reduced total production in 1921 to one-third of its 1913 level.

By the time the Civil War ended, the economy was close to collapse. The working class was decimated and exhausted; the peasantry sullen and discontented. Inflation was rampant and parts of the country were stricken by famine and disease. Normal exchanges between village and town had practically ceased. Control by the soviets was largely superseded by centralization and the setting up of a command structure on military lines opening the way for bureaucratic distortions. The consolidation of the party and state apparatus which began under War Communism did not end with it.

The end of the policy of War Communism was in response to the peasant opposition to the requisitioning of grain. A 'retreat' was called for, with the adoption in August 1921 of the New Economic Policy. In the face of peasant resistance and a tired and disillusioned working class, Russia did not have the resources, human or material, to make a forced march towards socialism. Above all, the failure of the revolution to spread, the ability of the capitalist states to survive the war and to begin the reconstruction of their own economies, shattered the hope that the working class of the advanced countries of Europe would come to the aid of backward Russia. Lenin and his colleagues were thus confronted with an entirely unexpected and unwelcome prospect. Although the Red Army had thrown back the forces of intervention, the new revolutionary regime was left alone and isolated, a pariah state in a hostile world for an unknown period until the revolutionary movement in the capitalist countries became strong enough to take power. Moreover, while the peasants had no wish to see the old regime restored and the return of the gentry, they were strongly opposed to the policies of War Communism and, as the source of the vital food supplies, held a strong card which the regime would ignore at its peril.

THE NEW ECONOMIC POLICY

If War Communism was determined by military considerations and had been accompanied by serious mistakes and not a few illusions, the New Economic Policy (NEP) came to grips with the grim realities of Russia's predicament. Like the policies which were to follow it, it accepted that, at any rate for the time being, Russia would be isolated. A compromise thus had to be made with the peasantry, and the dynamic of market forces and individual acquisitiveness had to be temporarily harnessed to the over-riding tasks of economic reconstruction, rather than of conducting a civil war. These were bitter pills for a Party committed to socialism to swallow, but there seemed to be no alternative. Clear differences began to appear within the Communist Party after the New Economic Policy came into operation; about how long the policy should last, and what should take its place. It was thus in the 1920s that the question of the type and tempo of industrialization appropriate for Russian conditions was debated at the highest level and with comparative freedom. All the issues pertaining to economic growth were discussed at length well before they began to interest Western economists.

Before 1914, Marxists had generally assumed that those countries in which capitalist development had reached the most advanced stage would be the ripest for revolution, and thus for the construction of a socialist society. The fact that the revolution had come first in one of the least-developed European countries, in which not the working class but the peasantry constituted the majority of the population, was disconcerting for many socialists inside and outside Russia. To some it seemed that the new regime would have to undertake the task of primitive accumulation assigned historically to the bourgeoisie and that the outcome would not be socialism but some kind of capitalism. This was obviously not the view of the Bolsheviks. At least until Stalin enunciated the doctrine of 'socialism in one country' at the end of 1924, all tendencies in the Party held that while Russia could take steps on the road to socialism, they were the vanguard of an international movement and that sooner or later the spread of revolution to other countries would enable them to break out of their isolation. Moreover, the Bolsheviks took the lead in splitting the socialist movement precisely on the point of activating the world revolution and breaking with the narrow nationalist conceptions of the old leaderships of the Second International, revealed on the outbreak of war in the summer of 1914.

It is sometimes forgotten by those who write the economic history of the Soviet Union that at this stage the tasks of the Soviet regime in Russia were seen as part of a larger strategy laid down by the Communist International. It was this strategy which was to resolve the dilemma provoked by the isolation of the first working-class revolution in a backward, predominantly peasant country. This belief made the retreat of 1921 more acceptable than it might otherwise have been.

Marxists were agreed, however, that a condition for socialism was the fullest possible development of the productive forces. This meant the application of advanced technology to agriculture as well as industry, the building up of modern large-scale industry and the raising of the skills of the working population through the maximization of educational possibilities. These were part means, part ends in making possible the improvement of living standards and the all-round fulfilment of the capacities of every member of society. It was agreed, moreover, that socialism, like capitalism, was by its nature an international system, particularly so because the abolition of scarcity as far as the essentials of life were concerned could hardly be brought about on the basis of the limited resources of any single country, however large, and certainly not of a backward country such as Russia.

For the Marxists, industrialization was an indispensable part of the march to socialism, a part which could begin in a relatively backward country, even one surrounded by hostile states. It required, of course, the nationalization of the major industries; not in itself socialism, but a step in that direction already taken early in the Russian revolution. Once the main industries were nationalized, the allocation of resources and decisions about what was to be produced could not be left to market forces. There would, in other words, have to be some centrally-determined plan. Here again, early on, the revolutionary regime in Russia had begun to set up central organs to direct the economy.

It can be said, therefore, that in Russia there was an inseparable and necessary connection between the building of socialism, and the beginnings of industrialization and planning. There could be no industrialization which was not planned; the object of planning was to make possible faster industrialization, which in turn, was a necessary basis for socialism; the plan was the instrument through which the material basis would be laid. Industrialization under these conditions was thus different in some fundamental respects from industrialization in the capitalist countries. Above all, it was to take place consciously and not in response to the blind forces of the market. Ostensibly, Soviet industrialization was intended to make possible the realization of the socialist goal, raising the living standards of the entire people by increasing the supply of use values; capitalist industrialization, on the other hand, had been geared to the drive for profit for the owners of the means of production through the increase of exchange values. Capitalist industrialization had been preceded by a phase of 'primitive accumulation', which included the forcible expropriation of the peasantry from the land,

and had been accompanied by the mobilization of an industrial proletariat constrained to accept a low level of consumption and harsh living conditions. The first generation or two of industrial workers derived few benefits from economic growth; and even if there were some, they were far less than those accruing to other classes. While recognizing the progressive character of capitalist industrialization and thus its necessity, Marxists had been equally at pains to demonstrate its dark side as part of the case for socialism. Presumably, therefore, if industrialization took place under socialist auspices it could be expected to have markedly different characteristics.

It should be remembered that the situation in the Soviet Union was by no means what socialists had expected. Not only was the country relatively backward, with a vast peasantry, but it had to face a hostile world, with an economy badly run down after years of war and civil war. The first task was to restore industry, repair the battered transport system, re-establish exchange between the country and the town and win the cooperation of the peasants. Only then could there be a resumption of industrialization or any hope of beginning the transition to socialism. In Lenin's conception of the NEP, temporary compromises would have to be made with capitalism at home by permitting market dealing and 'concessions' granted to foreign capitalists to operate on Russian soil until the revolution had spread to the more advanced countries.

By its control of the main industries, the monopoly of foreign trade, and the centralized bodies set up to control the economy, the state would be able to prepare the economic conditions for socialism. This meant not only reconstruction, but also making a start with long-term planning. The plan for electrification, enthusiastically supported by Lenin, and drawn up by a body of experts, began in 1921. In the same year Gosplan (the State Planning Commission) was set up to work out future economic plans. Such plans would clearly have to provide for investment in industry; just how much and where the resources were to come from remained to be decided and provided an essential part of the economic debates of the 1920s. Planned industrialization would require a high degree of centralized control. It would also require the accumulation of resources in the hands of the state. In the absence of foreign capital, these resources would have to come, to a very large extent, from the agrarian sector, from the peasantry who, under NEP, were once again able to produce for sale in the market once they had paid the 'tax in kind' to the state. There was an obvious contradiction, therefore, between the methods of the NEP and the requirements of planning.

In the first years of the NEP there were violent fluctuations in the relative prices of agricultural products and manufactured goods. Agricultural production had suffered less and recovered more quickly from the effects of civil war. The first year or two of the NEP saw agricultural prices rise more rapidly than industrial prices. In 1923 the opposite occurred; larger amounts of agricultural produce were placed on the market and prices came down while industrial prices were kept up. The result of what was called the 'scissors crisis' was that peasants withheld their produce from the market and refused to buy the high-priced industrial goods. In order to restore exchanges between town and countryside, state organs had to lower prices of industrial goods, but not before serious differences had arisen among those responsible for economic policy.

Many of these differences arose over the question of the policy to be adopted towards the peasantry. As a whole, the peasantry had gained from the Revolution, though mainly through its own efforts. Land had been seized from the gentry and redistributed, and the peasantry no longer had to pay rent to a landlord class. After 1924, taxes were fixed in money terms and produce had thus to be sold to meet this payment. On the whole, peasant families retained more of what they produced and, with the inflationary situation, were loath to sell unless there were goods which they wanted to buy. The way to induce the peasants to part with more of their produce seemed to lie, therefore, in increasing the output of consumer goods at prices which they were willing to pay. However, there was a danger that this would, in effect, enable the peasantry to determine the rate of industrialization. If the attempt was made to squeeze more out of the agrarian sector by turning the terms of exchange against agricultural produce, the peasants might strike back, as they had done during the scissors crisis, and refuse to sell. More to the point, if industrialization was to proceed once reconstruction had been completed, more resources would have to be channelled into heavy industry, meaning that there would be no corresponding increase in the output of consumer goods for some years. This meant that the peasants would be expected to feed the industrial workers in this branch of industry without receiving a corresponding return.

One wing of the Party, of whom Bukharin was the spokesman, wished to placate the peasantry by increasing the supply of consumer goods and accepting a slower rate of industrialization. Reliance would have to be placed upon market forces and material incentives, almost certainly to the advantage of the kulaks, the wealthier peasants, whose influence was already growing in the villages under NEP. Any attempt to squeeze more out of the peasantry by higher taxation or by manipulating prices against agricultural produce risked peasant hostility and reprisals.

In the disputes between factions within the Communist Party, following Lenin's death, Bukharin became the ally of Josef Stalin, the General Secretary and an increasingly powerful figure in the Party. The latter had, at first, gained the support of Zinoviev and Kamenev, two powerful party leaders, until serious differences arose over questions of policy, and especially over Stalin's theory of 'socialism in one country', first enunciated at the end of 1924, the year in which Lenin had died. Contrary to the generally accepted view in the Party during Lenin's lifetime, Stalin maintained that Russia had everything 'necessary and sufficient' for the building of socialism and did not have to depend upon the overthrow of capitalism in the advanced countries. Stalin's main support came from the apparatus-men of the Party and the state machine, anxious to consolidate their position and enjoy a quiet life after years of war and upheaval and with no stomach for foreign adventures. The failure of the revolution to spread led to disillusionment with the foreign Communist Parties and reinforced a strong nationalist current in the Russian Party which found an echo in the population.

The policy of 'socialism in one country' and the tendency towards bureaucratic control represented by Stalin, were opposed by Leon Trotsky and his followers, who formed what was known as the Left Opposition. This was later joined by Zinoviev and Kamenev and their followers, to form the United Opposition. Inner-party struggles reached their height in 1927; largely due to Stalin's control of the party machine, he was able to isolate, discredit and destroy the Opposition. The turn in economic policy, decided by Stalin in 1928–29, would not have been possible, and cannot be understood, in isolation from these political struggles.

Until the balance tipped decisively in Stalin's favour, in 1927, there was still a great deal of open and uninhibited debate about economic questions in the press and at Party gatherings. Planning was already on the way through the activities of Gosplan which published annual control figures to guide decisions by the industrial trusts and other state organs concerned with the economy. Although Stalin's views did not altogether coincide with those of Bukharin at this time, they were sufficiently close to make possible an alliance against the Opposition whose chief spokesmen were Trotsky himself and the economist Preobrazhensky. In the debates between 1924 and

1927, Preobrazhensky argued for a large-scale programme of rapid industrialization to be initiated as soon as possible. Just as capitalist industrialization had been preceded by a process of 'primitive accumulation', there was no alternative in Russian conditions to a similar pumping over of resources from the agrarian sector to industry without an equivalent return. Preobrazhensky described this as 'the law of primitive socialist accumulation'; it was, however, a theoretical concept worked out at a highly abstract level. As far as policy prescriptions drawn from it were concerned, they were intended to apply to the situation prevailing under the NEP. There was no intention to uproot the peasantry, to appropriate their land or to drive them into collective farms against their will. The 'law' simply meant that taxes and pricing policy should be used to transfer part of the surplus product of the private sector (of which peasant farming was the largest but not the only part) to the accumulation fund of socialized industry. It was assumed, also, that the latter would also provide for a portion of its own needs.

In its 1927 Platform the United Opposition set out its policies. These included: progressive taxes on the better-off peasants; support for the poorer peasants and peasants not employing wage labour against kulak influence; encouragement of agricultural cooperation, and the formation of collective farms on a voluntary basis to encourage maximum initiative from the peasants themselves. Obviously since this policy was not tried, its feasibility remains problematic; what is clear is that an alternative course to the one later to be followed had been put forward, but was rejected by the Stalinist leadership of the Party. As for the supporters of this policy, they were subsequently liquidated on Stalin's orders.

The Platform of 1927 advocated a policy of planned industrialization at a fast tempo. This would strengthen the relative position of the working class, enable agriculture to be supplied with machinery, undermine the position of the capitalist elements fostered by the NEP, make possible a raising of living standards and contribute to the defence needs of the country. At the time, this policy was rejected as being premature, if not actually wrong in principle, and the NEP continued more or less on Bukharinist lines until 1928.

Meanwhile, by 1926–27 industrial production had about reached its 1913 level. Existing industries were in need of new equipment and new branches had to be established. Whatever approach was adopted, it seemed certain that large-scale industry would have to play a leading role and that funds for accumulation would, therefore, have to be found. The planning authorities, Gosplan and

VSNKh, were strongly making this case. The outstanding question was how to bring the NEP to an end; but the real base of NEP was in the countryside. Could the wholehearted adoption of a policy of industrialization avoid breaking the pre-existing compromise with the peasantry, whilst transferring resources from agriculture to state industry along the lines recommended by Preobrazhensky and the Left Opposition?

The increased rate of capital construction in 1927–28 caused new strains, notably a 'goods famine', coupled with renewed reluctance on the part of the peasants to market their surplus grain (some of which they fed to livestock). Bukharin and those on the Right took this as a sign that too much pressure was being put on the peasants and that industrialization should be slowed down. With the Left Opposition already defeated, Stalin was now able to break with Bukharin and come forward as the advocate of rapid industrialization, while still attacking the Left for wishing to split with the peasantry. By the end of 1928, the Right had been routed and Stalin was talking about the need to 'catch up and surpass' the capitalist countries as being 'a life and death question'. Priority should thus be given to industrialization even though that might intensify the goods shortage for the time being and impose a strain upon the economy. What had been unacceptable two or three years before had now become acceptable because put forward by Stalin. It seems an inescapable conclusion that Stalin made this turn on political, rather than economic grounds, as part of a power struggle which he was determined to win.

THE FIVE-YEAR PLAN

The time was now ripe for the adoption of an ambitious Five-Year Plan for national economic construction which had been incubating in Gosplan for some time. Officially formulated in October 1928, it was not in fact presented and approved until the spring of 1929. The targets set and the tempos proposed greatly exceeded those of the maligned 'superindustrializers' of the Opposition in 1927. Even under the must favourable conditions they were bound to put a tremendous strain on the economy and on the working population. Although in the original Plan consumption was scheduled to increase, its most significant feature was the raising of net investment to a level between one-quarter and one-third of national income, three-quarters of which was to be in heavy industry. This was the beginning of the famous 'priority growth' of heavy industry, characteristic of the Soviet plans and even elevated into a 'law'. The justification for this priority was that until a machine-making industry was built up there could not be an expansion of consumer goods industry to make possible an increasing supply of consumer goods for a growing population. Thus resources had to be tied up for a considerable period of time in constructional projects of all kinds without making any contribution to the output of consumer goods. Present consumption needs were thus to be sacrified for the sake of the future. At the same time it was assumed that food and raw material supplies, as well as labour, would be forthcoming from the agrarian sector. It was here that the crisis broke.

Once the commitment to rapid industrialization had been made, there was little alternative to an onslaught on the peasantry, far more brutal than anything proposed by Preobrazhensky. From 1927, the government was having increasing difficulty in procuring grain from the rural areas. Relations with the peasantry deteriorated and the influence of the kulaks tended to grow. Various penalties were imposed upon peasants who failed to deliver grain. In retaliation, in 1929, some villages simply refused to supply any grain at all. The closing down of private trading and small artisan enterprises further antagonized many of the peasants.

The main issue was that just at the moment when the decision to industrialize called for regular and increased supplies from the agrarian sector, large numbers of peasants were refusing to cooperate. In a sense the regime was reaping the fruits of its previous policy of conciliating the peasants and even encouraging the kulaks – the policy associated with the now disgraced Bukharin (August 1929). As Stalin's stranglehold over the Party became more complete there was less and less scope for debate or discussion. Local officials tended to present a falsely optimistic picture because they feared being denounced as 'deviationists'. Inspired and personally led by Stalin, forcible procurements were organized in many parts of the Soviet Union in 1928–29. Then, without prior discussion or adequate preparation, Stalin launched the collectivization campaign, unleashing a storm in the Russian villages and bringing about an upheaval involving suffering and loss of life on a scale which has few precedents in history.

The first stage of collectivization, beginning in the summer of 1929, was ostensibly voluntary and concerned mainly the poor and middle-grade peasants. In practice, considerable administrative pressure was exerted on the peasants to form collective farms. The pace was accelerated, and the pressure increased; from November 1929, the whole process becoming increasingly arbitrary. At the same time, the policy was initiated of 'destroying the kulaks as a class'. Although this was supposed to be carried out by the poor and middle-grade peasants, as part of the class struggle in the village, it was generally spear-headed by workers' 'brigades' from the towns and the GPU (state security police). Kulaks were classified according to their degree of opposition to the regime. Some were arrested by the GPU, large numbers were deported, and others were assigned to poor quality land and not allowed to join the collective farms. Thousands of peasants who were far from being kulaks were classified as such, while others joined the collectives for fear of being treated as kulaks.

THE CONSEQUENCES OF COLLECTIVIZATION

The first mistake that Stalin and his supporters made was to under-estimate the tenacity with which the peasants would try to conserve the land they had secured as a result of the Revolution of 1917. They fought back against compulsory collectivization by slaughtering their animals, indulging in wild feasting, and by destroying property. The result was a disastrous fall in the numbers of farm animals, including horses needed for ploughing. This not only reduced the food supply directly, but it also meant a shortage of draught animals and a lack of manure for the newly-formed collective farms. Although the pace of collectivization was temporarily halted in the spring of 1930, and many peasants actually left the collective farms, the offensive against the kulaks was resumed in 1931–32. The human cost of the operation was incalculable. By the end of collectivization, millions of peasants had been deported hundreds of miles from their homes, many families were broken up and children abandoned. Large numbers of peasants were sent to forced labour camps. Others, for whom there was no place in the collectives, drifted into the towns to form part of the new labour army required for the Five-Year Plan. Many of the peasants who joined the collectives had done so against their will and resented the bureaucratic regime imposed upon them. They were, therefore, not interested in working hard or in making the farm a success. In any case, tractors and farm machinery were not available in sufficient quantities to raise the technical level of many collective farms above that of the peasant plots. Machines were often left to rust in the fields, tractors broke down and could not be repaired or fuel supplies were insufficient. Under the circumstances, there was a long running-in period for the collective farms. In the meantime there was an alarming fall in agricultural output.

Nevertheless, agriculture was now firmly under state control. It no longer had to struggle to extract a surplus from recalcitrant private peasants. What was produced on the collective farms was at the state's disposal. This does not mean that the method used to collectivize agriculture justified itself. Other ways were available which could have yielded equal if not better results without the terrible human cost and the legacy of peasant resentment which lingered on for decades.

It would be too simple to suppose that collectivization did at least provide the resources for industrialization. Between 1928 and 1932, rapid industrialization required a big increase in investment. Most of this seems to have been produced in industry through a reduction in the real wage and through the employment of forced labour on some of the large-scale constructional projects which were part of the Five-Year Plan. The urban labour forces more than doubled and the productivity of labour rose, perhaps by 40 per cent. Part of the increased labour force came from the previously unemployed in the towns, but the major part came from the peasantry. The rise in the productivity of labour depended upon machine technology, improvement in labour skills and greater intensity of work. Despite a fall in total agricultural output, a larger proportion of the surplus was available to feed the urban population and the increasing industrial labour force, although per capita consumption fell. In the early 1930s, food consumption in the countryside was also forced down. This hardly adds up to a favourable balance sheet for collectivization as imposed by Stalin nor does it justify the methods used.

INDUSTRIALIZATION

As with collectivization, the drive for industrialization, begun in the First Five-Year Plan, bore the unmistakable stamp of Stalin's methods. It was, in many ways, a grandiose improvization pushed ahead at breakneck speed regardless of human costs. The country was turned into a vast construction site from which sprang in record time a large-scale industry poised not to increase the output of consumer goods but to make more machines and, later, war material. Enormous hardships, more or less willingly borne, were imposed on the workers, and these were made worse by the effects of forced collectivization of the food supply, especially of meat, milk and other livestock products.

It has not been established that this was the only or the best way to industrialize an underdeveloped economy. Certainly there was no control or check from below on the way in which planning was carried out. Nor was any check imposed by market forces. The emphasis was upon quantity rather than quality, consumers had to take what was available and most necessities were in short supply. It was, in fact, a technocratic type of plan, imposed from above by an irresponsible bureaucracy.

Nevertheless, the Soviet planning system acquired considerable influence as a model. This was partly because Soviet propaganda emphasized success, concealed failure and said nothing about the forced labour camps, the unnecessary hardships and the repression of the Stalin era (though many admissions were, of course, to be made from 1956 onwards, including the true figures of agricultural production). The world depression, together with high unemployment levels in the capitalist countries, ensured the Soviet model a sympathetic reception in some quarters. Then, in the underdeveloped countries, the Soviet model seemed to have some direct application in showing how rapid industrialization could be achieved through planning. It was shown that planning could work, that high and unprecedented rates of growth could be achieved, that a society without landlords or capitalists was viable and could be dynamic. Impressive also was the spread of literacy, the creation of a disciplined labour force from the peasantry, and the training of hundreds of thousands of administrators, managers and technicians within a relatively short period of time.

THE HUMAN COST

All the same, the social costs were unparalleled in any industrialization before and since. In large part these were borne by the peasantry in the shape of 'dekulakization'. Many of the costs, however, had nothing to do with industrialization or with planning, but were part of the policy of repression employed by Stalin to maintain his place as head of the new bureaucratic stratum which had come to power. As a result, the repressive apparatus built up by the political police (GPU, NVKD, KGB) assumed wide-reaching and illegal powers. During the purges of the 1930s, millions of people were subject to arbitrary arrest, execution, imprisonment and deportation. The labour camps became an important part of the economy, employing millions of people on constructional tasks in the most inhospitable parts of the Soviet Union. To a considerable degree, the economy came to depend upon forced labour. Rather than being a necessary part of the planning system, or making a contribution to economic growth, the Stalinist policy of extra-legal repression had a negative effect on Soviet society which is still felt to this day.

Even critics sometimes imply that the methods of Stalinist industrialization were the only way in which a backward country like Russia could be industrialized within a short period of time. For good measure it is suggested that without the rapid build-up of heavy industry regardless of cost in the first two Five-Year Plans, the Soviet Union would have not been able to resist the Nazi onslaught when it came in June 1941. Such arguments prove to be a perhaps unconscious but sophisticated argument for Stalinism. There is no evidence that the high costs of industrialization were necessary or that there was no other way to plan industrialization. Stalin's opponents had argued since the 1920s that the danger of isolation made it necessary to build up a strong military-industrial base. The danger to the Soviet Union flowed principally from Stalin's own policies which helped open the way for Hitler's rise to power in 1933. Stalin weakened the Soviet Union by manoeuvring for alliances with the capitalist countries – a process culminating in the Pact with Nazi Germany in August 1939. Moreover, the purges had undermined morale, especially in the armed forces, and had removed many of the most talented commanders. It was significant that in some regions the peasants at first greeted the Germans as liberators and that many captive Red Army men joined the Vlassov army, set up by the Nazis, to fight against Stalin.

THE SECOND WORLD WAR

The war of 1941–45, by its scale and intensity, struck a heavy blow at the Soviet Union, destroying, as it did, much of the industry which had been built up with such sacrifices under the First Five-Year Plan. Defeat would have been certain but for the industrial base created in the interior, beyond the reach of the invaders. This enabled the tide to be turned and the already centralized, command economy lent itself to the mass production of weapons of war. Further sacrifices were imposed upon the civilian population behind the lines, while much of Soviet territory was devastated by the scorched earth policy and the huge battles between mechanized armies on a scale never before seen. Total human losses were estimated as at least twenty-six million while there were vast numbers of other casualties as well as homeless and displaced victims of the fighting.

Nevertheless, despite the unprecedented tasks of reconstruction which lay ahead, the Soviet Union emerged from the war as a major world power, stronger in relative terms than before. This was because of the temporary elimination of Germany and Japan and the effects of the war on Western Europe and on the British Empire. The bureaucratic regime of Stalin was not only able to consolidate itself in the Soviet Union, it was also able to extend its grip over Eastern Europe in a belt of buffer states defending its Western frontiers.

RECONSTRUCTION

The first post-war task was to rebuild the shattered economy in the occupied and war-stricken territories, priority being given to the industrial base. Preparations were thus rapidly put in hand to draft a Five-Year Plan for reconstruction and development for the period from 1946, which became the Fourth Plan. It was followed by a Fifth Five-Year Plan for the years 1952–55. Both these plans followed similar lines; essentially they were a continuation in aim and method of the pre-war plans and were heavily marked by Stalin's approach to economic questions. The emphasis was on the priority growth of heavy industry, great stress being laid on the high targets set for iron and steel, coal and petroleum, the output of which still seemed to measure the degree of industrialization of a country and its economic power. This required high rates of investment as productive capacity was built up, and further sacrifices for the civilian population in such matters as housing. Large numbers of constructional projects were put in hand using all available labour, including prisoners of war and political prisoners. Targets were set in quantitative terms – tons or numbers of articles – and industrial managers received bonuses on the basis of plan fulfilment.

It was once again a case of extensive industrialization, covering the country with constructional sites. The kind of problems encountered were those of shortage of supplies and of proportional growth of different interrelated sectors of industry. The high rates of growth recorded in the early post-war plans partly reflected the fact that wartime losses were being made good and that the country was still being endowed with basic production facilities. Moreover, official claims of plan-fulfilment in this and subsequent plans were based on inflated statistics, concealing short-falls in some critical sectors and the excessive number of unfinished projects. The exaggeration was particularly flagrant in the case of agricultural production, as was to be revealed by Khrushchev soon after Stalin's death. The hand of Stalin was also to be seen in grandiose schemes to transform nature by growing shelter-belts of trees, and changing the course of rivers (with disappointing results).

Stalin's successors took over the Fifth Plan at a time when the economy was facing new problems which the old methods were incapable of solving. While they inherited a powerful industrial economy, ranked as the second in the world, its strength lay mainly in heavy industry and was concentrated in old-style production technologies. In pursuit of aggregate growth, the 'steel-eaters' had not only neglected consumers, but newer types of industry such as petro-chemicals, plastics and electronics had also fallen behind world standards. The Soviet Union was still building the type of industry which would have been advanced in the 1930s when planning had begun. Research and development had been selectively concentrated on some fields, to the neglect of others. Agriculture had been sadly neglected and still bore the marks of forced collectivization in the lack-lustre performance of the peasantry and the shortage of livestock.

Tense struggles for power took place in the top leadership, and it took some time before changes could be made. Khrushchev eventually emerged as the dominant figure. Ebullient and irascible he saw the need for change and introduced some reforms, to no great effect. The Sixth Five-Year Plan, introduced in the crisis year of 1956, was abandoned after a year and replaced by a Seven-Year Plan. At the same time, whether to gain popularity or because he underestimated the weaknesses of the Soviet economy, Khrushchev improved on previous boasts to catch up and outstrip the capitalist countries in output and living standards. In an effort to overcome the grain crisis he launched the virgin lands project and sponsored maize-growing on a large scale. The expected results were not forthcoming and, after hanging onto power for several tense years, he was replaced in 1964 by Leonid Brezhnev as the head of a more orthodox bureaucratic team which grew subsequently old in office, to form, by the early 1980s, a veritable gerontocracy.

MODERN SOVIET INDUSTRIALIZATION

Under Brezhnev, the customary Five-Year Plans were resumed, and Soviet planning generally retained the centralized character which it assumed under Stalin, despite repeated 'reforms'. The development of manufacturing production continued to be regarded as the hub of industrialization; theoretically this has been taken to imply the incorporation of the latest technical and scientific achievements into production and the constant improvement of plant and equipment. In practice, partly because Soviet industry had already begun to fall behind under Stalin, this aim has not been realized throughout industry as a whole. Some older industries have become technologically obsolescent and some newer ones have been under-represented. The greater sophistication of advanced technology and the more complex organization required to make use of it, have imposed strains on the management structure. Meanwhile, the cracking pace of armaments competition with the capitalist world, as well as the increasing demands of consumers for more, better, and an increased range of goods, have made conflicting demands upon resources.

PRESENT-DAY PROBLEMS

By the 1960s, the Soviet Union could no longer boast the highest growth rate in the world. Growth rates in the more recent plans have been set at more modest levels, usually at 4 to 5 per cent for national income as a whole. To maintain these rates, considerable resources continue to be channelled into investment, and the consumer remains at the end of the queue behind the military and heavy industry. In an attempt to overcome deficiencies in some industrial sectors whole plants have been purchased 'keys in hand' from foreign firms, such as the car factory in Togliattigrad, equipped by Fiat.

There are no longer the virtually unlimited supplies of labour power available during the first Five-Year Plans, while additional supplies of basic materials such as coal, steel or oil become more costly to obtain. The phase of extensive development ended with the death of Stalin and no real solution has been found to the new problems presented by intensive development, able to satisfy consumer demand without sacrificing other goals. The rulers are no longer dealing with a new, raw labour force; and the repeated emphasis on material incentives has become something of a boomerang. Workers want better supplies of goods in return for their efforts. The regime's leaders are constantly calling for an improvement in labour productivity, apparently without very much success; yet it is admitted that the Soviet worker only produces about half as much as his American counterpart. The difference is accounted for largely by the level of mechanization and organizational efficiency rather than by the subjective attitude of the worker. The need, therefore, is for still more investment in labour-saving machinery. Meanwhile, demographic trends are reducing the supply of new, youthful workers – at the very time when new draughts of labour are required to develop natural resources in remote places such as Siberia and the North. There is, however, still an untapped labour reserve in agriculture. Approximately one-fourth of the labour force is still employed on the state and collective farms. In addition, every harvest sees a mass mobilization of city workers to assist in gathering in and transporting grain. With all the investment that has gone into the agrarian sector and grandiose projects, such as the opening up of the virgin lands, grain supplies remain inadequate except in years of exceptionally good harvest. Livestock products are still in deficient supply and of indifferent quality. Failure to solve the agrarian problem still dogs and restricts the bureaucracy. Because the difficulties still remain, it is impossible to shift labour from the land to relieve the growing labour scarcity in industry and resource-development.

It may be said, therefore, that the Soviet Union remains under-industrialized and suffers from a chronic problem of under-production. Labour scarcity has now become a major constraint on increasing output. All the same, there is evidence that labour is wastefully used in industry and in other forms of work. This may be because factory managers like to have a reserve of labour power to meet peak demands, for example, when the final effort has to be made to meet plan targets ('storming', as it is called). It may be because Soviet workers have a security of employment and cannot easily be dismissed. Also, lack of mechanical aids, such as fork-lift trucks or power-tools, means that many manual and menial jobs still exist, representing a waste of labour.

Despite the Soviet Union's record of growth, it is still in the process of catching up with the advanced capitalist countries in per capita terms. Although there are very advanced industries in the Soviet Union, in some vital sectors such as computers, plastics and oil technology it is behind the capitalist countries and depends upon them for machinery and technical know-how. The lag in the case of industries directly serving consumer needs remains particularly apparent, despite efforts in this sphere in recent years. Many consumer goods are unobtainable, in short supply or disappear into the black or grey markets. Soviet leaders repeatedly refer to 'shortcomings' in management and labour productivity, castigate the waste of productive assets, the disproportions between different sectors and the excessive number of incomplete projects in hand. Despite the attention of the press, and reforms in economic administration made over the years, these 'shortcomings' continue to figure in all discussions of Soviet economic performance.

Between 1964 and 1985, under a succession of ageing leaders, the economy of the Soviet Union settled into a routine which bordered upon stagnation. The rate of growth of production and productivity slowed down. Consequently, living standards improved only slowly and remained well behind those in the United States and Western Europe. Although Brezhnev and his successors spoke of these problems, especially the slow growth of labour productivity, the remedies either remained at the level of exhortation or failed to shift the economy into a higher gear. With inertia, complacency and even corruption in high places the public response was largely one of indifference and cynicism. Confronted by what was seen as a warlike threat from a rival system, military expenditure on conventional and nuclear weapons constituted a major drain on resources, absorbing perhaps 12–14 per cent of GNP. Undoubtedly, unlike the case with many consumer products, military procurement officers were able to insist upon the highest quality standards. The development of ever more sophisticated weapons systems absorbed scientific and technical manpower as well as industrial capacity which might otherwise have gone into much needed industrial investment to increase the output of consumer goods. However, the quality of defence supplies as well as the achievements in space research showed what the planned economy was capable of.

While some part of the responsibility for the faltering economic performance of the 1980s can be blamed on the arms burden, it was clearly not the only reason. Much of the explanation was to be found in the overcentralized, bureaucratic and irresponsible planning system still basically unchanged from the Stalin era. Although that was clear enough to many Soviet economists and even to the party leadership, it was not clear along what lines it could be improved and reformed, and even less how widespread popular enthusiasm could be harnessed to the task. Moreover, the economy was not in a state of collapse; it continued to grow, if more slowly than before. Its failures and inefficiencies were daily becoming more obvious. In its own interests the bureaucracy had to find ways of dealing with these problems. It needed to find some way of at least limiting the drain of armaments on the economy – which required some form of agreement with the United States. It also needed to improve the efficiency of the planning system while seeking to involve large sections of the population in an effort to modernize the economy with the promise of higher living standards, and perhaps greater political freedom.

These tasks devolved upon the new general secretary of the party, Mikhail S. Gorbachev, who took over in March 1985. He initiated a reform programme which stirred worldwide interest and promised to bring changes in Soviet life on a scale not known since the 1930s. In some ways the new leader continued reform efforts begun by his predecessors, but he did so on a wider and more ambitious scale and in an atmosphere of greater freedom of discussion and criticism. His aim was to speed up economic growth; a new version of the old slogan of catching up with the capitalist world. This was to be done through a whole series of reforms of the planning system and industrial management aimed at providing greater flexibility, more room for innovation and initiative and greater discipline. Changes in top personnel were intended to restore confidence in the leadership. How far the Gorbachev reforms will go remains to be seen. It seems likely that the basic planning apparatus will be retained, but that more power will reside with plant managers. What is envisaged seems to be a re-arrangement of the economic hierarchy, specifying responsibilities more clearly and offering more scope for initiative. More controversially, certain private and cooperative business activities have been legalized; they include a wide range of services, repairs and handicrafts, the aim being to satisfy consumers. In many cases activities carried on illicitly have now been legalized. There are strict limits on these new types of private enterprise, particularly as far as those eligible for employment are concerned.

More important for the long run will be the extent to which the changes in the planning system will facilitate the tackling of the major economic problems confronting the Soviet economy in the closing years of the twentieth century. These comprise, notably, the modernization of the older sectors of industry and the building up of entire new sectors based upon applied science and new technology. This will require a heavy burden of investment comparable to that in the early Five-Year Plans and, at least in the short term, will limit the output of consumer goods which can be expected. Resources will have to be channelled into machine-building and construction to carry out this tremendous task of modernization and re-equipment. It will require much technological borrowing and capital import from the advanced capitalist countries. The question arises, then, of how such imports can be paid for. In most fields the quality and variety of Soviet products will have to be greatly improved if they are to compete on the world market. Here, too, there is need for renewed detente to make possible the diversion of resources from arms production into the productive sectors of the economy. Gorbachev thus has a twofold task: to reform the economy while improving relations with the capitalist world.

SOVIET INDUSTRIALIZATION AS A MODEL

During the 1930s, a characteristic model of industrialization appeared in the Soviet Union, which was in sharp contrast with what had gone before. This model was adopted by, or imposed on, the East European countries which came into the Soviet orbit after the Second World War. It was the model followed in China after 1949 and still has an influence there despite the Maoist repudiation of some of its features and subsequent concessions to market forces. Plans in countries which remained basically capitalist, such as India, have been influenced by techniques first used in the Soviet Union. Nevertheless, today it is widely recognized, even in the Soviet Union, that the model has defects and it is now unlikely to be imitated elsewhere. In summarizing these defects, it may be said that they stem from excessive centralization, the concentration of power in the hands of an irresponsible bureaucratic regime, and disregard for consumer needs. These defects have led to others and have been compounded by waste and mismanagement on the part of the ruling bureaucracy. This is not the place to consider whether some different course would have been possible, or what changes should be made in the planning system, but only to appraise the role it has played historically.

EVALUATION AND INTERPRETATION

Thus it might seem good enough to say that the Soviet system did make possible the industrialization of a still backward country, and did so at a rapid rate. Nevertheless, since the sacrifice in human terms was so great, it might well be asked whether the end result was worth it.

Another point of view sees post-1928 industrialization as taking over where Tsarism had stopped at the time of the First World War. Some historians have spoken of a 'second take-off' (the first being the 'great spurt' of the 1890s). A comparison between the two suggests that there were important qualitative as well as quantitative differences. Industrial growth under the Tsarist regime had not brought about a fundamental structural transformation of the entire economy, nor is there proof that it would have been able to do so; rather did industrialization generate forces which made a political overturn of some kind virtually inevitable. This was because the political system and the social relations of the old regime blocked the all-round development of the productive forces, the further surges of growth on a wide front necessary for successful and complete industrialization under conditions of backwardness. Even without involvement in a war which taxed it to breaking point, it is difficult, then, to see how the old regime could have long survived into the twentieth century. If not a proletarian, then a bourgeois revolution, sooner or later would have occurred; the question remains, however, whether a regime of the latter type could have solved the problems it would have inherited. As it was, the successor regime claimed to be based on the working class, but it could not avoid shouldering the tasks of modernization which in more advanced countries had devolved upon the bourgeoisie. The strain of carrying out the tasks of a bourgeois as well as of a socialist revolution in a backward country, without support from abroad, notably from proletarian states in the more advanced countries, created the specific historical conditions for the rise of the Stalinist bureaucracy and for all the terrible, and needless, sacrifices which followed. There was nothing inevitable about this process; it was the outcome of a political struggle in the Soviet Union and of a particular constellation of international forces.

With the victory of Stalin, industrialization was given a particular course and governed by a particular mechanism of planning (or pseudo-planning) which, in its main features, has been conserved to this day. Once industrialization had begun in this form – at breakneck speed and under conditions of virtual seclusion from the world market – some specifically Russian factors have to be taken into account. The first of these centred around the fact that some basic industrialization (more than in China by 1949, say) had already been achieved. Once reconstruction had been completed during the early 1920s, this was clearly an asset. Foreign workers and technicians in the Soviet Union at this time were often struck by the modernity of the plant inherited from the past, often comparing favourably with that with which they were familiar in the more advanced countries. Not only was there this technical basis, but there was also a cadre of skilled workers and administrators. One of the features of the 1930s was the rapid increase in the number of qualified engineers, technicians and managers. Of course they had to have teachers, but, although some of these were foreigners, most were Soviet citizens. Moreover, the Russian intelligentsia was highly educated and contained many remarkable personalities. There was, of course, a brain drain of those hostile to the new sytem. Others stayed, although they might not altogether agree with the system; they carried out their professional work or even cooperated with the planners. The high level of debate on economic and political questions which took place while discussion was relatively free in the 1920s inside the Party, and in the planning organisms (where there were many non-Party experts), reflected the quality of this intelligentsia. Much of this human capital was wantonly squandered by Stalin in the following decade; and intellectual standards in some fields suffered, with adverse economic results. Stalin supported charlatans like Lysenko in biology and blocked the development of cybernetics. On the credit side, the new regime put considerable resources into campaigns of mass literacy and into education and training of all kinds, thus raising the educational level of the population as a whole. This investment has clearly paid off; a lesson which some countries, such as India, have failed to learn, to their cost.

Just as Tsarist Russia was able to benefit from the advantages of the latecomer, by taking over modern technology and importing the latest plant and machinery from the most advanced countries, so the Soviet Union was able to do the same even when it was pursuing a policy of economic isolation. Industrialization in the 1930s would not have been possible without such borrowing and the purchase of plant and machinery which Soviet industry at that time was incapable of producing. This practice has continued (as, for example, in the cooperation with foreign firms in the building of complete new factories). Indeed, the Soviet Union was unable to insulate itself from the world market even in the time of Stalin. As the economy has become more complex and diversified its dependence has grown and participation in the international division of labour has been accepted as necessary and desirable. Rapid growth would not be possible on any other terms.

On the other hand, Soviet industrialization did not make use of foreign financial aid, nor did it borrow on any appreciable scale as other industrializing countries have done. Imported machinery and other goods have thus had to be paid for with materials or manufactures which might otherwise have helped to raise consumption levels at home. In any case, until recently, foreign capitalists were reluctant to lend to a regime which threatened their system (at least in their view) and which had repudiated Tsarist debts as one of its first actions (thus freeing itself from a considerable burden).

Self-reliance has been a feature of Soviet industrialization. This has been facilitated by the very size of the country, by the variety, and in some cases the richness, of its natural resources. However, these resources were (and are) not as abundant as is sometimes supposed. They are often located in peripheral areas; their extraction often poses enormous difficulties because of harsh climatic conditions and their transportation to manufacturing centres is costly. In the earlier period, forced labour was sometimes used; although it was not necessarily economical. Only a regime of the Stalinist type could have used such methods. Grandiose schemes followed from the nature of the regime, regardless of the human cost. Stalin, deified by the Party, promised to change the climatic conditions of entire regions by the growing of shelter-belts; Khrushchev initiated the 'virgin lands' scheme in an effort to solve the grain problem. The former did not come off; while the success of the latter was dubious. Khrushchev's successors denounced his 'harebrained schemes' and have themselves been more cautious. It is doubtful whether they could resort to the high-handed methods of Stalin.

Irresponsible bureaucratic control not only imposed an enormous and unnecessary human cost on the Soviet masses, but also led to incalculable material waste in carrying out the huge constructional projects of the early Plans. Despite these heavy overhead costs, a powerful industrial base was built up, often seeming to become an end in itself during the Stalin period. The surplus product sweated out of the workers provided a large part of the investment required for growth. Agriculture, likewise, was sacrificed. At times, consumption standards were almost intolerably low and still compare unfavourably with those in the advanced capitalist world.

The ruling bureaucracy took pride (and still does) in gigantic modern plants, quoting the statistics of industrial production to justify its stewardship. The privileged of the regime never go short and receive a disproportionate share of what consumer goods are available. They have their *dachas* (country retreats) and limousines, while for many people housing conditions remain poor and queues and shortages are a fact of life. However, it is probably doubtful whether even in the worst times there was such inequality as is common in most 'developing countries' today and it may be less than in the advanced capitalist countries. Nevertheless, by the 1930s, the privileges and prerogatives of the ruling bureaucracy were great enough for it to be reasonably claimed that the principles of the revolution of 1917 no longer applied. The type of industrialization adopted by Stalin, as the representative and chief of the new ruling layer, had made this inevitable. In fact, no alternative pattern of consumption or style of life to that of the advanced capitalist countries was then, or subsequently has been, proposed. Soviet industrialization was seen as a process of catching up, not of transcending. It was to provide people with what was already available to many in capitalist society; the privileged were served first, others in accordance with the value put on their work. The supply of goods was, however, more or less the same. The Soviet people want what is already available in capitalist department stores and supermarkets. Warsaw Pact generals sip Coca-cola while watching manoeuvres.

Perhaps for history Soviet industrialization will be best remembered simply by the fact that within the space of a generation it transformed the predominantly peasant and still relatively underdeveloped land of the Tsars into a modern industrial giant, second only to the United States in aggregate industrial production. In economic terms this was made possible by an unprecedentedly high rate of investment, a claimed twelve-fold increase in the net stock of capital between 1928 and 1967. The pre-war build up of basic industry could be said to have yielded its main results, after reconstruction of the damage resulting from the Second World War, in the following decades of steady, rather than spectacular, growth. According to official claims, by 1978 the Soviet Union accounted for 20 per cent of world industrial production, against only 5 per cent in 1928. The immense build-up of the means of production, represented by such figures, required the creation of a huge new working class, now approximately one hundred million strong, from a people previously made up predominantly of peasants only a generation or so away from serfdom. Rapid growth was also facilitated, in the past, not only by the flow of new recruits from the countryside, but also by a high rate of population increase and the greater participation of women in the labour force. Once this labour army was harnessed to means of production incorporating modern technology, and endowed with new skills, there is no mystery about how the Soviet economy was able to grow as it did.

It has been shown, however, that the process of industrialization remains incomplete, the resources pinned down in a still inefficient agriculture remain excessive, labour productivity lags well behind the best capitalist levels. As for the economic mechanism itself, this raises a whole area of theoretical discussion. The plans are centralized, imposed from above after the fashion of a command economy, and leave little or no room for the masses to make their wishes felt, despite official claims to the contrary. Attempts have been made to improve them by various reforms, notably by encouraging more initiative on the part of plant managers, and by laying down more refined criteria for the carrying out of plans. In practice, however, the bureaucracy is unable to remove the defects of the existing planning mechanism or to overcome the frequently denounced 'short comings'. Even with computers and modern input-output techniques a faultless plan cannot be drawn up. The problem with the plan is that it is remote from the people whose activities it determines. It is not a response to their individual and collective requirements. That is a political rather than an economic weakness, and one which can only be overcome by substituting democratic control from below for centralized decision-making by an all-powerful technocratic-bureaucratic centre. In discussions about over-centralization and the introduction of greater regulation through the market, the human and political aspects tend to be overlooked. The question really is whether industrialization is to be geared to the needs and wishes of the people, or is to provide what the planners think they should have. It is not only a problem in the Soviet Union. It remains to be seen how far Gorbachev (or his successors) will be capable of promoting a permanent new course while modernizing the planning system.

CHAPTER FOUR
India's industrialization: problems and pitfalls

The experience of industrialization in India is characteristic of the difficulties faced by a newly-independent underdeveloped country. Industrialization in India has taken place as a conscious policy of growth under the leadership of an indigenous political elite, after a long period of colonial rule. While some problems were specific to India, arising from the inherited social structure and cultural patterns, many were comparable to those found in other countries at a similar stage of development. In particular, India has tended to become the test-case for economic development without social revolution, within the framework of a mixed economy. Indian planning has not set out to supersede private ownership and the operation of market forces. The country remains part of the capitalist world market in a relationship which is clearly dependent, especially where finance and technology are concerned. While it is clear that there could be no replication of the industrialization path of the advanced countries, points of similarity, as well as contrast, do arise with other countries at different periods, notably Japan, China and the Soviet Union. They will be apparent in the following case study.

At the time of independence in 1947, India was undoubtedly an underdeveloped country with one of the lowest per capita incomes in the world. About 75 per cent of the population was engaged in agriculture which contributed 50 per cent of national income. Factory industry employed about 2 per cent of the working population and contributed only 6.5 per cent of the national income. In addition, about three times as many people worked in cottage and workshop industries contributing some 9.6 per cent of national income.

Despite the predominance of agriculture, the very size of India gave the industrial sector some significance. It was a basis to work on after Independence. However, the question clearly arises as to why industrialization had not advanced beyond a preliminary stage under British rule. This question cannot be separated from a further one which concerns the disappointing overall performance in the subsequent decades, despite further build-up of industry. The answers to both these questions seem to lie in the lack of structural transformation to remove blockages in the way of development, especially in the agrarian sector, and in the lack of a resolute policy to carry out the proclaimed aims of the government – to abolish poverty and to create a more equal society. As a result, the vast mass of the Indian people, who have shown astonishing patience, have experienced little or no improvement in their welfare, while the gains of the economic growth so far achieved have been garnered by the fortunate minority.

To understand the problems of Indian industrialization it is necessary to examine the results of British rule. When this was imposed over the sub-continent from the latter half of the eighteenth century, the new rulers displaced the former Moghul conquerors while leaving intact the traditional economy or, at least, only slowly undermining it. The Moghuls, as a military aristocracy, had been mainly interested in extracting the agrarian surplus by means of the land revenue. This surplus, instead of being used for productive purposes, served to maintain the military establishment and the consumption of the mainly urban-based ruling class. The Moghuls were not interested in owning and improving land after the fashion of the English land-owners. Ownership rights remained with the village community, itself a largely self-sufficient productive unit, carrying on agriculture under conditions where there were few means and little incentive to invest in improvement.

The surplus represented by the land revenue gave rise to urban handicrafts of a luxury type carried on mainly by labour-intensive methods in small units of production. There was, however, little interchange between town and country. Most of the needs of the rural population were met by local craftsmen, often part of the village community receiving payment in the form of a share in the product. The Hindu caste system regulated everyone's place in society and an intricate division of labour had grown up on the basis of a multitude of sub-castes, or *jatis*. Higher castes, besides enjoying social prestige, were also, generally speaking, the economically better off. At the bottom of the scale were the pariahs, or untouchables, who formed an hereditary pool of labour for the performance of unclean, menial and manual tasks. Besides the priestly Brahmins, warriors and peasants, the caste system also provided for merchants who were able to enrich themselves and accumulate capital within the pores of Moghul-dominated India.

Merchants, whether from the Hindu trading castes or from other communities, were circumscribed in their operations by the conditions of Indian society. The market in the villages was small in the absence of much disposable income. There was more scope for profit in monetizing the agrarian surplus and in catering for the needs of the ruling class. There were also some opportunities in foreign trade. Once merchants had become wealthy there was probably some social pressure on them to consume lavishly or to hoard. There were limited possibilities for investment in industry and additional risks to be faced. Merchant capital was hardly likely to venture further than the buying up of the output of traditional craft industries. The abundant labour supply discouraged technological innovation. There was no standardized mass market, transport costs were high, and thus there was no incentive to produce on a large scale. During the eighteenth century, the export trade came to be dominated by foreign merchants. Soon India was to experience the effects of the industrialization of other areas in the swamping of the market with machine-made low-priced textiles and a demand for primary products. This not only hit the Indian craftsmen who were working near the ports and even some way into the hinterland, but also meant that exports could not act as an engine of growth, and that Indian capitalists were faced with powerful competition from foreign capital. Economic policy had meanwhile passed out of Indian hands and was shaped by the interests of the British Raj.

The British had no positive policy for Indian economic development, but they did not deliberately set out to restrict it. Although some 'deindustrialization' accompanied the extension of their rule, it is doubtful whether India was on the way to becoming an industrial country. Of course, a Japanese-type development was now ruled out, and by the early nineteenth century India had become a captive market for Britain as well as a source of revenue, through the land and other taxes, to pay for the new military-bureaucratic structure. A brake was put on whatever autonomous forces for change may have existed, and Indian development was now very much determined by the relationship with the world market arising from British imperial control. This meant that a smaller proportion of people found employment in industry than might otherwise have been the case, while the relative weight of agriculture tended to grow (a process which continued to some extent into the twentieth century). The way to industrialization was thereby blocked, though it does not follow that industrialization would have taken place had India not come under British rule.

THE BEGINNINGS OF CAPITALISM

Under the conditions which prevailed in India in the early nineteenth century, there was no possibility of the artisan-craftsmen taking control of a larger share of production, accumulating capital, and becoming capitalists and employers of labour. On the other hand, some of the barriers to capitalist development which had existed under the Moghuls had now been broken down. A greater degree of law and order prevailed. Improved transport facilities brought about greater economic integration. The growth of import-export trade gave opportunities for the Indian merchants to extend their operations in the home market in a subordinate capacity and in spheres which the British did not enter. The steady rise of the Indian merchant class, recruited from traditional Hindu trading castes and other communities, was a feature of the period. By the 1850s, some members of this class were seeking outlets for their capital in industrial investment. The first cotton mills were set up by Bombay merchants in the 1850s. In the meantime, however, the cheap cotton textiles of Lancashire had taken a firm grip on the Indian market, so had some other imported manufactured goods. Equipment for these mills, as well as for railways and other installations built by the British, came from abroad. The old urban luxury industries of Moghul times had disappeared or declined and the new rulers largely consumed imported wares and in so doing influenced the consumption style of wealthy Indians as well. But the mass of the people remained poor, the internal market for textiles, dominated by Lancashire, was made up of many small purchases. Local industries were affected in different ways; many adapting themselves to changing demand and using new materials. Certainly they were not destroyed by a huge influx of imported manufactures which most Indians would have been too poor to buy.

The effect of the changes made in the land system was to generalize private and contractual relations. Land became a commodity, instead of a communal asset which was part of an unchanging way of life. The way was clear for the growth of tenancy though without an immediate change to capitalist agriculture. The new landlords created by British legislation were primarily interested in obtaining a share of the surplus, not in reorganizing production. While the direct cultivators slipped into debt and dependence they had to support absentee landowners, intermediaries and moneylenders who made no contribution to agriculture but enjoyed social power and prestige. Although by the twentieth century agriculture showed many variants, from the capitalist plantation employing wage-labour, the large market-orientated farm, to the dwarf holdings of the poor peasants, there was no sweeping change as a result of British rule. Many of the traditional features of village life showed remarkable continuity. However, while many peasants were concerned mainly with survival, others made an adjustment to market opportunities. The result was considerable stratification and the existence in many places of a dominant group of better-off peasants and landowners, generally from the higher castes, together with a mass of 'dwarf-holders' and landless or semi-landless villagers.

The object of the British Raj was to ensure that the colony should pay the heavy bill for its administration and defence and provide a source of profit through trade. The East India Company had originally been interested in selling Indian products, such as tea and opium, in foreign markets. With the growth of industry in Britain, the once important export of Indian cloth came to an end and India was opened up as a great market for Lancashire's machine-made textiles. After the Mutiny and the winding up of the Company in 1857, India was drawn more closely into the world market, then dominated by Britain. The building of railways, the improvement of ocean shipping and the opening of the Suez Canal in 1869 speeded this process, and at the same time confirmed India's economic dependence. The Indian market was kept open for British imports, facilitated by the railways, and growing world demand encouraged investment in primary production either from plantations or by the commercialization of peasant agriculture. It was no part of the design of British administrators to develop the country economically, but their policies, what they did as well as what they refrained from doing, helped shape the economic structure. At this period the modern sector was mainly concentrated in the port cities which grew as centres of import-export trade. They drew in foreign capital to build docks, harbours and warehouses as well as constructing railways. As they became centres of population, so they attracted service trades and industries, as well as British banks and commercial firms. Since India was not regarded as a colony of settlement, this population was predominantly Indian and the growth of the port-cities, more than anything else, with the possible exception of education, was a vehicle through which Indians were introduced to modern – European and capitalist – forms of organization.

Thus it was that, while on the one hand the development of the port-cities had an enclave character, they also fostered a symbiosis between Indian merchant capital and foreign capital. They introduced Indians to the ways of European society and were the gateways through which the forces that were to transform Indian society could flow. Thus the way in which these cities grew was not altogether alien to India; indeed, they opened up new opportunities to Indians for trade and employment, enabling them to acquire knowledge of Western business methods and industrial techniques. The British could hardly have prevented this even if they had wanted to. As it was, Indian merchant capital was complementary to British capitalism in India; Indians were needed in subordinate positions in the administration as well as the army. British firms had to train Indians for a variety of jobs of a kind not available in the old society. Indians were able to learn from and emulate their masters; in the long run it was inevitable that they would come into conflict with them.

This process of culture contact, emulation and conflict took place unevenly and was spread over a considerable period of time. At first it affected mainly communities outside the Hindu or Muslim mainstream (such as Parsees or Jains) or Hindu merchant sub-castes to whom it offered new possibilities of profit-making. Indian family businesses were active in assembling primary products for export, or merchandizing imported manufactured goods in the hinterland. British capital occupied the commanding positions in foreign trade, shipping, banking and insurance. Successively, throughout the nineteenth century, other business groups, mainly from traditional trading sub-castes (especially from the north-west, like the Marwaris and the Gujeratis) pushed forward, consolidating what became a distinctively Indian capitalist class. As elements in this class grew wealthier and more self-confident they moved into new fields, including industrial investment, where it was more difficult to avoid a collision with the alien rulers. It was the latter who determined policy in such fields as the tariff, railways, the currency and the purchase of government stores. Moreover, the Raj constituted a heavy drain on India's resources and this blatant fact began to sharpen nationalist feeling.

British capital was drawn to India in search of profitable investments, but the openings were relatively few. Apart from railways, which gave a guaranteed rate of return, investors had to face unpredictable risks. Primary production was the safest bet for British capital, perhaps with some processing to follow. There was little scope for investment in industrial production serving the home market, or in production for export, which would be in competition with British exports. The main articles, apart from those locally produced, purchased by the peasant masses, were textiles. The Lancashire industry had tapped this market very successfully in the earlier part of the nineteenth century. A limited amount of British capital did go into the Indian textile industry, but the Indian-owned mills, until 1914, produced mainly the coarser varieties of cotton textiles. These were exported to countries where they would not be in direct competition with the Lancashire exports. Neither the civil service nor the British capitalists in India had any interest in building up a self-supporting industrial structure in the colony. British capital was orientated towards the world market and it was in trade that money was to be made. Teaching Indians modern technology was no part of the white man's burden; they would have to fend for themselves. Political power and influence were used to favour British firms or to discriminate against Indians (as in shipping, for instance), but otherwise the policy of the Raj was not a positive one. In short, within the overriding interest of Britain in India as part of the world Empire of the time, capital flows were left to market forces.

In other words, whether that capital derived from British or Indian sources, it obeyed the law of profit. Fields which might seem too risky, or to promise too low a return to Europeans, might be attractive to Indian capital, given the lack of alternative outlets arising from the policy of the Raj. As long as we are talking about the trading castes and communities, there seems to have been little inhibition derived from religious scruples or cultural restraints which could have influenced business dealings. There was a long-standing trading tradition and the Indian merchants were able pupils. On the other hand, the social stratification by caste, which was especially prevalent in the rural areas, did have some negative effects, though it is difficult to disentangle them from those which arose from poverty. The caste system and religious feeling probably limited the area of recruitment for entrepreneurs, though it did not prevent peasants from being rational calculators if they were producing cash crops. Merchants, traders and money-lenders were often strangers, alien to the communities among whom they did business.

What deterred more Indian capital from investment in industry were basically the same factors that accounted for the lack of British investment: low income levels, high distributive costs, doubtful risks and lack of tariff protection. Also, in some industries, relatively large amounts of capital would have been required and investment would only have been profitable if there was some hope of an export market (as there was, for instance, in cotton textiles and especially jute). The linkage effects (that is, the influence which growth in one industry or sector exerts upon others through their interdependence) of railway construction were largely felt by Britain. The lack of a machine-making industry was not necessarily a result of British policy, as there would have to be a substantial user industry to make investment in it worthwhile. It was a long time before Indian capital was adequate in volume to diversify into more advanced branches of industry, and not until after the First World War that it was able to do so on an appreciable scale. Even after the Second World War it was not able to do so on a scale adequate to initiate a full-blooded programme of industrialization. Hence the acceptance of state planning.

It should be remembered that the British Industrial Revolution made itself felt in India largely by its disadvantages; that is to say cheap manufactured goods took over the market under the protection of imperial rule. As we have seen, industrialization in India was not an autonomous process; it came in as an import, or rather some of its components (like the railways) were imported on a piecemeal basis with different results from those in the country of origin. By its very nature, British capital was incapable of promoting Indian industrialization; it was simply not profitable to do so. The alternatives were much more attractive, especially investment in trade and in primary production. These were safer and more profitable than industrial investment could have been. Investment in this form, however, kept India dependent and underdeveloped. This was not a deliberate policy imposed by the Indian civil service but rather one which arose inevitably from the relationship between a backward country and the most industrialized country of the time, under conditions of imperialism. A lopsidedness was imparted to the Indian economy as the necessary legacy of British rule. India acquired some of the features of advanced capitalism but without that thorough reshaping of agrarian relations and society as a whole which had accompanied the rise of capitalism in the metropolis. It was the kind of situation Marx had in mind when he spoke of a country which 'suffers not only from the development of capitalist production, but also from the incompleteness of that development'.

British imperialism thus permitted a limited growth of capitalism in India and the emergence of a local class of capitalists searching for profitable opportunities. Market factors determined the pattern and amount of investment within the context of foreign rule and the peculiarities of India's social institutions and culture.

In the second half of the nineteenth century, a factory industry had been established in cotton and in jute. Both flourished commercially, largely on the basis of exports. They used local raw materials and a low-paid industrial proletariat was recruited from the villages. The machinery and chemical products were imported, mainly from Britain. In the cotton industry, a leading role was played by Indian capital (though British capital was certainly not absent) but the jute industry was mainly British controlled. Indian capital was partly channelled through managing agencies; that is, British firms having a contract to manage the factories. These industries demonstrated a number of important points. It became evident that Indian capital was not reluctant to go into industry where profits could be expected. In addition British capital was not deterred by the thought of competing with firms at home; Indian mills were, in any case, equipped readily by British machine-makers. Moreover, it was shown that Indians could manage modern industrial establishments and the bait of regular wages could draw poor peasants into factory work in India as well as in Europe.

At the same time, as has already been seen, objective factors in the Indian environment limited the kind and amount of industrial investment likely to be profitable. Industry could not count on tariff protection or any other special benefits from the state. The successful industries were in consumer goods (jute, of course, was largely used as packaging material) but were not dependent upon home demand (although, in the case of cotton, demand began to increase in the early part of the twentieth century). The result was that, although before 1914 India was perhaps unique among underdeveloped countries in having an organized sector (factories) partly under native ownership, as well as railways, ports, banks and other attributes of a modern economy, these remained localized in their influence. To put it another way, they had not initiated a genuine process of industrialization or fundamentally transformed the agrarian structure.

Indeed, although part of agricultural production was hinged to the market, there was no shift of population out of agriculture; if anything the proportion of the population dependent on the land tended to rise. The existence of some advanced industries did little to raise per capita incomes or to initiate economic growth. Indian capital was too weak to transform the Indian economy. British capital could have financed large-scale industrialization but had no incentive to do so. British capitalists looked upon India as a captive market and a supplier of raw materials and foodstuffs to the world market. As for the British governors of India, they were concerned to maintain the imperial interest through the raising of revenue to meet the military and financial commitments they had made on India's behalf but without her consent.

RESULTS OF THE FIRST WORLD WAR

The First World War drastically undermined the relationship established in the nineteenth century between Britain and her Indian possessions. During the war, India provided manpower and material which had to be paid for out of revenue raised in the country. At the same time, the curtailment of imports opened up fresh possibilities for the investment of Indian capital in manufacturing industry, and a number of new factories were set up in fields such as glass and chemicals. The demand for munitions gave a boost to the small iron and steel industry founded partly for nationalist reasons before the war. Wartime inflation and speculation arising from scarcities offered further opportunities for capital accumulation by Indians while worsening the financial position of the government. The cotton industry took advantage of the situation to build its sales in the home market in the face of growing Japanese competition in the Far East. The war-time experience strengthened Indian capital, reinforcing the demand for protection and a more positive government policy towards industry. In 1916 an Industrial Commission was appointed to enquire into possible new openings for the profitable employment of Indian capital and to see what assistance the government might give. Although its report made in 1918 envisaged a more active part for the state in industrial development, little came of its recommendations. The ending of the war and the placing of industrial matters under Provincial jurisdiction by the Government of India Act of 1919 both contributed to the lack of any tangible follow-up.

The war brought about an all-round weakening of British imperialism and undermined the old relationship with India. At the same time it intensified the conflict between Indian and British economic interests and strengthened the nationalist movement, enabling it to sink popular roots and make more radical demands. Concessions had to be made, especially in the shape of tariff protection for Indian industries on a selective basis.

In the 1920s Britain could no longer export capital to India at the pre-1914 rate. At the same time, the continued flow of interest and other receipts from India helped to mask the weakening of Britain's financial position. Although India continued to be a sheltered market for old-style exports facing sharper world competition, and remained the largest single market for Britain's exports down to the 1930s, its importance in relative terms declined significantly. By the end of the 1930s, Britain supplied a little over 30 per cent of India's imports compared with more than twice that figure before 1914. The new growth industries in Britain showed little interest in the Indian market while industries like cotton were now facing stiff competitive pressure from Indian producers.

Meanwhile, India's role as an earner of foreign exchange to bridge Britain's deficit with the rest of the world had virtually ended. Britain still had a substantial financial stake in India and the Indian army remained crucial to the strategy of British imperialism but the links with India had changed in nature and were weaker than they had been. Britain's economic difficulties were greatly to the advantage of Indian capitalists, some of whom had done very well out of the war. They sought to play a greater role especially in industry, but found that the imperial connection posed a barrier to their aspirations. Businessmen thus tended to become more committed to the nationalist cause because only a government of their fellow countrymen could offer them the conditions for the accumulation and investment of capital which they desired. On the one hand, the financial burdens imposed by British rule became more oppressive, on the other hand British interests in the relatively small but crucial sector of organized industry were still predominant if declining.

The world depression of the 1930s hit India hard, as an exporter of primary products, through a fall in prices and the deterioration in the terms of trade. The general slow down in the economy reduced demand for such products as coal. On the other hand, import-substitution continued to buoy up home-market demand for cotton and some other manufactures. The Government of India tried to handle its financial problems by a policy of deflation and by holding the rupee at a parity which Indian critics declared to be over-valued. These measures could only worsen the effect of the depression. The export of capital from Britain to India was arrested and some repatriation of capital took place. Even the extension of tariff protection could do little to overcome the sluggishness of the economy.

If India did not experience the depression as severely as did the advanced capitalist countries, or experienced it in a different way, it was because there was no large industrial sector or a predominantly commercial agriculture. The basic problems of the Indian economy were not transitory ones of a cyclical nature but were a product of secular stagnation and the poverty and low purchasing power of the peasant masses. While depression in the early 1930s worsened the position of industrial producers, the recovery in the following years mainly benefited industrial producers and the better-off urban consumers. Indeed, there was some expansion of home-market demand and Indian entrepreneurs responded with investment in new industries as well as in the more traditional ones. The period saw the appearance of a more definite ideology of industrialization in business circles, as well as among the mainly intellectual leaders of the national movement. The two sections tended to draw closer together on the basis that India's problems could only be overcome by the building up of an industrial base and by its diversification. Strangely enough, the figurehead of the National Congress, Mahatma Gandhi, stressed the dangers of large-scale industry and the virtues of small-scale handicraft production within the framework of the self-sufficient village.

Despite Gandhi, powerful objective forces were working against any general adoption of his proposals. Although some Indian businessmen, as well as Congress leaders, wore homespun and did their daily stint of spinning or weaving, in practice they accepted that industrialization was the corollary of independence. If there was any doubt on this question it was to be dispelled by the experience of the Second World War.

RESULTS OF THE SECOND WORLD WAR

Standing as it did between two theatres of war, and then directly threatened by Japan, the full strategic importance of India for the

British Empire was revealed. For the strategists in London, India was to be a source of manpower, a military base camp, and also a source of supplies for the armed forces, in accordance with its resources and potential. A massive contribution to the war effort was demanded and imposed, against considerable nationalist opposition. Part of the expenditure involved was met by the government of India from taxation and loans; Britain's share was credited to Indian accounts in London. As a result of these transactions, by the end of the war, not only had India's debt to Britain been wiped out but the sterling balances had reached the sum of about £1,300 million. The Second World War therefore resulted in a fundamental change in the financial relationship between the metropolis and the colony. India was no longer a debtor, but a creditor, and there had been an irremediable deterioration in Britain's world position.

In the course of the period 1939–45, India experienced the consequences of war economy: inflation, civilian shortages and the setting up of a network of government controls. Large armies had to be maintained and supplied and there was a considerable growth in industrial production as a result. Moreover, some kinds of production were encouraged in India to meet the needs of the imperial war effort. The inflation was a consequence of increased government demand financed by an increase in the money supply; most goods were in short supply and their prices soared. Industry received lucrative contracts for materials and equipment on government account. There was no corresponding flow of civilian goods onto the market to match the money incomes created. Merchants and industrialists found unprecedented opportunities for profit, while price rises, shortages and actual famine worsened the lot of the people, most of whom had little or no interest in the outcome of the war.

Industry was harnessed to the war machine by an array of government controls, similar to those operated in Britain and the other belligerent countries. In contrast with its past, rather passive role, the government now encouraged new types of industry, placing contracts at guaranteed prices and purchasing practically the entire output of some industries such as leather, footwear and wool textiles. Only limitation of capacity and the difficulty of obtaining new machinery and equipment from abroad – India's lack of a machine-making industry was now revealed as a serious weakness – prevented the growth in output from being far greater. There were also scarcities of materials, of skilled labour and technicians. The government was thus reaping the fruits of past neglect. When short-run considerations prevailed, no attempt was made to establish the more advanced types of production, such as motor vehicles, ships and aircraft, and projects put forward by Indian entrepreneurs were turned down. Consequently, the war accelerated industrial growth without bringing about a structural transformation. The wartime need for primary products also tended to reinforce India's traditional position in the international division of labour.

The experience of the Second World War proved to be frustrating to those Indian businessmen who had hoped that it would provide an opportunity to diversify the economy and especially to build up a heavy industry. Nevertheless, it did enable them to extend their operations and to accumulate capital on a scale which would not have been possible in peacetime. Further, Indian capital was able to consolidate its position relative to British capital. With Britain now in debt to India, the Raj had ceased to be the paying proposition it had been. The growth of nationalist feeling, and with it the power of the Indian National Congress and the All-India Muslim League, made it improbable that the old relationship, under which India paid excessively to be governed by foreigners, could ever be restored. British rule could not have been maintained without the use of military force and at enormous cost. At the end of the war the decline in the strategic and economic importance of India for Britain, in itself made such an attempt futile.

THE BRITISH WITHDRAWAL

As this was accepted by the British government, so the steps were taken which paved the way for a peaceful handing over of power to the two rival nationalist movements. Consequently, when the final departure of the British took place, although it was followed by horrendous communal blood-letting and disorganization resulting from large-scale population movements, there was no social revolution. The nationalist leaders who assumed control of independent India and Pakistan, took over the existing machinery of government in a peaceful transition. Despite the rhetoric, in most respects social and economic life went on as before. In the main, the new leaders assumed the role of the former masters of India, taking over the top rungs of the administration and, apart from measures against the princes, leaving the existing distribution of property and power as it had been under the Raj. State power was now exercised by a new elite, drawn from the intelligentsia and property-owning classes, most of whom were from the higher castes. Congress rule, once it had become established, led to an alliance between the urban-based bourgeoisie, with its specifically Indian characteristics, and the rural notables consisting of the better-off peasants and landowners, also in the main from the higher castes.

In the absence of a revolution of the type which took place a year or so later in China, there was no change in property relations. Land reform was left to the provincial governments and in practice brought few changes. Where agrarian revolts took place they were suppressed. The deeply-rooted problems of Indian society which the new government inherited were seen as matters to be dealt with by legislative reforms and administrative intervention, rather than through the involvement of the mass of the population itself. The passivity and resignation of the peoples of India, temporarily broken during the struggle against the British, now seemed once more to predominate as hopes of significant changes were not realized.

PLANNING

To be sure, the Congress government adopted economic planning from an early stage, with the intention of speeding up the industrialization of the country. Even this was not a great innovation; it was only spelling out a long-held tenet of nationalist doctrine, that the state's proper role was to promote industrial development and not to remain indifferent to it, as had been the case under the Raj. Seen as an administrative measure to be applied from the top downwards, the kind of planning initiated in India remained lifeless at the grass-roots level. It was an intellectual exercise to be translated into practice by bureaucrats, largely remote from the concerns of the people. In its early stages, at least, the need for a plan was accepted by business as well as by Congress politicians and great hopes were placed upon planning in the period of euphoria and national consensus which followed the achievement of Independence.

The antecedents of Indian planning can be found in the discussion during the 1930s provoked by such examples as the Five-Year Plan of the Soviet Union and Roosevelt's New Deal. The influence of Marxism, and perhaps more of Keynesianism, can be seen as contributing to its theoretical side. There seemed no way in which an economy suffering the effects of colonialism and underdevelopment could industrialize through market forces alone. The investment effort required, especially in the field of heavy industry, public utilities and general infrastructure, was beyond the capacity of private capital. On the other hand, businessmen recognized that without such an effort there would be very definite limits to private investment and accumulation. Congress set up a National Planning Committee, presided over by Jawaharlal Nehru, in 1938, but its activities were brought to an end by the war. A number of prominent industrialists put forward what was known as the Bombay Plan in January 1944. It resembled Soviet plans in its emphasis on heavy industry and on the central importance of achieving rapid rates of growth. Not only did it influence the plans drawn up after Independence, but it was also significant in showing that an important section of India's capitalist class endorsed central planning. However, the Bombay Plan, and rival plans put forward by the Gandhians and the trade unions, were little more than statements of intention. Neither the theoretical framework nor the administrative machinery for planning were worked out until after independence.

In its Industrial Policy Resolution of April 1948, the new regime made it clear that it envisaged a positive role for the state, mainly in the key and basic industries, leaving the rest of the industrial field in the hands of private enterprise. Indian planning was thus to take place as part of a mixed economy. This was the understanding on which the Planning Commission was appointed in March 1950. Its main task was to draw up a draft plan for the five-year period 1951–56. Like subsequent plans, it set forth a number of desirable social goals which planning was to ensure. These include adequate livelihood for all, together with a proper distribution of wealth and income. It assumed that through planning, India could take on the attributes of a welfare state setting a minimum standard below which no one should fall. In the first place, however, it was necessary to deal with the adverse results of wartime dislocation and of partition, for which projects already existed in the ministries concerned. Although the plan was intended to lay the foundation for more rapid economic growth, the amount of new public investment was on too modest a scale to initiate a real industrialization drive. Priority was given to raising the output of food and raw materials and taking up the unused capacity in consumer goods industries.

The actual results achieved in the five-year period differed from the plan targets in a number of respects. They were assisted by favourable monsoons which eased the food supply position.

Although India was able to draw on the sterling balances, little foreign aid was forthcoming. Actual investment outlays were less than those proposed, especially in some important fields such as irrigation, electricity supply, iron and steel and aluminium. The overall result was a rise of 18 per cent in national product and an increase of about 30 per cent in industrial output. The planners were encouraged to set more ambitious targets for the next plan; it had also become clear that a more concerted industrialization drive depended upon state investment in the heavy industries.

The shift in emphasis between the First and Second Plan was reflected in the new Industrial Policy Resolution adopted in April 1956. While in some ways it only reiterated the 1948 resolution, it spelled out more clearly the commitment to industrialization on the basis of a mixed economy. The Resolution claimed to represent the adoption of a 'socialist pattern of society' and enumerated a series of industries involving investment on a scale which only the state could provide. These industries were to be progressively state owned, or the state was to take the initiative in establishing new undertakings. Those industries not explicitly mentioned were to remain within the sphere of private ownership. The resolution also called for the coordination of the two sectors, following the view of the First Plan that 'private enterprise should have a public purpose and there is no such thing under present conditions as completely unregulated and free private enterprise'.

The language of the resolution reflected a compromise between the socialist phraseology of the Congress intelligentsia and the practical necessities of Indian businessmen. The latter were in no position to project or finance a programme of industrialization; only the state could do that. For electoral reasons, to avoid being outflanked from the Left, the Congress leadership had to avoid giving the impression that it was opening the gates for capitalist development. Conflicting interests and pressures became more intense in the years which followed. Many businessmen and Congress supporters became openly hostile to creeping socialism from the state sector. At the same time, in the practice of the mixed economy the state sector seemed to be the servant of private interests. As government policy became increasingly sensitive to private interests it became evident that the state sector was not to be the commanding height from which a socialist policy could be implemented. Nehru himself declared that as long as privately-owned industries were well managed 'we see no need for nationalization at any time'.

The resolution envisaged a certain intermingling of the private and public sectors, as well as the possibility of joint enterprises between the state and Indian or foreign business capital. As far as planning was concerned, however, the state could obviously only determine the allocation of investment and resources and the targets for output in those industries which it controlled. Since the state industries would be mainly in the producer goods sector, those consumer goods industries likely to benefit most from an expansion of demand and to be most profitable in the short run, were to be left in private hands. Such industries would only be developed so far as they promised to be profitable; as long, that is to say, as there was an expanding market for their output. So far as the state industries brought about an increase in the rate of economic growth and raised per capita incomes, they would contribute to the profitability of the private sector. On the other hand, there was no compulsion for those who accumulated capital as a result of rising real income to invest it in socially desirable ways. The pattern of investment, and thus of production, in the privately-owned consumer goods industries would be determined by the laws of the market and would reflect closely the distribution of income. This was to be shown in the outcome of subsequent plans.

What could be achieved in the way of industrialization from the method of planning adopted in India was thus limited from the outset. But it was even more constricted by the social structure of the country: the vast inequalities already in existence, and the fact that, so far as industrial goods were concerned, the mass of the people had a minimal amount of purchasing power, or none at all. Unless something was done to improve the levels of their incomes practically all the gains of industrialization would go to the higher income groups.

However, every plan, including the Second Plan, announced as among its main objectives the reduction of inequalities in wealth and income to be achieved through state action and redistributive taxation. What the planners failed to perceive was that the kind of economic measures they proposed (which emphasized economic growth, however investment was allocated between producer goods and consumer goods) could not reduce income inequalities and might even tend to increase them. Only direct social measures could counteract and reverse such a trend. It had to be accepted either that the balance between the state and private sectors proposed in the oddly-named 'socialist pattern', made the social goals of the Plans unattainable, or that there had to be direct action against the existing unequal distribution of property and income. To assume that economic growth if maintained long enough would end poverty and unemployment and bring about a more equal distribution of income was a vain pretension. There was an inherent conflict between the declared 'socialist' objectives of the Plans and the methods employed.

THE SECOND PLAN AND AFTER

The planning models used from the Second Plan onwards were greatly influenced by Soviet examples as regards the allocation of investment and the expected consequences for output. In the Soviet Union, however, planning operated on the basis of a totally nationalized industry and a collectivized agriculture. In India, the professed aim of the Congress government was to steer a middle course between capitalist methods and those used in the Soviet Union. The Plans may be appraised individually against their own stated aims and from a technical point of view it may be judged how far they achieved them. Here the main emphasis will be on the plan period as a whole from 1956 onwards, to determine how far they made possible the industrialization of the Indian economy.

It may be said at the outset that although India claimed to have embarked upon 'democratic' planning, this meant no more than that there was a parliamentary system, and that the degree of compulsion embodied in the plans remained consistent with the maintenance of private property. In practical terms it was a policy of counterfeit socialism; this could be determined by the failure of successive plans to carry through a structural transformation, or to change the distribution of wealth and income in a more egalitarian direction. Planning has remained remote from the people, since they have had no share in drawing up the plans or any part in carrying them out except as executants of commands from above. True it could be claimed that there has been a lack of sustained pressure from below to promote far-reaching changes, or that such pressures have been contained within the repressive framework of the state. Most significantly there has not been a determined drive from above to bring practice into line with the professed intentions of the plan. Land reforms have not been carried out on a significant scale; income distribution has not become more equal; poverty and unemployment remain endemic. Yet, in terms of overall aggregates there has been growth both in industry and in agricultural production. Thus a kind of industrialization has been taking place in India under the aegis of the Plans, and the remainder of this chapter will attempt to characterize it more precisely.

MODERN INDIAN INDUSTRIALIZATION

In the absence of a powerful home-market demand, which could only have come had there been a structural transformation of the rural sector, industrialization in India had to begin from the top. After the First Plan, therefore, the planning effort was concentrated on building up the capital goods sector. At the time, this seems to have been acceptable to businessmen, who had long bewailed India's deficiencies in this respect, and to nationalists, since a heavy industry seemed to be a necessary step towards economic independence and a basis for a long-term programme of industrial development. It was assumed that adequate supplies of food would be forthcoming, that one-fourth of the finance required would be available from foreign sources, and that no more than one-fifth would come from deficit financing. The increased consumption resulting from the incomes generated by government outlays would come to a large extent from the cottage and small-scale industries of the traditional type. Indeed, from this period dates a steady expansion of small capitalist businesses. The medium- and larger-scale firms in the private sector were subject to government licensing of capital issue and plant construction. Customs protection and foreign exchange restrictions safeguarded high-cost import-substitution industries from being swamped by foreign competition. Controls operated in a rather negative way to limit the operation of the laws of the market, giving rise to a bureaucratic apparatus with some corruption and considerable evasion. Businessmen became increasingly averse to these controls and sections of business came out in open opposition to the planning system.

The Second Plan encountered difficulties. India's resources in foreign currency were rapidly drained away; the food supply situation deteriorated; and inflationary pressures began to display themselves. Continued industrialization thus became dependent upon foreign aid, mostly in the shape of loans. Foreign assistance, while also needed to make good the deficits in the food supply consequent upon poor harvests, may be seen as an alternative to curtailing investment in heavy industry, squeezing consumption more, or making a radical alteration in policy (especially in the agrarian sector). It operated, therefore, to preserve the political institutions and distribution of social and economic power as they had emerged after the handing over of power by the British in 1947. In any case, the priority accorded to heavy industry, though designed to increase self-reliance in the long run, required heavy imports of plant and machinery (about two-fifths, in fact) while the growth of the indebtedness meant that there was a need to increase exports. By the end of the Second Plan, in 1961, over one-fifth of the cost had been financed by foreign assistance.

Industrial production went up by 41 per cent in the course of the Second Plan the main gains being in electric power generation, iron and steel, fertilizers, cement and coal. Supplies of factory-made consumer goods for mass consumption increased scarcely at all. Moreover, instead of increasing at the expected 1.5 per cent per annum population growth had averaged 2.5 per cent.

The Third Plan, which covered the period 1961 to 1966, followed similar lines to its predecessor in its emphasis upon the building up of the basic industry complex for the production of industrial material and capital goods. It aimed to raise national income by 5 per cent per annum, and to achieve self-sufficiency in food-stuffs. The Plan document made the references which were to become mandatory to the aim of combating unemployment, overcoming poverty and making possible greater equality of opportunity and a better distribution of income, wealth and economic power. Plan technique had improved, personnel had been trained and the plan machinery had been run in but objective difficulties were looming larger.

THE THIRD PLAN

The Third Plan, on much the same lines as its predecessor, envisaged continued industrialization, promoted by high rates of investment in the public sector and with heavy industry leading the way. In the outcome, however, the plan experienced severe setbacks and the results were disappointing: there was a falling off in the rates of growth of industrial production and per capita real income. Two bad harvests upset the objective of self-sufficiency in food grains, and India became dependent upon US grain supplies under Public Law 480. Overall, the amount of foreign aid utilized was twice as much as the Second Plan; India's dependence upon foreign aid now seemed to be irrevocable. The major goods of mass consumption (such as cotton, sugar and vegetable oils) showed virtually no increase in output although population growth continued as rapidly as before. On the other hand, the kind of factory-made goods bought by those with higher incomes were being produced in greatly increased quantities. The 'demonstration effect' was working; with it foreign firms and imported technology began to play an enhanced role in industry, with government approval.

More ominously, India's pretensions as a great power inheriting the role of the Raj in the region caused friction and conflict with her neighbours: a border clash with China in 1962 and war with Pakistan in 1965. This imposed a heavy defence burden for modern weaponry, as well as for a standing army of about one million with another 800,000 police and para-military forces. The war with Pakistan led to a virtual cessation of economic aid and forced the devaluation of the rupee. Instead of going on with the Fourth Plan, already in preparation, the government declared a 'plan holiday' and until 1969 the Fourth Plan was replaced by annual plans. In any case, there was a shift away from the earlier form of planning. An influential section of business re-asserted its confidence in market forces, denounced the interference of the bureaucracy in economic matters and called for greater reliance on incentives to private investment. There was a down-grading of the Planning Commission as a source of policy. In formulating economic measures more emphasis was laid upon the states rather than the centre. While the central government did not hesitate to intervene in the food market and in banking greater support was given to increasing production even if that meant concessions to private enterprise and foreign capital. Increasing pressure was coming from such institutions as the World Bank to curtail ambitious public sector programmes and give more scope for private enterprise with priority to agriculture, notably through the introduction of high-yield seeds and the package making up the 'Green Revolution'. The social goals of the Plans were conspicuously neglected in practice.

The plan holiday period was generally one of retrenchment. Existing core projects were completed while the commencement of new investments with a long completion period was deferred. Foreign capital import and aid were resumed following rupee devaluation. Considerable excess capacity now appeared in the capital goods industries established during the earlier plans. The cutback in public investment did not see private investment filling the gap. A serious problem throughout this phase of Indian industrialization was the reluctance of private capital to enter into new industrial projects on the requisite scale. Some private industries were adversely affected by the curtailment of government spending; there were bankruptcies and unemployment. Imported goods, including plant and machinery, became dearer in rupee terms. This gave some incentive for import-substitution, especially in those goods consumed by the top 10 or 15 per cent of income-receivers. Real wages stagnated or even fell. Overall industrial production rose by only 12 per cent from 1966–69, while per capita income was virtually stagnant and actually below the 1964–65 level. In any case, in India, per capita income figures have scarcely more than a symbolic value and reveal practically nothing about the welfare of the great majority of the people. The benefits of planning so far had been imperceptible as far as they were concerned.

The new Plan, launched in 1969, was intended to change this state of affairs by increasing the rate of growth in industry by utilizing existing capacity more fully and starting new projects. The aim was an industrial growth rate of 8–10 per cent annually, together with an increase in agricultural production and the elimination of dependence upon food imports. More scope was to be allowed for the private sector, notably through the relaxation of controls. This time, the intention of doing something for the rural poor and the underemployed and unemployed was spelled out even more plainly than in previous plans. Once again, however, it has to be reported that little progress was made to overcome poverty and the additional jobs created by the Plan absorbed only a fraction of the newcomers to the labour market. The new Plan was also intended to halve the amount of investment financed from foreign sources by cutting down on non-food imports and increasing exports. As much as 78 per cent of the new investment projected was to be raised without resort either to foreign borrowing or deficit financing.

The hopes placed upon the Fourth Plan were almost totally frustrated by shortfalls in investment and production at home, the effects of the second war with Pakistan and the adverse changes in the world economy. The combination of the slowdown in world trade and production, the four-fold increase in oil prices, and currency instability, together with the internal difficulties, hit the economy hard, slowing down growth, aggravating inflation and accentuating a social-political crisis which culminated in Mrs Gandhi's declaration of a state of emergency in 1976. In the event, then, the growth rates attained in the 1969–74 period were below those estimated in the Plan. This tendency to fall below anticipated targets, indeed, a general slowing down of growth was to be characteristic of the 1970s during the Fourth and the Fifth Plans.

A retrospective view of this decade provides an opportunity to draw some conclusions about the course of India's industrialization so far. Politically there seems to have been a general down-grading of the Plan and a growing dependence upon market forces with pragmatic government intervention in such fields as food distribution. While the building up of some basic industries was seen from the start as the main motive force for industrializing the economy as a whole this has clearly not worked out in practice. The industries concerned have not imparted to the economy, as a whole those high rates of growth characteristic of the Soviet Union and Japan. The Fourth Plan aimed at a rate of 12 per cent per annum in organized industry and the Fifth Plan aimed at 8 per cent. Growth rates recorded were 3.25 per cent in the period 1965–70 and around 2.75 per cent in 1970–74. In the mid-1970s, national income was growing at about 3.6 per cent per annum. While these rates could be considered respectable compared with those of some advanced countries during the same period they fell a good deal short of what was necessary to make even a dent in the problems of mass poverty and unemployment.

Instead of the basic industries being the locomotive for growth and the promotion of a structural transformation, the main trends in the economy seem to be determined by factors operating in the opposite direction. The slow-down in growth has been most apparent in iron and steel, mechanical engineering and cement, while the fastest rates of growth have been scored by consumer goods industries geared to the top end of the market, from synthetic fibres and cosmetics to air conditioners and refrigerators. As already noted for an earlier period, mass consumption industries have remained relatively stagnant. In other words, market forces have taken over. The product-mix of industry corresponds to purchasing power in a society with an extremely unequal distribution of income. There is a large enough market made up of the minority (10 or 15 per cent) with discretionary purchasing power for industrial products to encourage investment in certain kinds of production. At the same time, most of the rest of the population can afford few, if any, of these products. Industrialization has thus not drawn the population as a whole into its orbit; it has stopped short of a structural transformation. Steel mills, modern factories, banks,

107

offices and luxury flats rear up against a background of unrelieved mass poverty and abysmally low living standards. It would be unduly optimistic to expect that the modern sector will gradually absorb the 'traditional' sector. In fact there is no sign that the proportion of the population in the modern sector is growing at all.

It can only be concluded that the Plans have failed to achieve their professed and repeated objectives of abolishing poverty, overcoming unemployment and bringing about a more equal distribution of income, wealth and social power. They have produced a partial and lop-sided form of industrialization which only sharpens regional and class disparities and social contradictions. India has not found a successful alternative to central planning of the Soviet or Chinese types, nor is it an advertisement for the ability of capitalist methods to transform an underdeveloped country. Whether there has been too much planning or not enough, the hopes held out for 'the socialistic pattern' – really a mixed economy with capitalist relations of production still dominant – have not been realized.

Dissatisfaction with the results of planning, especially the alleged inefficiency, lethargy and corruption of the state sector, brought 'liberalization' into favour after Rajiv Gandhi became prime minister. It followed a re-thinking of industrial policy which reached back to the mid-1970s. The main target of the reform policy was the system of licensing and import controls intended to direct industrial growth into the desired channels by encouraging infant industries, conserving foreign exchange and assisting the process of import-substitution. It was also aimed at the complex system of price controls applied to some products. The private sector had long been chafing under the restrictions of the licensing system and calling for its reform. Policy-makers were influenced by the fashionable swing towards free-market economics in the Western countries and the comparative eclipse of Keynesianism and of economic planning.

Gandhi's reforms certainly gave Indian capitalism a boost, notably through an investment boom, including the importation of foreign technology on a much greater scale than before. Industrial growth was pushed up to 9 per cent in 1986–87. The main, if not the only, beneficiaries of 'liberalization' have been the top 10–15 per cent of income-receivers who make up the bulk of the consumer market for manufactured goods. In short, in a programme of reforms which stopped well short of the privatization of the state sector, the rich have got richer and, as before, the mass of the population remains outside, or only on the fringes of, the consumer market. In a country like India it appears that the supply-side theory that if business is offered the freedom of the market it will generate new wealth which will 'trickle down' to the mass of the people just does not work, at least not for decades. While the policies of Rajiv Gandhi have produced rapid growth in some sectors and made possible an investment boom, the effect can be expected to wear off after a short time, resulting, perhaps, in over-shooting and excess capacity. It may be argued that liberalization has not gone far enough and that it must be followed up by the dismantling of the state sector and its handing over to the big corporations which dominate the modern private sector. To do this would be a political gamble of the first magnitude which seems unlikely however well-founded much of the criticism of the way in which state industry is run may be.

As it is, every surge of growth, such as that produced by Rajiv Gandhi (threatened in any case by drought in 1988), only exposes the contrasts and contradictions of Indian society, heightening its tensions, provoking sectarian rivalries and communal conflicts. Not the slow working out of market forces but direct measures of policy seem to be the only possible way in which the problems of poverty, underemployment and unemployment can be dealt with. It is significant that the recent industrial boom saw not the creation of new jobs in manufacturing industry but an actual fall in employment resulting from technological upgrading. A sustained rise in the number of urban jobs can only come when the millions of rural poor gain access to the consumer market.

REASONS FOR FAILURE: THE LACK OF AGRARIAN CHANGE

Successful industrialization, whether capitalist or not, has been associated with fundamental changes in the agrarian sector. Such changes have made it possible to increase the output of food and raw materials while releasing labour from the land. In the earlier stages of industrialization this means at least a relative decline in the rural population. Improved technique in agriculture also raises incomes and/or makes a larger proportion of the rural population dependent on the market as sellers of farm produce and/or labour power, thus contributing to the growth of the home market for manufactured goods. In general, then, there is a shift from less productive to more productive occupations, a movement from the land to the cities. These processes may take place in a variety of ways, such as the classic preparation for capitalist agriculture in the case of English enclosures or, at the other extreme, the collectivization of peasant farms in the Soviet Union. In other cases, agriculture has been modernized without imposing such severe sacrifices on the peasantry. Under the pressure of market forces operating to push marginal cultivators off the land and to attract surplus rural population into urban occupations by the pull of higher earnings, it may take place relatively painlessly. Other variants are possible, such as the encouragement of cooperative farming and the development of small-scale rural industries. In actual historical cases, however, a proletariat generally has been constituted from the rural population because there was a more or less corresponding growth in the market for labour power through the growth of industry, whether in response to market forces or to a central plan.

The point is that under Indian conditions the complementary changes in the agrarian sector have simply not worked out. The proportion of the labour force in agriculture has remained roughly stationary during the Plans at about 72 per cent, and has grown considerably in absolute numbers. At the same time, farm income has gone up in real terms (by 65 per cent between 1951 and 1971) while the number of 'dwarf holders' (below five acres per family) and of landless labourers has grown. There are, at the same time, enormous regional disparities between prosperous states such as Punjab, Haryana and western Uttar Pradesh, and poor ones such as Bihar, Mysore and Orissa. Rural India has followed the pattern already shown for the country as a whole: a relatively affluent minority has experienced definite gains from economic growth while the incomes of the great majority have shown little or no rise and may indeed have declined in the past decade. Thus the mass of the rural population can afford to buy little if anything in the way of manufactured goods or, in the case of land-holders, inputs which could raise the productivity of the land. While the internal market is kept relatively small there is also little incentive to move off the land; those who do generally join the many-millioned army of the urban jobless.

The Congress government which took power after Independence did not justify the expectation that it would carry through an agrarian reform as the basis for improving the lot of the vast majority of the population. Under the new constitution this matter devolved upon the governments of the states; there was no national policy and thus no uniformity in dealing with the agrarian problem. The main line of the reforms introduced was to abolish the *zamindari* and similar landowning systems resulting from British legislation, and to do away with functionless intermediaries between tenants and landowners. The existence of an enormous variety of different forms of tenure made the introduction of reform a protracted process. In any case, the landowners were to retain land in 'personal cultivation'; but the meaning of such phrases was unclear. Where there were limits on the amount of land which could be held, the landowners were generally given plenty of time to hand over part of their land to family members or front men. Where land was taken over, compensation was paid. Evasion of the laws, laxity and corruption in their execution limited their effectiveness. There were no sweeping changes, no genuine redistribution of land to those with insufficient land or none at all, and no alteration in the balance of social and economic power in the villages. Politicians in the state parliaments as well as in New Delhi were too dependent upon the support and cooperation of the landowners and village notables to attempt to make any serious inroads into their privileges. Voluntary transfers of land were also mainly of token significance.

Half-hearted as these reforms were, they did lead to the abolition of intermediaries in large parts of the country, break up some of the big estates and provide some tenants with more security than they had enjoyed before. These changes simply made possible a fuller development of capitalist relations. Further, former *zamindars* and big landowners turned to commercial leasing or farmed part of the land themselves. The better-off peasants, belonging to dominant castes, already a powerful group in many parts of rural India, were able to consolidate their position. Unevenly and at different rates in various regions of the country, agricultural capitalism spread. The government assisted the process by irrigation, land reclamation and the spread of technical knowledge. Improvements of this kind assisted the expansion of production but tended to increase the disparities between the big landowners and better-off peasants and the 'dwarf holders', share-croppers and landless labourers who made up the majority of the village population. Rural change has taken many different forms; the general tendency has been to substitute capitalist relations for the old feudal and patriarchal relations between landowners and peasants.

From the mid-1960s this process was accelerated with the adoption of the new agricultural strategy based upon high-yield seeds, artificial fertilizers and water control. This so-called 'Green Revolution' was sponsored by the government under strong external pressure from the World Bank and other institutions who saw social and political stability in the future tied up with the creation of a prosperous class of rural capitalists. To an extent this policy has worked, at least in those regions where the new capital-intensive package could be utilized, that is to say on not more than 25 per cent of the cultivated area. Landlords and strong peasants with capital have gained; improving land under cultivation, acquiring more land, investing in tractors, pumps and other machinery and employing more hired labour. Market forces, whether or not directly connected with the 'Green Revolution' have, at the same time, further undermined the position of small peasants – owners as well as tenants, turning some into share-croppers or wage-labourers. However, there has been no corresponding increase in the demand for labour either from rural industries or from the towns. In a rough and uneven way capitalism has done part of the job that it has done in other countries in the past, but it has not prevented the pauperization of a large part of the rural population, especially in those regions little affected by the 'Green Revolution'. Agricultural output has been increasing at a rate of about 2.6 per cent per annum, against only 0.8 per cent under British rule. It has slightly more than kept pace with the growth in population. In fact, in years of good harvest there have been surpluses of food, not because of absolute overproduction but because the poor have not been able to buy all they need to ensure an adequate calorific intake (and this despite government interference in the provision of foodgrains).

POVERTY

Agrarian development in India, while significant in terms of production, has not complemented industrialization to the same degree as in the countries of developed capitalism. While in the favoured regions a rural elite has prospered on an all-India scale there are two hundred million more rural dwellers whose poverty prevents them contributing to the home market and whose labour is not required in industry. They eke out a bare existence from scraps of land or from performing manual and menial tasks; from an economic point of view they are superfluous to requirements. It is doubtful whether development on the present lines, even over a long period, will provide much relief for these underemployed and overexploited millions, or draw them into the development process as productive members.

Mass poverty in India, in the cities as well as in the rural areas, is sometimes attributed to the 'population explosion'. To be sure, the population of India has grown at an unexpectedly high rate of about 2.5 per cent per annum. In broad terms it could be said that advances in production are eaten up by increasing numbers; but this is not really so. A disproportionate share of total output goes to the 10–15 per cent of the more affluent people in town and country. Growing population mainly adds to human misery at the bottom end of the scale; additional family members are no real problem for those whose incomes are rising. Moreover, it is easy for politicians and planners to evade responsibility for their policies, or lack of them, by taking cover behind the high rates of population increase. The compulsory birth control and sterilization programmes which took place during the Emergency were a panic attempt to deal with a situation which had arisen from decades of evasion and perhaps a fear of the social reckoning likely to arise from overpopulation.

However, population is not an autonomous factor; it grows out of and is influenced by complex forces some of which are susceptible to alteration through policy measures directed to the economy. The experience of the advanced countries shows that a slow down in population increase accompanies rising incomes. It may be said, of course, that India cannot wait that long or that such a happy situation will never be reached. Indians, especially in the rural areas, have children because they soon contribute to family income, are a kind of insurance for old age, or are necessary for cultural and religious reasons. It would also be true to say that high birth rates and large families depend upon the acquiescence of the women of India, 80 per cent of whom are still illiterate. It is not only that lack of education makes it difficult to understand and practise birth control techniques, it is also because society provides no incentive to apply them. As long as educational opportunities are not widely available and women see few alternatives to motherhood, high rates of population growth are likely to continue. On the other hand, if primary education were available to all women within a decade or two a durable downward trend in birth rates might begin. India is now living with her failure to grasp this nettle some thirty years ago. The problem is one of policy options, not of some natural and unalterable laws of population or of unchangeable cultural traits. There is still an alternative to a continued frightening increase in numbers or an ultimate Malthusian catastrophe.

The taxation of the rich, the carrying out of agrarian reform and the tackling of the problems of underemployment and

113

unemployment have all been marked by an absence of political will at the top and in adequate pressure from below. The tendency has been to avoid dealing with root causes and to treat symptoms, and even then to do so without conviction. This lack of determination obviously has to do with the distribution of power and influence in India. The bourgeoisie, closely allied with the privileged elements in the countryside, cannot play the same historical role it has played in the past in other countries. This is true even in the general field of industrialization. The erection of some modern large-scale plants in heavy industry, the enlargement of the infrastructure with public money, and some assistance to capitalist agriculture do not suffice to create a modern economy out of what was left by the British Raj in 1947. Without a much more concerted drive for industrialization on a wide front and including fundamental agrarian reform, neither the structural transformation of the economy nor a self-generating process of growth is possible today. As it is, the benefits of the industrial development which has taken place in India since Independence have not yet reached the masses and the call to abolish poverty remains unanswered. Industrialization in India has thus been a limited success; one more example of growth without development.

CHAPTER 5

China: the slumbering giant awakes

Since China is by far the largest country in the world in terms of population size, it is not surprising that her attempts to industrialize have attracted considerable world attention, especially because they have been accompanied by social and ideological upheavals of an unprecedented character. While deeply influenced by the Soviet model, the Communist regime, after the Revolution of 1949, under the leadership of Mao Tse-tung, adopted novel approaches to the problem of industrialization in a predominantly agrarian and backward society. His successors, while departing from the guidelines he laid down, have embarked upon a programme of modernization which necessarily has industrial growth as one of its key strategies. As the population continues to grow, there is a desperate race to raise output as in other countries similarly placed, but it is carried on by methods which are specifically Chinese.

China evolved its own form of civilization in an historical process which extends back over at least four thousand years. In that time, intricate cultural patterns were developed which had immense staying power. For most of that time China was ahead of Europe in its social organization and culture with its own political system. In the later European Middle Ages, the countries of north-west Europe began to move ahead with accelerated speed, adopting the capitalist mode of production and entering on the road to industrialization. Nothing like this took place in China as an organic and autonomous process. By the time that Europeans began to batter on her doors seeking profitable trade, they had the advantage of a superior technology and military power as well as of superior economic organization. Although China avoided colonial status, unequal treaties were imposed by the European metropoles, bases were ceded and the country was effectively divided up into spheres of influence. The foundations of the old order were undermined and China entered the twentieth century a prey to external pressures and internal turmoil. The old empire finally gave way in the revolution of 1911 but the new republic failed to establish a viable, centralized regime, falling into warlordism and civil war, compounded by Japanese invasion and war (1937–45) from which the well-organized Communist Party with its peasant armies and programme of social revolution emerged triumphant in 1949.

From an historical point of view, the first problem is why, having developed to such a high level, China showed no signs of embarking on a process of industrialization before the intrusion of the Europeans? Why was it that despite the relatively advanced state of scientific knowledge and technology and an intensive agriculture China showed no tendency to generate those forces which make for capitalism? Why did it fail to find its own way to raise income levels and promote sustained growth? Why was it that labour-saving machinery and factory methods of production were not developed in China? Why did China, at least, not follow, or even precede, Japan in adopting them when they were introduced into Asia in the nineteenth century? Why was it that the main initiative for economic change came from outside, from the Europeans, rather than from within the old order?

These are important and difficult questions and scholars specialized in the field are by no means able to provide complete or agreed answers. Clearly, there must have been factors in Chinese society which inhibited change and growth beyond a certain point, a built-in inertia resisting even the strongest pressure. There was nothing unique about the conservatism of traditional China; it was, indeed, a means of self-preservation for the dominant social strata. The leading role of an educated body of officials, recruited by examinations and steeped in the Confucian classics, which gave ideological sanction to the established order, was an important factor in resisting change. The mandarin officials were interested in upholding law and order, in protecting the interests of the rich and powerful, since this was the best way to maintain their own position. There were no movements comparable to the Renaissance or the Reformation in Europe to challenge orthodoxy, upset the social order, encourage a more individualistic attitude or to stimulate discovery or invention.

THE OLD ORDER

The Chinese economy under the last two dynasties, the Ming and the Ching, the latter being that of the Manchus who ruled until 1911, had reached a relatively high level of sophistication but it was, in essence a regulated economy, not one determined by the laws of the market, Necessarily its basis was agriculture and, as under European feudalism, the surplus product extracted from the peasantry provided the support for the upper class of officials, scholars and gentry. Over a large part of China, rice was the main crop; cultivation was thus highly labour-intensive and required water control involving complex structures and devices. Land ownership was unequal, with landlords and richer peasants in each locality dominating a great mass of small owners and landless or semi-landless peasants. The division of plots of land on inheritance was widely practised and tended to keep the average size of holdings small. The upper classes derived their income from the surplus produced by the dependent peasantry through rents and taxes, not from a manorial type economy or the labour of slaves or serfs.

Throughout much of Chinese history, land had been relatively abundant, so that expansion took the form of new settlements. By the eighteenth century, however, probably because political conditions were more settled and new crops and improved methods of cultivation had spread, the population began to grow more rapidly. This tended to make labour still more abundant than it had been before, and increased the number of peasants with inadequate amounts of land or none at all. This population upsurge, a major factor in modern Chinese history, has continued virtually without interruption down to the present day. In the eighteenth and nineteenth centuries, population pressure on the land did not necessarily lead to a decline in per capita income levels but it did seriously limit any increase in them. Both in agriculture and in industry – mostly carried on by artisans and in small workshops – advantage was taken of the abundance and cheapness of labour to employ large amounts of it, relative to land and equipment. China was a labour surplus economy by this time with labour-intensive methods generally prevailing.

Under these conditions, traditional forms of production, which would have been relatively advanced compared with Medieval Europe, and even in the eighteenth century remained so compared with many parts of the world, held their own and changed only slowly. The practice of using large amounts of labour in agriculture, on constructional projects and in industry was reinforced by continued population growth. With abundant supplies of labour available, there was a deterrent to any search for labour-saving technology. Existing methods of production were capable of meeting any increase in demand and there was no rapid growth in markets to provide a stimulus. The social surplus, concentrated in the hands of the state and ruling class, was enough to support large cities and urban industries, a merchant class and bankers, but it still came essentially from agriculture. What was lacking was any new factor or force to promote a change in the established order, which had tended to perpetuate itself over the centuries.

Merchants or financiers who built up large fortunes aspired to pass into the gentry class or to see themselves or their sons become government officials. For their part, the gentry landowners had no incentive to change the existing set-up which secured them in their privileged position. Markets were large but fragmented. Long distance trade was mainly in luxury and semi-luxury goods for the upper classes. The market for goods of everyday consumption was local and narrow, based as it was upon a mass of peasant households with limited purchasing power. Trade and industry also tended to be closely regulated by officialdom, after the fashion of European mercantilism. While there was considerable scope for merchant capital, and the merchants at this time probably had a stronger position in Chinese society than is sometimes suggested, there was little scope for the investment of capital in industrial production. This was less a question of regulation or control than of a simple lack of incentive, especially as the abundance of labour deterred investment in machines or labour-saving methods. Lucrative outlets for merchant capital could be found in other directions. Financiers and bankers could earn high rates of interest lending to officials and the gentry and, at a lower level, to the peasants at usurious rates.

The major part of the surplus produced by the mass of peasants and artisans above their subsistence needs was scooped up by the state, local officials and the gentry. It took the form of direct taxes, in money or in kind, indirect taxes and various other levies and payments. Part of this revenue, to be sure, found its way into productive uses, such as the maintenance of waterways, roads and flood control, but probably most of it went to the upkeep of a vast bureaucracy and army, or into the coffers of gentry families. Largely this was a one-way traffic: funds and goods flowed from the provinces to Peking, or from the rural areas to the provincial towns.

The flow in the opposite direction was on a reduced scale; the towns were not industrial centres but the administrative headquarters of the ruling class.

Considered as a pre-industrial economy, on a comparative basis, China was at a high level of development by the eighteenth and nineteenth centuries; but it had achieved that level long before and showed no signs of a qualitative shift to a more complex structure or to a higher rate of growth. There was no independent middle class, or bourgeoisie, of the European type, owning individual private property, investing in trade and industry or practising the professions. The Chinese merchants were more like those to be found in medieval Europe or any other similar society; they played only a subordinate role, despite their riches, and their interests tied them to the established order. As for the scholar-officials, they, likewise, were identified absolutely with the existing social order and not likely to be the seed-bed for a critical or reforming tendency on the scale, for example, of the European Enlightenment of the eighteenth century. There was no reason for them to reject the received Confucian doctrines which sanctified their role.

The vastness of China, as well as the relative ease of transport over much of the territory by means of the river system, gave its policies an inward-looking character. There was little need for, or interest in, foreign contacts and trade, and still many inner frontiers to be opened up. Foreigners were treated disdainfully; trade with them was not prohibited (as in Tokugawa Japan) but was only carried on with them because they had come to China. Chinese merchants of the Ching period seldom ventured abroad in search of trade.

All in all, there were no indigenous forces or pressures prior to the nineteenth century that were in any way strong enough to promote fundamental change in the Chinese economy. Though change was not absent, it was constricted by the whole nature of traditional Chinese society, as well as by the lack of any incentive to change the existing relations between the factors of production or any class which could take the initiative in such a change. That is why, although pre-industrial China did possess some of the 'prerequisites' for economic growth (looking at it in retrospect) – markets, money, merchants, banking – they could not be turned to account. No inventors or innovating entrepreneurs appeared able to promote an industrial revolution. China was fated to receive the new modern technology as an import from the hands of foreigners. It did so, at first, in a largely passive role.

Europeans began to draw China into the world market on

a significant scale in the eighteenth century, just as the industrial revolution was beginning in Europe. As the British East India Company extended its territorial domain in India, it came to dominate the trade with China, being especially interested in finding there a market for Indian opium to pay for the Chinese tea and silk it was shipping to Europe. When the Chinese government decided to resist a trade which was debilitating its subjects and depleting its revenues, the British went to war in 1840. In any case, by then the Manchu regime was in a state of crisis and in no position to rally the people for a national war against the foreigner. After two years of desultory warfare it made peace at Nanking in 1842 and from then on a new era in Chinese history began. Britain imposed an indemnity on China and acquired Hongkong as a base for trade. A number of other Chinese ports were to be opened up to foreign trade. This was the beginning of the treaty ports system under which the United States, as well as the major European powers, imposed treaties on a weakening China, giving their subjects extra-territorial rights in these ports. In 1857 Anglo-French forces launched the Second Opium War at a time when the Manchus were facing the most serious challenge to their rule from the Taipings, a vast peasant revolt which might have led to the renovation of China, only defeated in 1864. As a result of their victory over China, by the Treaty of Tientsin Britain and France were able to impose even more stringent terms. Besides legalizing the opium trade, the treaty opened up ten more ports to Western trade. Merchants, missionaries and others were permitted to travel into the interior of China and Western control of the customs system (first imposed in 1854) was extended. The process of bringing China's economy under foreign control had begun and was to continue, but the rivalry between the countries concerned, together with the size and remoteness of China, saved it from becoming a colony or being partitioned between the powers. Instead, foreigners established themselves for business purposes in the treaty ports and staked out spheres of influence in the interior, as the need arose.

FOREIGN INFLUENCE

Thus, unlike Japan, China was unable to offer any real resistance to the foreign intruders and was forced to accept an inferior position. Their hold on the treaty ports gave the foreigners access to the interior, control over external trade and bargaining counters for winning more concessions. To develop their trade they had to depend upon Chinese nationals who knew the language and the country to act as middlemen, assembling products required for export and finding markets for foreign imports. These were the *compradore* capitalists whose interests and fortunes were now bound up with foreign trade and cooperation with foreign businessmen, rather than with the independent development of the national economy.

The opening up of China by force, placing the foreigners in a privileged and dominating position, had contradictory effects on its development. Foreign traders were interested in immediate profits, but they also had to finance an infrastructure of transport and other facilities to extend their business. In fact they were the vehicle through which modern technology and business practices reached China and took root. Inevitably at first the country was seen principally as a source of primary products such as tea, silk and bristles and also as a market for cheap, machine-made, foreign goods. As a result, some branches of agriculture began to grow, while old-style artisan industry suffered from foreign competition. Overall, China now became increasingly exposed to world market forces; tea exports were hit by the new plantations in India, silk by Japanese competition. Price trends and changes in world supply and demand conditions now began to influence China for good or ill. An adaptation had to be made to foreign imports by shifting to new lines. Cotton-spinning, a hand industry, declined, but hand weaving for a time was able to expand using cheap imported machine-made yarn.

From the 1860s Chinese officials made some attempts to introduce modern industry and to develop mining and shipping on Western lines. Without a thorough renovation of government and a new national policy of the kind which followed the Meiji Restoration in Japan, such measures proved to be abortive. Officials saw in these enterprises more a source of squeeze for themselves than a means of guaranteeing national survival; it was an attitude which was to be persistent not only until the fall of the Manchus in 1911, but throughout the nationalist regimes which followed down to 1949. Corruption in one form or another appeared to be endemic.

Meanwhile, although during the second half of the nineteenth century some Chinese entrepreneurs came forward to found new businesses with imported technology and on modern lines, they did not do so on a sufficient scale to initiate a process of industrialization.

In 1895, following defeat in the war with Japan, the establishment of foreign-owned industries was legalized and another indemnity had to be paid. In fact, foreign capital had already begun to find its way into industrial production. Now even more advantage could be taken of one factor China possessed in abundance: labour. It was on the basis of low wages that foreign-owned industries were set up in the treaty ports, especially Shanghai. These industries were not so much directed at the Chinese market, although there was a good deal of import-substitution, as at production for export. It was a type of industrialization with which Asian countries were to become familiar. Foreign capital also flowed into railway construction, shipping and banking. The object of this investment was not to make possible the balanced growth of the Chinese economy but to open up profitable opportunities for foreign capital, chiefly in trade. This was done by opening up the interior and linking it to the ports. Thus the Chinese economy developed in a typically colonial, and one-sided, relationship to the world market. Foreign investment, followed by some native capital, went mainly to peripheral areas – Manchuria and the treaty ports – and had only limited linkage effects on the interior. Over much of the country, the agrarian economy continued to stagnate or even to decline, while population growth was taking place at a rapid rate. Part of the surplus population in adjacent rural areas moved into the treaty ports and other industrial areas to form a cheap labour force for industries often owned by foreign capital. Enclaves of capitalist industrialization were created without close organic relationship with the economy as a whole. On the other hand, they had a 'demonstration effect' for other parts of China and strengthened modernizing forces. Some Chinese were able to acquire new skills, though management posts were, at first, generally held by foreigners. They enabled the *compradore* class to grow and flourish, and encouraged some Chinese entrepreneurs to emulate the foreigner, even to the extent of setting up factories and importing machinery from the West. Native capital could also be mobilized through the banking systems. In the towns an industrial proletariat came into existence, while radical new tendencies began to emerge among the intelligentsia as it was exposed to foreign influences.

In the final analysis the role of the treaty ports, and thus of foreign capital, remains problematic. Did foreign capital merely exploit China and hold back development? Or was it the exogenous force without which the economy would have continued to stagnate?

As has been seen, the Manchu regime was unable to undertake the task of national regeneration performed by the elite of Meiji Japan. The defeat of the Taiping rebellion removed another interesting alternative: the overthrow of the old system by a movement from below, with possible development along bourgeois-democratic lines. Subsequently, the nationalist movement grew in response to foreign intervention and control, but came on the scene too late to prevent it. The slow development of China compared with the Western world fated it to a long period of dependence; at the same time the Western intrusion provided new models and new means of achieving them before the old models had lost their potency. There was nothing to stop the import of the most modern machines or the most advanced ideologies into a China still hidebound by tradition, itself embodied in the officials and gentry of the old regime. By the early twentieth century the challenge of modernization was taken up, first by the nationalists, inspired by Sun Yat Sen, and, when their efforts finally collapsed, by the Chinese Communist Party after 1949. The latter inherited the unfinished tasks of its predecessors. Under whatever auspices industrialization took place in a backward, overwhelmingly agrarian country like China, it was bound to necessitate increased output from the land and a flow of labour from the agrarian sector into industry. On the other hand, it was unlikely that the impetus would come from agriculture, say by its transformation on capitalist lines. Landowners were not turning over to estate-farming for the market, nor was there a class of large capitalist farmers. In the late nineteenth and early twentieth century, Chinese agriculture seems to have been in an intermediate position: it was neither so resistant to change as to consititute an absolute barrier to growth, nor dynamic enough to initiate it. Whoever owned the land, cultivation was overwhelmingly in the hands of the peasantry, mainly using family labour. There was, on the whole, no problem of large estates nor of serfdom. Land was held as private property and could be bought and sold; holdings were usually divided up on inheritance. Land was an investment for both the gentry and the urban rich, for the income it offered and the status it conferred. The income was drawn from the produce of the peasant received in cash or kind, not by taking hold of the land as a means of production and revolutionizing techniques through the investment of further capital. There was, then, a problem of landlordism of a parasitic character, of exiguous holdings and of pressure on the land where population density was high. Landowning was therefore unequal; much land was held by absentees. Some peasants were able to consolidate their holdings by purchase; others, who owned little or no land, might rent it from the gentry or from other owners who had no desire to cultivate it themselves. Peasants who fell into debt, as a result of crop failures or other disasters, might have to relinquish their land; more likely they stayed on as tenants, while paying off their debts to the landlord-usurer. Expensive family ceremonies might also cause the peasants to fall into debt or tenancy. Gentry and others with spare money might lend it on mortgage to distressed peasants, exacting their pound of flesh from the gruelling toil of the cultivators.

In a country as vast as China, generalizations about the agrarian regime, or anything else, are subject to regional variations. There were differences, for example, between the wheat- and sorghum-growing regions of the North and the predominantly rice lands of the South. Some areas had long been opened up to trade by proximity to towns and then to the treaty ports which meant a market for food and demand for labour. Others, in the remote interior, suffered from poor soil or inclement climatic conditions, generated little in the way of surplus and remained desperately poor.

Where markets did exist, there is evidence that the peasants took advantage of the opportunities, producing more for sale, turning to new crops and adopting improved methods. The peasant was susceptible to monetary incentives where they were offered. In many places there was a struggle for survival, made all the more acute by population growth, as the twentieth century progressed. There was also chronic political instability: the breakdown of the Manchu regime, the Revolution of 1911, the failure to build a strong centralized regime, together with the endemic warlordism and civil war in the period from the 1920s onwards, all of which could not have failed to have a disastrous impact upon many parts of rural China. Local rulers imposed new and often unwarranted exactions upon the peasants; military commanders seized their stocks, their animals and their poultry. Young men were conscripted into the warring armies. Public works vitally necessary for water control tended to be neglected, heightening the risk of flood or drought. The Nationalist government, whatever its intentions, was unable to arrest this process of decay or to carry through badly-needed agrarian reforms. This arose largely from the fact that government depended for support on the local gentry and other interests who were opposed to changes likely to diminish their social power. All these factors were noted by the Communists and taken up in their propaganda directed towards the peasantry and all who suffered from misgovernment and corruption.

Until the social disintegration which accompanied civil war in the 1930s there were signs that the land system was accomodating itself to growing commercialization and the growth of industrial centres. The fact that many, if not most, peasant families, held some land, as owners or tenants, may have facilitated this. On the other hand, there were wide differences within the peasantry and where production for the market was carried on, these differences tended to widen. Some peasants turned to commercial agriculture and accumulated capital, if only on a small scale, in a way reminiscent of the Russian kulak. Continued population growth meant more mouths to feed and more sub-division of holdings, many of which were already exiguous. The ruling class was more interested in securing part of the surplus than in finding ways to increase the total output from the land, and there was little incentive for them to do otherwise. In any case, the peasantry would probably have resisted a movement from above to recast the land system in the interests of the larger owners. Their ability to improve productivity was limited by lack of knowledge, lack of capital or addiction to traditional ways – all familiar problems in underdeveloped countries. Moreover, within these constraints, agricultural production, using labour-intensive methods, was highly productive per acre, comparing favourably, for example, with Tokugawa Japan. The typical village remained highly self-sufficient, with local crafts or household production supplying most needs. The absence of any transformation of the agrarian sector closed one avenue for faster economic growth. However, with population growing, in the long-term agriculture was running into an impasse.

The stimulus to growth from the treaty ports was not strong enough to promote rural change outside a restricted hinterland. Manchuria was a special case: the institutional background was different from that of China proper and labour was more scarce relative to land. The coming of the railway opened the way for the commercialization of agriculture and laid a basis for industrialization; the Japanese took full advantage of this when they seized the territory in 1931. Elsewhere, in the 1930s, the most notable feature was the failure of the authorities to formulate or impose a programme of modernization in response to foreign penetration and to win popular support for it. The measures taken were mainly half-hearted and localized in scale.

One explanation of China's disappointing performance is that it had been drawn into the world market in a subordinate position as a result of the Opium Wars and was not therefore able to strike out on an independent path. The Manchu regime was thus forced to allow foreign capitalists to acquire a dominant position in the treaty ports from which they exercised a stranglehold on the entire economy. The failure to develop industrially in the middle decades of the nineteenth century meant that when the new imperialism of the great powers turned to Asia in the last quarter of the century, China was once again a helpless victim. By contrast, Japan escaped the earlier imperialism of free trade thanks to the policy of seclusion before 1858; established a strongly nationalist policy of modernization after the Meiji Restoration of 1868; and in the last quarter of the century joined the imperialist pursuers at China's expense. In Japan's case, the unequal treaties imposed by the Western countries were of shorter duration and proved less onerous. The success of the Restoration policy enabled Japan to become accepted as an equal trading partner while China was incorporated into the world market as an inferior. This role made it still more difficult for industrialization to take place, since the initiative had passed to foreign capital in the treaty ports. Outside these peripheral areas there was no incentive for private capital, Chinese or foreign, to invest in manufacturing industry. The poverty of the peasantry limited the size of the home market, as did the cost of transport in a country of vast distances. The richer consumers wanted high-class goods, either made by small-scale craft industry or imported. In the absence of any other propelling force, the initiative lay potentially with the state. Manchu China was not a modern centralized state and lacked the will as well as the organization either to resist foreign encroachments altogether, as did the Japanese in the Tokugawa period, or to turn the technologies of the West to advantage with a national programme such as that of Meiji Japan.

Elements of modern capitalist economy were certainly introduced into China, but mainly under foreign control. For a long time Chinese entrepreneurs were content to exploit trading opportunities in a subordinate position, either to foreign capital or to the state. Thus a form of bureaucratic capitalism did take shape under the Manchu regime and was continued during the years of Kuomintang rule in the form known as 'official supervision and merchant management'. Factories and some mines were established in this way, but they were mostly local enterprises or produced arms and stores for official use; they were adapted to the traditional framework, much like the state industries of seventeenth- and eighteenth-century Europe, and could not act as a dynamic, transforming force. In particular, this form of bureaucratic capitalism could not penetrate and undermine traditional relations in the rural sector and lead the way towards a more commercial or capitalist type of agriculture. Meanwhile, outside a few areas, the old, labour-intensive, small-scale forms of industry continued to survive, or even to grow, with little incentive for the introduction of technical change.

There is, it must be said, a danger in an analysis like the foregoing of unconsciously imposing a European yardstick on a non-Western country like China. Why should China be expected to follow the Western model? Is there not an implication that every step along the Western road was in China's interests? A case could be made out that the European impact was destructive, leading as it did to a century or more of turmoil, and being motivated by such discreditable causes as the opium trade. There is no reason, it could be argued, why China should have followd foreign models, either voluntarily or under compulsion. Perhaps the old order could have reformed itself and carried through a modernization programme of its own, given time. Perhaps China could have worked out a response to the Western challenge along the same lines as Meiji Japan. There is no way in which such questions can be settled. Whatever may be said in defence of the foreign intrusion, and in particular about the influence of foreign capital, technology, business management and enterprise in preparing the way for the industrialization of China, it should be pointed out that industrialization had not seriously begun before 1949. Certainly, by then, whether or not the foreign intrusion had done more harm than good, it had practically destroyed the old China. What was to replace it?

Whatever the rights and wrongs of history, when Chinese nationalism became a political force it looked to foreign models and ideologies in order to escape the stranglehold of foreign imperialism. This was the paradox of most of the non-European dependent countries when they sought to assert the right of nationhood in the twentieth century. Besides, once China had been opened up by Europeans and brought into contact with the world market there could be no going back; an irreversible process had begun. To become a unified national state China had to follow the European model and in particular it had to industrialize; on the other hand, it could not slavishly follow any foreign model if it were to do so successfully. Answers had to be found to specifically Chinese problems. This lesson was to be impressed on the Chinese Communist Party when it came to power in 1949.

That industrialization was a central part of the policy of turning

China into a modern and socialist country and of assuring its national independence was axiomatic. It was possible to reflect upon the experience of the European countries, of the Japanese enemy and of the Soviet Union, the latter being taken by many Chinese Communists as their mentor. After all, the Soviet Union presented the only example of the industrialization of a backward agrarian country on a planned basis. Although China began at a lower level of industrial development, the Soviet model appeared to be directly relevant. Moreover, although Stalin had not been enthusiastic about the taking of power by Mao Tse-tung and his party, there was no doubt that the latter held the Soviet economic policies and methods in high regard. In the absence of any alternative model, the early steps on the road to planned industrialization, taken after 1949, closely followed those which had apparently proved their worth in the Soviet Union during the 1930s. In any case, after years of war and civil war a period of reconstruction was necessary. In the absence of aid from any other quarter, China had to depend upon plant and equipment provided on loan by the Soviet Union, and the assistance of Soviet technical specialists and advisors. It seemed, therefore, that Chinese industrialization would be a carbon copy of that under- taken two decades earlier in the first two Soviet Five-Year Plans.

Indeed, the influence of the Soviet model on the planning structure and economic policy, overwhelming at first, remained significant through all the vicissitudes in Sino-Soviet relations and the break with the Soviet Union and is still discernible today. However, it was soon discovered that the Soviet model was not entirely suitable for China's stage of development and that it tended to produce side-effects, notably the growth of a bureaucratic hierarchy, which Mao Tse-tung, and some of his close followers, found unwelcome and dangerous for the health of the revolutionary regime. Other party leaders, no less powerful, though they might share Mao's suspicions of Soviet motives, whether on theoretical grounds or for practical reasons, opposed any wide divergence from Soviet-style planning and management. The stage was soon to be set for the surfacing of those sharp differences within the leadership and the various changes in policy which took place during Mao's lifetime and after his death.

THE NEW REGIME

The initial tasks confronting the Chinese Communists on taking power were those of reconstruction and stabilization after years of war, civil war, economic dislocation and runaway inflation. Having acquired considerable mass support and a great fund of goodwill by their lead in the struggle against Japan, and the reforms carried out in the Liberated Areas, they were able to restore production and bring inflation under control within a comparatively short time. The party cadres introduced new standards of honesty and efficiency into everyday administration. Many Chinese from the urban middle classes and the intelligentsia threw in their lot with the new regime.

The mass of the people were peasants and it could be claimed that peasant support had been crucial for the success of the Communist Party and the armed forces which it controlled. Agrarian reform was a top priority and was extended in 1950 to all areas of China on the lines already adopted in the Liberated Areas. Reform consisted essentially of a redistribution of land at the expense of the gentry landowners and richer peasants, thereby creating, over the next two years, a more uniform pattern of working peasant proprietors in the country as a whole. In the course of carrying out the reform, a vigorous campaign was launched against the big landowners and village exploiters; large numbers were arrested, tried and punished, frequently with the death penalty, by revolutionary tribunals which had the character of mass meetings. This agrarian reform may have seemed in contradiction with the ultimate aims of the new regime in so far as its first result was to consolidate small-scale peasant landowning.

However, during the struggle for power against the Kuomintang a conciliatory policy had been adopted towards the 'middle' peasant, the one most likely to have surplus crops. In the same way, Mao had made a distinction between the 'national' bourgeoisie and the *compradore* bourgeoisie who were regarded as agents of imperialism. While this may have been a shrewd tactical move at one particular juncture, it left some serious problems. In agriculture, for instance, production based upon small holdings was likely to become a breeding ground for petty capitalism, as in rural Russia after the Revolution of 1917. It was also likely to mean that peasants would consume more of their own produce and be less willing to supply the needs of the towns for foodstuffs and raw materials. Yet rapid industrial development depended upon agricultural surpluses. In part the problem was overcome by the levying of a tax at the rate of 17–19 per cent on the peasant's harvest. Even so, although an increase in production was claimed, it fell short of needs; the problem of how to extract a larger surplus from agriculture remained.

In the light of Soviet experience in the 1920s, the obvious solution to the procurement problem was collectivization. By pooling the land and farm equipment, and by mobilizing the vast labour reserve of the countryside, it would be possible to raise productivity and production and thus provide resources for accumulation as well as food for the population. In a backward and still mainly agrarian country, which was committed to a socialist policy, there seemed no other way in which industrial investment could be stepped up from its own resources. However, Soviet experience also showed that the peasants might resist such a move and might respond to any attempt at collectivization in the same way as their Soviet counterparts had done in the 1930s, by slaughtering farm stock and destroying equipment. Those in the leadership of the Party who were familiar with Soviet history perhaps knew that Soviet collectivization had not been an unqualified success, that it had been carried out at the expense of the deportation and death of millions of peasants dubbed as kulaks and had led to a disastrous fall in farm output. True, many of the Chinese kulaks had already been disposed of in the course of the agrarian reform, but in places a distinct stratum of better-off peasants still remained. Consequently, a section of the leadership held back from collectivization, not wishing to antagonize the peasantry – from which the mass of the Liberation Army was drawn – and arguing that it should at least be postponed until the means were available to raise the technical level of the collective farms above that of small-scale peasant cultivation. These differences were not made public at the time but were only revealed later during the campaign against the so-called 'capitalist-roaders'

Meanwhile the new regime had taken over the state industries already in existence and had nationalized foreign-owned businesses. Other private enterprises, those of the 'national' capitalists, remained in existence, subject to state supervision and increasing taxation, during the early 1950s, the final nationalization drive taking place in 1955–56, but even then still leaving some private capital in joint ventures. In some factories, too, the former owners and managers were kept on for the time being. The Korean War made it necessary to turn industrial capacity and skilled manpower to war production once again, and also created a need for food supplies for the army in Korea. However, these were familiar problems and were less of a drain than might have been supposed.

Together with the Stalinist style of planning, the Chinese Communists also adopted the policy of 'socialism in one country' which assumed the building up of a near enough self-sufficient industrial base. This required large-scale investment in industries producing means of production (Department I in the Marxist terminology), to provide basic materials for industrialization such as steel, coal and heavy chemicals as well as machinery for its own plant and to equip consumer goods industries (Department II). Industry would likewise have to supply the tractors, farm machines and fertilizers necessary to raise the technical level of the agrarian sector and thus enable it to feed and supply with raw materials (such as cotton) the whole expanding industrial complex. At first sight this seems to present a vicious circle to any backward country without foreign aid. How can it make the heavy equipment needed to build up the producer goods industries unless it has such industries in the first place? How can agriculture produce a surplus unless it is supplied with the manufactured inputs and unless the peasants are supplied with consumer goods? Where are these goods to come from unless Department II expands output? The Soviet example suggested that consumer needs would be left unsatisfied during a more or less prolonged period in which priority was accorded to Department I.

Such questions would have to be worked out by the decision-makers: the central leadership of the Party. However, post-1949 China was hardly in a position to embark upon economic planning forthwith. It needed statistical and other information, trained personnel and a clear conception of where to begin. Planning began at a much lower level of theory, data and expertise than it did in the Soviet Union in the 1920s where Gosplan was able to mobilize a wealth of information and talent. Like the Soviet Union, Communist China could count mainly upon the hostility of the capitalist world, and even normal trade was unlikely to be resumed. On the other hand, the Soviet Union was now the second largest industrial power and China counted on its aid as well as on that of the East European countries. However, those countries had their own problems arising from the war and its aftermath; and China could not expect that such aid would be lavish.

It was clear that at this stage, objective conditions pushed China into dependence upon the Soviet Union. The adoption of the Soviet planning model based upon the priority of heavy industry, made it inevitable that some plant and equipment would have to be obtained from outside and the only possible source was the Soviet Union. This is not to say that in the circumstances there was not a sound rationale for this policy. Soviet plant and equipment provided the way out of the vicious circle. While a period would be required in which consumer goods production could not be greatly increased and in which, for lack of machinery and fertilizers, agricultural production would not be likely to increase rapidly, the initial injection of Soviet equipment would, in time, provide the means for these and other sectors to grow. Growth had to begin somewhere and Soviet aid in establishing mainly heavy industry, both in material form and the know-how and example of the experts and technicians who helped to build and run-in new plant, could give it that start. The danger was that peasants and consumers generally would react unfavourably to a more or less prolonged postponement of any substantial improvement in their living standards. Hence the need for propaganda campaigns to rally support and to provide ideological satisfactions when material ones were in short supply.

PLANNING

The First Five-Year Plan covered the period 1953–57, although it was not finalized until the early part of 1955. Until then there was a period of transition in which the planning apparatus was being put into place and objectives were being worked out in negotiation with the Soviet Union. Meanwhile, the economy functioned on a series of short-term plans. The Five-Year Plan set ambitious targets, notably the doubling of industrial production with a high rate of investment and emphasis on the priority growth of heavy industry. Very much the centrepiece of the Plan was the building of new giant plants equipped with Soviet machinery on the model of the Soviet Plans of the 1930s. Having adopted this aim, it was virtually inescapable that the current Soviet style of management would also be adopted. This gave wide powers to the plant director over production and discipline while obliging each plant to fulfil targets laid down by the state. The practice of one-man management and centralized control prevailed throughout the planning system and produced a rigid, bureaucratic hierarchy. Additional payments and bonuses were widely used as incentives for the fulfilment of targets and the efficient carrying out of work.

The one-man management system and other methods established by the Plan generated some opposition within industry, largely because they conflicted with previous practice or were simply not workable in the many small factories which made up the old private sector. Amalgamations were necessary and such firms were taken over by the state. There were other reasons, too, for opposition, but the main ideological objections only became known later as Chinese and Soviet views conflicted on a wide range of issues. In any case, Chinese Party officials were not agreed among themselves.

When Sino-Soviet differences began to surface from about 1956, economic policy became an issue; later, differences within the Chinese leadership itself also became plain. One-man management came under attack for creating powerful, privileged bureaucrats, and the organizational methods as a whole for laying too much emphasis on material incentives and stultifying initiative. The debate was symptomatic, in part, of tensions within the Chinese leadership. Also, no doubt, there had been opposition on the part of workers and lower-echelon managers to the new Soviet-style methods. Underlying the discussion was the increasingly evident fact that the Soviet model could not simply be transferred lock, stock and barrel to a country in which conditions were very different. For example, China had an enormous labour reserve and a still backward agrarian sector. Large-scale industry, concentrated in a few areas, left untouched the problems of modernization in the country as a whole, while absorbing enormous resources. The whole planning enterprise was remote from the concerns of the mass of the people and brought no appreciable improvement in living standards. It was perhaps inevitable that the Soviet model would have to be tried before it could be found wanting. Once the glamour of it had worn off, and it was discovered that it provided no ready answers, the way was open to seek other solutions. Even so, there was no question of the complete abandonment of the Soviet model, many aspects of which had, in fact, proved their worth or could not easily be replaced. However, with the rapid worsening of the relations between China and the Soviet Union and the final break between the two countries, all Soviet aid was withdrawn in 1960 and the Soviet technicians went home. China had to go it alone but a high degree of self-sufficiency was a central feature of Stalin's policies, and he was to remain a highly esteemed figure in China.

Somewhat belatedly, more or less empirically, once Soviet support had been cut off, alternative strategies for industrialization had to be devised. High on the agenda for economic policy was the agrarian question which had by no means been solved by the reform of 1950. As long as the land remained in the hands of small peasant proprietors there was a limit to the increase in output which could be obtained, and thus in the surplus available to make possible more investment elsewhere. It was basically the same problem raised and fought out in the Soviet Union in the 1920s. Either the rate of industrialization had to be governed by the quantity of products the peasants were willing to supply voluntarily through the market in exchange for consumer goods, or a larger proportion of the product of agriculture had to be siphoned off directly, through compulsory levies or by collectivizing the peasant lands. In addition, there was the question of tempo: how fast to go. There was also the question of how to make best use of the almost inexhaustible labour reserve in the countryside.

Evidently, these issues of economic policy caused wide rifts in the leadership, though for a long time the differences were fought out behind closed doors and even now it is difficult to know their exact nature. Ever since Mao's death there has been no real opportunity to know what the actual policies of the defeated were. As it was, the advocates of rapid collectivization, led by Mao Tse-tung in his first major intervention in economic policy, won the day. They were not prepared to wait until the collectives could be provided with equipment, farm machinery and other aids. Instead, the peasants' labour was to be mobilized on cooperative lines and an effort was to be made to harness their loyalty to newly-formed collective farms rather than to the family or the village. The collectivization drive, like the later formation of communes, was consciously directed at reforming social structures and individual psychology and was never simply regarded as a means of increasing production. It was accompanied, therefore, by an intensive campaign to convince the peasants of the advantages assumed to follow from the new system of agriculture and to educate them in the new form of social living. Opposition was encountered not only in the villages, but also from a section of the Party leadership; nevertheless collectivization was pursued step-by-step, from lower to higher forms of cooperation and was completed by 1957. At this stage collective farm administration closely followed the Soviet model but, as it turned out, it was destined to be superseded after only a few years by a still more grandiose project.

THE GREAT LEAP FORWARD

As the period of the First Five-Year Plan came to an end, important decisions had to be made about the future shape of economic development. There were bitter disagreements within the leadership, not resolved until mid-1957 with the triumph of Mao Tse-tung's line and the launching of what was known as the Great Leap Forward. Despite the relative success of the Plan it was evident that a series of such Plans would be required to overcome China's economic lag. Besides, a narrow emphasis on economic achievement could result in a tacit agreement to leave old institutions in place and to accept greater inequality and the consolidation of a bureaucratic stratum and privileged groups through the operation of material incentives. The Maoist view seems to have been that revolutionary goals were being forgotten in the search for ecomonic efficiency.

The Great Leap Forward was intended to make a sharp break with the past as well as to project an alternative economic model more closely attuned to China's needs as assessed by Mao himself. It called for the mobilization of the entire population, starting with the great majority living in the rural areas. The collective farms, which had only been in operation for a few years, were to be merged into much larger units to be known as the Peoples' Communes. In a five-month period in 1958, the 740,000 cooperatives (or collective farms) were regrouped into some 24,000 communes, each comprising about 5,000 households. The pooling of resources was intended to make possible the provision of communal kitchens, dining rooms, schools and other facilities. The economy of labour in cultivating the land would make it possible to recruit huge armies of labour for flood control, irrigation and similar projects aimed to increase the productivity of the land and combat flooding and droughts, those agelong scourges of the peasantry. At the same time the communes were encouraged to take over or set up a multiplicity of industrial projects on a small-scale, including the famous backyard furnaces for the making of iron and steel. From the economic point of view, the aim was to transform China's main resources – her teeming millions – into a productive asset, and to realize the communist dream of combining different forms of labour and harnessing it for the common good.

The unprecedented scale and novelty of the effort represented by the Great Leap Forward attracted worldwide attention, evoking both enthusiasm and revulsion. At first, aided by favourable harvests, the new policy seemed to be a success, but in 1959 and 1960, climatic adversity and natural disasters afflicted China and resulted in harvest failures and food shortages. Even apart from these misfortunes the communes were running into difficulties. Such a massive change in agricultural organization, coming so shortly after the formation of the collective farms, could hardly fail to cause administrative and organizational problems which must share the blame for the fall in agricultural output. The herculean efforts demanded of peasants and workers, especially the leading cadres, could not be sustained. Machinery and equipment were worked to the limit and when breakdowns occurred there were no replacements. Although the encouragement of small-scale rural industry to supply everyday needs was sound in principle, some of the projects initiated by the communes, such as the backyard furnaces, were technically unsound and led to waste. Moreover, the acceleration of production by the methods of the forced march, without central direction or national plan, was bound to run into trouble. Incompetent direction, inadequate coordination, lack of raw materials or spare parts, or sheer physical exhaustion all contributed to a growing crisis in production. While the Great Leap Forward had as its centre one important, positive gain, the mobilization of China's immense labour reserves for large-scale projects, it was not the way to promote sustained economic growth or industrialization. In fact, it created chaos in some sectors and drove the economy near to breakdown.

As the Great Leap Forward ran out of steam so the methods behind it tended to become discredited, strengthening those elements in the Communist Party leadership which were opposed to Mao Tse-tung, and leading, temporarily, to the adoption of a more cautious strategy. By the end of 1960, Soviet aid had come to an end and this contributed to a reduction of emphasis upon heavy industry. Now there was a growing tendency to decentralize light industry and an effort was made to step up the production of fertilizers. More attention was paid to the quality of production rather than volume. Reorganization of the communes took place, curtailing some of their more ambitious activities while restoring private plots, and thus, as it were, rehabilitating the family as a productive unit alongside the commune. In the factories, the former managerial structure, which had been superseded during the Great Leap Forward, was regaining favour. Once again emphasis was placed upon material incentives. The centralized planning system was, to a large extent, restored. The strategy now pursued seemed deliberately to negate the aims of the Great Leap Forward; Mao was in eclipse. It seemed that China had settled down to a long period of steady but not spectacular industrialization on more orthodox lines. Not for long, however; the calm of these years presaged a yet more spectacular turn in policy: the Great Proletarian Cultural Revolution as it was styled.

THE CULTURAL REVOLUTION

Once again Mao took command; the new strategy, like that of the Great Leap Forward, was not exclusively economic in nature. Indeed, it set out to put politics in command, to sweep away most of the landmarks of traditional China, to revolutionize the educational system and generally to eradicate from society all the vestiges of the past which conflicted with the formation of a new man. In practice, also, it was aimed very directly at those in the Party leadership who had prompted the policies of the First Five-Year Plan, who were half-hearted about the Great Leap Forward, and whose influence had largely shaped the retrenchment called for in the early 1960s. The accusation now made by Mao and his supporters was that these policies opened the road to the restoration of capitalism in China, the road already followed by the Soviet Union since the death of Stalin in 1953. A tremendous nationwide propaganda campaign was launched to make it appear that Mao had acted just in time to prevent the 'capitalist-roaders' headed by former President Liu Shaochi, from taking power. The main weapon of the defeated faction, who were not allowed to express their policy publicly, was said to be the appeal to material appetites, an improvement in living standards or what was described as 'economism'. In the place of material incentives, Mao offered service in the public interest, self-sacrificing effort for the revolution, mass participation and the correct 'proletarian line'. It was clear from the turmoil which accompanied the Cultural Revolution that Mao's policy was by no means universally accepted.

The implication of the new line for economic policy was not as clear as it had been during the Great Leap Forward as the emphasis, particularly in the early stages, seemed to be upon tearing down all reminders of the old social order rather than instituting new practices. In any case, rapid economic development was not the priority aim. It was soon evident, however, that a change was intended in economic policy in the pursuit of other goals. There were a number of features which became identified with Maoism: a move away from centralized planning and from one-man management towards a more decentralized administration, the ending of piece-wages and bonuses for individuals and the placing of moral incentives in the foreground; 'enterprises must become places to train people as well as produce goods' was the slogan advanced. While these methods gained some sympathy outside China and appeared to offer an alternative to the over-centralized Soviet planning system, as a way

137

of advancing towards socialism they proved to be economically disastrous. Production in the factories was disorganized by attacks on the old management or by disputes between the workers. Prolonged political struggles, and in some places pitched battles, took place between rival factions. The educational system was disorganized and research practically stopped. Many leaders and cadres identified with previous policies were denounced and sent in disgrace to perform manual work in remote areas. Youthful Red Guards and other activists moved about the country by train or bus while raw materials and essential goods no longer reached their destinations on time, owing to the disorganization of the transport system.

Whatever else it did, therefore (and many of its results proved to be short lived), the Cultural Revolution certainly checked the momentum of industrialization. During 1967–68 there was an actual fall in output of up to 20 per cent. Little new capital investment was put in hand and the supply both of consumer goods and chemical fertilizers fell back. It seems that 'moderate' elements in the leadership intervened to keep production going in defence industries, and that agriculture was not too seriously affected. Moreover, the setting up of new management structures and the downgrading of material incentives, whatever their justification, had the effect, in the short run, of bringing down production. But then the goal of increased production was regarded as 'economism', tantamount to a return to capitalism.

After about three years the Cultural Revolution had run its course and by 1969 there were desperate appeals in the press to increase production again. In fact, despite the years of upheaval and turmoil and the human suffering involved, none of the basic problems facing China were any nearer to solution nor, in reality, had the differences within the leadership been finally resolved, despite Mao's apparent victory. Questions such as what kind of planning should be pursued – the relative priority to be accorded to industry and agriculture; the tempo of growth; the structure of management; of material incentives versus other sorts for greater production; of whether it was better to be 'red' than expert – all remained posed as starkly as before. Although food production does not seem to have been badly hit by the turmoil, a big effort was called for to restore and increase industrial production. Indeed, the Maoist purity of the methods used tended to be less important than the results, though the achievements and sacrifices of particular groups of workers were still held up as models. The point was that an undoubted contradiction existed between the needs of productive efficiency and the Maoist goal of the Cultural Revolution. An influential section of the leadership, although temporarily muzzled (or giving unwilling lip-service to the Party line), had quite different views to those of Mao as to how China's problems should be solved. Events were to show that they were biding their time for a comeback which was not to be too long delayed. It was brought nearer by the failing powers of the 'Great Helmsman' and by the dislocation brought about by the Cultural Revolution he had inspired, though the excesses were tactfully blamed onto others.

In any event, in the early 1970s expansion began to be resumed on more orthodox lines. A number of new plants were built for chemical production and steel-making and the petroleum industry was developed using much imported machinery. Corresponding but not spectacular improvements were made in commune agriculture, while a more relaxed attitude was adopted towards the cultivation of private plots by the peasantry. Organization was evidently less rigid than originally intended and work tasks were allocated in such a way that families and village groups could still be identified. Although accurate information is scanty, food supply seems to have kept pace with population growth and there was a steady increase in the output of industrial crops. Clearly, with population growth continuing at a high level, despite propaganda for birth control, there could be no relaxation in the drive for production; the margin between food production and the mouths to feed remained uncomfortably narrow. Moreover, significant differences in food supply and well-being between different parts of the country had not been overcome. Some areas were extremely poor and showed little improvement. There were also wide differences between the more prosperous communes and those which had less fertile land or faced difficult climatic conditions.

THE NEW ORTHODOXY

Changes on the political front, beginning with the Tenth Party Congress held in August 1973, heralded a swing back towards more orthodox economic policies. The following years saw the radicals reasserting themselves in a number of propaganda campaigns. In 1976 came the death of Mao Tse-tung and the subsequent arrest of the so-called 'Gang of Four' representing the radical wing who were now made scapegoats for the difficulties following the

139

Cultural Revolution, while a number of its prominent victims were rehabilitated and some found their way back into power. A relatively unknown provincial official, Hua Kuo-feng, took Mao's position, evidently hoping to preserve continuity, but his reign proved to be transitional. The real force behind the post-Mao transformation of policy was one of the old guard discredited during the drive against the 'capitalist roaders', a former Mayor of Peking, Teng Hsiao-ping. Teng had an alternative programme, a determination to carry it out and the personality and standing in the party which enabled him to assume control.

In the years following Mao's death, Teng and his supporters called for the repudiation of the Cultural Revolution and for the adoption of new policies. In the course of a bitter struggle in the summits of the party they succeeded in defeating Hua Kuo-feng as well as the hard-line Maoists. A new coalition committed to thorough-going reform took over. Mao's economic policies were criticized and rejected. They were seen as having slowed down the growth of production and the improvement in material conditions, which many people saw as the purpose of the revolution. The keynote now became what was called 'modernization': concentration on the development of the productive forces by every technological and organizational means. This was precisely what Mao had denounced as 'economism'. In practice, Mao's policies had led to political turmoil, victimization of critics, a stagnant level of consumption and bureaucratic abuses. Their popular basis had been eroded and where ideology had apparently failed, Teng and the pragmatists were able to move in.

From 1977, and at an accelerating rate from 1982, the unwinding of many of the changes wrought by the Cultural Revolution went on side-by-side with a review of the country's needs and possibilities – priority was to be given to the achievement of faster economic growth – together with the improvement of living standards. More emphasis was laid upon food production; short-term objectives took precedence over the long-term re-shaping of society and of human psychology which had previously been dominant. Technical experts, specialists, teachers and others who had been disgraced during the Cultural Revolution were re-instated. Foreign models of economic development were studied carefully and, within a few years, China was opened to the outside world on a scale and in a way which would have seemed unbelievable in Mao's time.

The communes, which had been the centre-piece of Mao's agrarian policy, were effectively dissolved. Responsibility was shifted first to the production team (generally the former village) and then, in 1983, to the family unit. Subsequently, in most parts of the country, there has virtually been a return to family farming, a major concession to the peasantry. The state makes contracts with the peasants to ensure supplies of food for the towns and raw materials for industry; the rest of production goes to satisfy household needs or can be sold in the market. Under the slogan 'get rich' introduced in 1979, peasants have been encouraged to produce more for sale and they have been freer to diversify production in accordance with market demand. 'Household responsibility' has taken over from the commune, with families allocated tracts of land. Income was more closely geared to output, thus tending to more inequality between different areas and regions and between households within the limits of the former commune. With this went the passage of much farm machinery and draught animals into the ownership or management of private households, especially in the richer agricultural regions. Similar changes were introduced into industrial management, which reverted to something more like the Soviet pattern introduced after 1949 and superseded at the time of the 'Great Leap Forward'. More authority was now placed in the hands of the plant director and his managerial and technical associates, and the hold of the Party was tightened up. The idea of educating the workers and giving them some participation in the making of decisions was now subordinated to production efficiency. Hitherto Chinese planning had laid down fairly rigorous guide-lines for each enterprise in what was called the 'five-fixed' system. That is to say, the following were prescribed by the plan and had to be adhered to: the type and quantity of the product; the number of workers, the amount of raw material and the sources of supply; the amount of fixed and circulating capital; and the cooperation between enterprises necessary to fulfil the targets. The post-Mao tendency was to give the plant directors greater discretionary powers in obtaining means of production as well as in disposing of the finished product. At the same time, there was a return to incentive and bonus payments to stimulate increased output. Discipline was tightened up and norms laid down for the workers or teams and a more rigid division of labour was also imposed. Propaganda media called for the study of scientific management and of the advanced technology of the capitalist countries.

Each enterprise was now encouraged to keep down costs and increase returns and accounting profits were taken as an index of performance. Where the new methods of management were introduced, plants were permitted to retain 5 per cent of the planned profits for their own use, together with 20 per cent of any excess. The level of profits determined the scale of bonuses for the managerial personnel and the workers. Failure to make profits would result in loss of bonuses and other sanctions. Enterprises which made satisfactory profits were rewarded in other ways, for example, by being given priority in the supply of new machines or raw materials. The state's accumulation fund could now be seen to be tied directly to the profitability of the individual enterprises. Legal codes and judicial procedures necessary for the enforcement of the new system of management were brought into operation. On the economic side, the system of pricing came to be a more accurate reflection of supply and demand considerations. There was, therefore, some effort to combine planning with regard for market forces in a move towards an economy resembling the Yugoslav system of 'self-management'. All these changes, and others of a like kind, such as the introduction of more stringent financial controls over industry, ran contrary to the Maoist canon of putting politics in command. Their general tendency was to emphasize material incentives and productive efficiency at the expense of distributive justice, greater social equality and increased popular participation. The influence of the Soviet model by no means disappeared, even during the Cultural Revolution. Five-Year Plans continued to be adopted, the shape of the planning system and the emphasis of policy on building a powerful industrial base, could all be said to reflect Soviet practice. By the end of the 1970s, with the departure from Maoist principles, the similarity between Chinese and Soviet planning once again became closer despite the continued political antagonisms.

Chinese policy has always been nationalistic, it has stressed self-reliance perhaps with the grim warning of the unequal treaties in mind. Soviet aid was willingly accepted after 1949 and the import of Soviet plant and equipment, as well as the presence of Soviet experts and advisers (numbering some 7,000), gave the initial stimulus for planned industrialization. This aid was made available on loan and had all been paid for by 1964. Subsequently China has imported machinery from capitalist sources, but this has had to be paid for and has required credit from foreign commercial banks. At the end of the 1970s, as part of the new economic policy, large orders were given to foreign firms some of which were later cancelled or scaled down for financial reasons. Nevertheless, the principle has been accepted that China should extend its trade and other links with the world market and buy the technology necessary to carry through the industrialization programme. The main constraint is that Chinese exports have not been able to grow on the scale necessary to pay for large-scale imports without foreign credits. The Chinese leadership obviously feels that heavy indebtedness to foreign banks will lead to political dependence. Even so, a law passed in 1979 permitted foreign firms to invest up to 25 per cent of the capital for joint ventures in China, with an undertaking that they will be free to repatriate their profits. Foreign-style consumer goods are now given wide publicity even when they are not available, presumably as part of the incentive policy aimed to encourage individual effort.

The aim of self-sufficiency, or something approximating it, is, as we have seen, an inheritance from the Stalinist policy of 'socialism in one country'. The strains of China's industrialization reflect the application of this policy, notably in the building up of a heavy industrial base. During the early years after 1949, Soviet aid did something to alleviate the strain. After the split, 'self-reliance' was stressed even more; on the other hand, it led to greater emphasis being laid upon agriculture and decentralized rural and small-scale industry, which was reasonable, given Chinese conditions. In practice, however, China has not been able to insulate itself from the world market. For instance it has had to import food grains to make good bad harvests, and the current modernization programme depends largely for its success upon the ability to obtain, and pay for, foreign technology. It is now accepted that China cannot be self-sufficient and that there is much to be learned from foreign experience, including that of other Asian countries such as Korea and Japan. China's economic interests have always come before support for revolutionary movements in other countries.

A RELATIVE SUCCESS?

Nevertheless, Chinese experience in modern industrialization depended upon a successful revolution fought out with much upheaval and violence. It made possible a complete reorganization of the agrarian system, without precedent in other countries, as well as the nationalization of the industrial sector. At the time of the revolution, per capita income in China ranked it among one of the poorest countries of the world. It had less industry than Russia had inherited from Tsarism and a poorly-developed transport system.

The technical level of production, outside the modern plants in the former treaty ports and Manchuria, was extremely backward. The population was huge and continued to grow. Considering the low starting point Chinese performance has been respectable. One estimate puts the growth rate between 1950 and the late 1970s at 6–7 per cent per annum and the growth in industrial production at 10 per cent per annum. After some slowing down, industrial output rose to an average of 11.7 per cent per annum between 1983 and 1986. Industry has accounted for a steadily increasing proportion of gross domestic product. The figures suggest that industrial output is about twice as high as that of India on a per capita basis. Nevertheless, China remains a poor country, while the changes of recent years have increased social inequalities.

The leadership has not hesitated to use violence against its enemies to achieve its ends. Under Mao it deliberately resorted to massive social upheavals involving unprecedented disorganization of production in order to carry out its policies. Bitter conflicts have been fought out inside the leadership. For years after the Cultural Revolution, the educational system was in chaos and thousands of the most highly-trained professional people in the country were disgraced and sent off to do menial work, if not imprisoned. It is difficult to say how much support all these changes had from the mass of the people, or whether they simply acquiesced. Certainly the regime, whoever has been in control, has tried to carry the people along by mass campaigns of persuasion and propaganda. When criticism has been permitted it has been sharp and pertinent and has attracted much interest and support.

The old landlord, bureaucratic and *compradore* classes have disappeared. Rule is in the hands of the party and state bureaucracy which enjoys the privileges of office and power and no doubt lives rather better than the mass of the people, although how much better it is difficult to say. In any case, the rural masses have not been relieved of back-breaking work; probably their life is more secure than it was in pre-revolutionary days and they can perhaps feel that they are reaping the fruits of their endeavour, or that they are contributing to the growth of the land in which their children will enjoy a better life. In the factories it is doubtful whether industrial work has been made any more pleasant than under capitalism. Especially under Mao, an attempt was made to associate the workers more closely with the running of the enterprise and to win their cooperation through a sense of participation in a common effort. Since his death there has been some back-pedalling;

the emphasis has been not upon changing the methods of work but upon increasing the output of goods to be brought about by offering material incentives.

Social inequalities may be less apparent than in the advanced capitalist countries, the Soviet Union or developing countries like India, but undoubtedly they exist. All visitors remark that the cadres can be distinguished by the cut of their uniforms, their bearing and style of life. Despite the claim to be fighting bureaucratism, it is evident that a bureaucratic stratum does exist and rules, and that it has become more distinct from the masses since the death of Mao. All policy measures are accompanied by unremitting propaganda campaigns, and quite contradictory lines have been plugged within years or even months of each other, to the probable confusion and bewilderment of many. Popular participation is not so much a spontaneous thing as the harnessing of the masses to applaud leaders, or to undertake tasks about which they have not been consulted.

The average Chinese may have more say about how he does his job than a worker in a capitalist factory, but it cannot be said that he possesses democratic rights in any real sense despite the flourishing, at times, of the *dazibaos* (wall posters and inscriptions). The tendency is to demand obedience and passivity from the masses, in the hope that this will lead to better living standards. The degree of toleration of dissenters has varied; in times of mass campaigns there has been little or none.

The repudiation of Maoism after 1976 has meant the substitution of material incentives for revolutionary fervour. The powers of the managers of state enterprises have been extended. In the urban areas the bulk of industry is in the hands of the state; the non-state sector only employs about 4 per cent of urban workers. Private trade is mainly to be found in the service sector. Outside the towns, however, there has been a proliferation of small-scale privately-owned enterprises producing simple consumer goods. Private industry could only employ up to five people outside the owner's immediate family. In Wenzhou, near Shanghai, an enclave of privately-owned businesses has been permitted. Despite the claims of some observers that China is returning to capitalism, the 'commanding heights' of the economy are still firmly in state hands. At the same time, the situation remains very fluid with considerable debate within the leadership regarding the country's future course. The increased scope for market dealings and the emphasis on material incentives have led to widespread graft and corruption among officials. A new element of risk and insecurity has been introduced, with pools of unemployed labour in the towns and the concomitant growth of criminality. Inflationary pressures have also become disquietingly manifest.

The most controversial aspect of the post-Mao era has been the greater integration of China into the world market. This has not just been a question of trade. The state has sought closer relationships with foreign capital. It is now accepted that continued industrialization means borrowing foreign technology and having closer relations with capitalist countries than in the past. This has required some wholly new departures. More links have been established between Chinese producers and their foreign trade partners. Every source of foreign credit has been actively pursued and assistance and advice have been obtained from United Nations agencies, foreign governments and American consultant firms. Above all, foreign investment has been encouraged in many sectors of the economy, some by foreign corporations, others by 'overseas Chinese' mostly from Hong Kong. Since 1979 there have been four 'special economic zones' on the south-east coast in which foreign investment in export-oriented industrialization has been encouraged. These enclaves of foreign capitalism made it possible to employ low-wage Chinese labour to compete with other South Asian exporters. Close ties have been established between firms operating in these zones and businesses in Hong Kong (prime centre of Asian capitalism which will be returned to China in 1997). Many of the concessions to foreign capital made in the 'special economic zones' were extended to fourteen coastal cities in 1984. Eventually the whole of coastal China was made as attractive as possible for foreign capital. This policy, with its risks of growing capitalist influence, remains controversial, though it clearly has the support of the Teng leadership. They see it as a means of speeding up industrialization by adopting foreign technology and capital to widen an industrial base still concerned predominantly with servicing the national ecomomy.

Industrialization in China is identified as a national task, making demands on every individual. This gives it a unique character. However, the decisions are taken in the ruling circles of the party, and are not the result of public discussion. Propaganda seeks to enlist mass support and mobilize the masses for the tasks in hand, creating a sense of solidarity which, may, to the outsider, seem like nothing but regimentation. Industrialization in China has other specific features. It has been carried out largely without foreign help. Besides building giant plants and mobilizing labour on a large scale for constructional projects, small scale, decentralized types of industrialization have also been favoured. The encouragement of industries working for local needs, usually of a labour-intensive type, would seem to offer a model which other developing countries might follow. It means some degree of local or regional self-sufficiency, taking the strain from an over-stretched transport system. However, it is probably a second-best, justifiable in the short run, rather than as a permanent policy. It enables the simple consumer needs of a predominantly agrarian society to be met, but would seem to be a costly and inadequate way of meeting more sophisticated needs. such a policy of rural and small-scale industry may enable other resources to be channelled into the building up of producer goods industries to provide the industrial base for future growth. Although much attention has been paid to light industry, the need for heavy industry to grow, if modernization is to proceed, is clear enough. What impedes the growth of heavy industry is technological weakness and lack of resources for accumulation. Despite continuous industrial growth the industrial workforce in 1976 amounted to only 26 million.

The great bulk of China's population remains tied to the land in an agriculture whose output barely keeps pace with population growth. Whatever the achievements of Chinese industrialization, therefore, it has still not yet succeeded in raising the living standards of the mass of the people. It would seem that this basic task has now taken precedence over the development of new and more equitable forms of living which seemed to be the ideal of the Mao period.

CHAPTER 6
Brazil: dependent industrialization

Brazilian industrialization since the 1930s can be taken as an example of what is described as the Import-Substitution Strategy, widely followed in Latin America. In other respects, however, Brazil can hardly be considered typical of the region. Most obviously, it is Portuguese not Spanish by culture and language; it also has a large black population descended from African slaves. It has the advantage of being the largest country in Latin America, occupying almost half the land area and having the largest population. This means a diversity of natural resources, many still not opened up, and a potentially large home market. In principle this makes Brazil a country which could support a large and diversified industrial base. The question is, how far have these potentialities been realized?

During the period after the Second World War, industrialization proceeded rapidly, resulting in one of the highest growth records in the world. However, while it can be claimed that the foundations for industrialization were being laid in the nineteenth century, Brazil is very much a late-comer to the world scene of industrialization. The reason for this is to be found in its history as a dependent country. Brazil was politically dependent upon Portugal until it became a sovereign state, then economically dependent, first upon Britain and then upon the United States. Its history is reflected in the secular problems inherited from the colonial past. Despite the industrial build-up of recent decades, endowing it with an advanced modern sector, large areas of the country remain backward and the population desperately poor. For centuries Brazil has been a primary-producing country, highly dependent upon foreign demand, and remains so. Recent growth has depended to a large extent upon an inflow of foreign capital, making Brazil one of the most highly indebted countries in the world. The economic vicissitudes of the present century have aggravated social strains and contradictions, held in check by authoritarian regimes based upon the military. Although there has been an impressive advance along the road of industrialization, widely hailed as an 'economic miracle' in the late 1960s and early 1970s, it has not overcome the poverty endemic in much of the country. Progress has been extremely uneven and remains fraught with difficulties. An excursion into the past is necessary in order to understand Brazil's contemporary problems.

PORTUGUESE COLONIZATION

Brazil became important to world history when the area was discovered and colonized by the Portuguese conquerors during the sixteenth century. At that time Portugal was a small country in decline; Brazil was a vast and varied territory sparsely populated by loosely-structured 'Indian' communities. These were able to put up little resistance to the intruders who, though small in number, came equipped with European technology and weapons of war. The object of colonization at this time was, of course, material enrichment in the quickest manner possible: by the search for precious metals and the plunder of the existing societies' wealth. When these methods reached their limits or proved unsuccessful, the next best thing was to turn the local inhabitants into a labour force for the production of staple products for sale in the European and world markets. In this respect Brazil was, for a long time, something of a disappointment. There was plenty of virgin land and tropical forest but no instant riches for the Portuguese invaders. In addition to this their hold on the region was, for some time, disputed by other European predators: Spanish, English, French and Dutch. The first staple product of value was dyewood, in demand in Europe for the textile industry. Then came sugar, which the Dutch, during the period in which they occupied part of Brazil (1604–54), built up into a flourishing industry.

Sugar was to prove to be the principal engine of growth for the colonial economy of Brazil during the early seventeenth century. Unlike dyewood which was cut out of the forest, it required capital investment to equip the sugar-mills, plenty of land cleared for cultivation and a reliable labour force able to work in a tropical climate. On the whole, the original Brazilians resisted work for their new masters; some were hunted down or killed off in battle, many succumbed to Old World diseases against which their bodies had no resistance. For a labour force, the white settlers had to look elsewhere, namely to Africa, where Portugal also had colonies. Like other plantations in the New World, those of Brazil were manned by black slaves. Slavery was to last in Brazil until 1888 and provide the labour force for the sugar, coffee and other plantations upon which the wealth of the Brazilian landed oligarchy was based.

In 1654 the Portuguese succeeded in expelling the Dutch from Brazil, and the latter took their capital and skills to the West Indies. Sugar production continued in north-east Brazil but the development of other, low cost, supplies from the Carribean made it less profitable than before. Nevertheless, the sugar plantation economy proved to be resilient to price fluctuations; the owners simply accepted a lower income or found other sources. For example, a cattle industry grew up to supply the food needs of the settlers and the plantation labour-force. Some other crops, such as tobacco, were also introduced. Slaves and the surviving Indians employed in European enterprises, supported themselves by subsistence agriculture; and this was always an alternative for the less successful European immigrants. As time went on, some internal trade developed in agricultural products or simply-made articles for everyday needs. Export staples, principally sugar, enabled plantation-owners and the merchants who handled the trade, to import better-quality goods from Europe. Expansion was clearly linked to the production and export of staples and depended very much upon the course of external demand. The surplus extracted from slave labour on the plantations was largely realized in the sale of exports and the return flow of other commodities from abroad. The internal market was limited both by high transport costs and also by the presence of a large labour force made up of slaves whose subsistence needs were provided for by their masters. Even when exports boomed, as they sometimes did, the linkage effects were limited; it meant that a larger surplus came back to the slave-owners in the form of imported commodities (or credits). The tendency was to consume, rather than to invest most of the surplus. So far as it was invested it went into buying more slaves and making more land clearances. The cultivation of plantations occupied some, but not all, of the population, for there were other forms of cultivation mainly of a subsistence nature. Subsistence farming was adopted by runaway slaves who were able, in some places, to establish their own communities, at least temporarily.

From the seventeenth century onwards, Brazil experienced a series of booms; or, more accurately particular regions experienced such booms. When these ended, as they inevitably did, the region concerned would find its income sharply curtailed, because it no longer produced an export staple in demand on the world market or because the price had fallen to a less remunerative level. In such cases, the area would tend to stagnate, withdraw in upon itself, and turn more to low-productivity agriculture, whether using slave or other dependent forms of labour, or that based on family subsistence cultivation. In any case, there would be a falling off of imports into the region and stagnation or contraction of the market for manufactured goods.

One such boom which brought temporary riches came as a result of the discovery of gold, and later diamonds, in the inland plateaus during the 1690s. Gold, of course, was exactly what the settlers were looking for in the New World but its discovery did little to stimulate the economy of Brazil. When the mines were exhausted, the region in which they were situated reverted to a subsistence economy, consisting to a large extent of Europeans who had initially been attracted by the gold rush. As for the gold which was extracted, much of it found its way to Britain in return for goods sent to Portugal, or to Brazil, and it contributed more to the rise of the City of London as a financial centre than it did to the development of the producing country.

The French Revolution and the wars which ensued were to have a dramatic effect on Brazil, activating its economy and ending in the break with Portugal. During the eighteenth century, Portugal and her colony, following the Methuen Treaty of 1703, had been brought into a satellite relationship with England. In return for the reduction in the duty on Portuguese wines entering England, English manufactured goods, notably textiles, were admitted into Portugal and her colony.

During the wars which followed the French Revolution, Portugal became a battleground and a prize. Occupied by Napoleon's troops, it was cut off from Brazil. Following this, in 1808, Brazilian ports were opened to foreign traders. Two years later by a treaty signed with Britain, her goods could enter the country on payment of a lower rate of duty than that imposed on goods from other sources. With the occupation of Portugal by French troops the King and the Court moved to the colony.

THE BRITISH INFLUENCE

These upheavals created conditions favourable for British trade and enterprise to establish a predominant position in Brazil. British ship-owners and traders were virtually the only foreigners in a position to benefit from the opening of Brazil to trade. The establishment of the Portuguese court in Brazil meant that revenues formerly sent to the mother country were now spent in, or from, the colony. Although this may have stimulated some local industry of a luxury or semi-luxury type, organized on artisan lines, it opened up a wider market for the kind of goods which only industrializing Britain could supply.

The separation of Brazil from Portugal in 1822 resulted in its becoming, to all intents and purposes, part of Britain's informal empire of free trade, a status which it retained until the First World War. Brazilian development over that period of almost a century has therefore to be seen in this context.

Of course, Brazil was not ruled from London. The dominant slave-owning class was still sovereign and there was friction between it and the British government. A major bone of contention was the slave trade which the former had an interest in maintaining, but which the latter wanted to ban. This conflict has to be seen in the light of changes in the Brazilian economy consequent upon the changes in the world market following the French Revolution. In the 1790s the great French-owned sugar plantation economy of Haiti was put out of action by a slave revolt. This caused an increase in sugar prices and opened up new opportunities for the Brazilian planters. However, they could only take advantage of these opportunities if they could be sure of the labour supply, hence their desire to keep open the African slave trade. British interests, centred on the West Indies, were, from the 1830s, against the continuation of the trade, which was finally abolished in 1850.

During the early nineteenth century there was increased world demand for some other Brazilian staples, including cotton and leather. British trade enjoyed a privileged position in both directions, as British manufactured goods secured a strong position in the Brazilian home market and benefited from any rise in the incomes of the planters. The City of London became the source of credit and loans. In short, after independence from Portugal, the new state became economically dependent upon Britain.

The years after 1815 saw a general fall in the prices of primary products on the world market which put an end to the commodity boom. When the new Imperial regime took over it had to grapple with a series of difficult internal problems, partly financial, partly political – the discontent of some provinces – as well as with the conflict with Britain over the slave trade. By the 1830s, however, a new staple was coming to the fore which was to have a decisive role in shaping Brazil's subsequent economic development. Coffee had been introduced as a crop in the eighteenth century and during the time of the wars in Europe, had become an important export staple. Coffee plantations, organized with slave labour, were carved out of virgin forest lands mainly in south central Brazil in the hinterland of Rio de Janeiro. Cultivation of coffee later spread to the state of São Paulo, which was to become the main coffee-producing, and most prosperous, region of the country, with Santos as the port of shipment.

Coffee-growing required large amounts of land as well as the intensive use of labour on the plantations. Land was abundant enough and the slowdown in other parts of the economy made slave labour available. In contrast with the sugar-planters, the coffee-planters were more commercially-minded and entrepreneurial in their attitudes. They were able to take initiatives in business and establish their dominance in political life. Policy was thus made to serve the interests of coffee: a commodity for which there was an expanding demand from most advanced countries during the nineteenth century (with the exception of Britan where demand was actually falling). The coffee-planters wanted cheap labour and other inputs and also the necessary infrastructure of railways, ports and handling facilities. They were in favour of 'development' of a certain kind and anxious to see Brazil emulate the civilized (i.e. European) world. As long as investment in coffee was profitable, however, there was no reason why they should be interested in industrialization. Indeed, export earnings enabled them to buy whatever they needed in the shape of manufactured goods from abroad, notably from Britain. Imports were cheaper and of better quality than local products, if they were available at all. It was easy for them to accept the free-trade doctrines of British political economy and to assume that Brazil's comparative advantage lay in producing coffee.

This was all the more so when Britain adopted a full free-trade policy from the 1850s onwards, the beginning also of an upsurge in the world economy which boosted demand for Brazilian coffee and other primary products. Throughout this period, British manufactured goods held sway in the Brazilian market and there was little scope for local producers except in filling in the gaps. Unlike the situation in North America where the interior of the continent was being opened up by a class of free farmers producing for the market and having purchasing power, much of which was used to provide their households with everyday articles of consumption, most Brazilian production was organized on the plantation system. Apart from that, in other regions, the agriculturalists were too poor to buy much of anything. In other words, the home market grew only slowly. The linkage effects of coffee-growing were not unlike those of sugar production in the past. There was some demand for locally-produced food and rough textiles for the slaves, inputs such as sacks or tools which had to be purchased, purchases of furniture and luxuries for the plantation-owners – but none of these things offered much of a prospect for industrial investment. Most manufactures continued to be imported. European immigration was not greatly attracted when there were still abundant opportunities in North America. Some immigrants might find jobs on the plantations as overseers, on the railways, or in the growing business sector in the towns; otherwise they might end up as poor subsistence farmers, a labour reserve for the large landowners. Moreover, the existence of slavery tended to down-grade manual labour for an employer.

The abolition of slavery was a necessary part of the modernizing process which Brazil was undergoing as the economy moved forward in the third quarter of the nineteenth century, in the wake of world prosperity. Britain was the model and mentor for the changes Brazilian society was undergoing at this time, through commercial and cultural contacts and the many British people handling business in the country. Whatever the moral motives of the anti-slavery campaign, abolition was also a response to a chronic labour scarcity appearing in the more rapidly growing areas such as São Paulo. Pressure was also coming from the wage and salary earners in the towns. Slave labour tended to be immobile; it remained in stagnant areas while employers elsewhere were crying out for labour. Its existence discouraged immigration and also tied up capital. However, abolitionist sentiment in the country, strongly backed by Britain, undoubtedly grew and, especially with its abolition in the United States as a result of the Civil War, the continued existence of slavery was seen as an obstacle to modernization. During the war with Peru (1865–70) many negro slaves had been released to serve in the army. After it was over, in 1871, the Law of the Free Womb was passed whereby children born to women slaves were to be freed on reaching their twenty-first year. In the following decade, discipline on the plantations began to break down and in places there were mass desertions. Urban officials and the military became increasingly reluctant to play the ignominious role of rounding up the chattels of the big landowners. More and more slave-owners freed their slaves; by 1877–8 this became increasingly common as the only means by which plantation owners could retain their labour force. Clearly, the days of slavery as an institution were numbered, The final act of emancipation in 1888, which granted the slaves their freedom without compensation to their owners, was something of a formality.

The immediate future of the slaves depended very much upon the area in which they found themselves; in some places the labour market was overstocked, while in others there was a labour scarcity. The influence of slavery on work habits both of former slaves and free white workers did not disappear overnight. No doubt the effects of slavery are still discernible in Brazilian society today: descendants of former slaves are to be found chiefly on the lower rungs of the social ladder. Slavery introduced a large black element into the population of Brazil and while colour discrimination was markedly less severe than in the United States it existed (and exists) nonetheless. As for the immediate economic impact of abolition it seems not to have been very pronounced one way or the other. In the long run it probably contributed to an improvement in the quality of the labour force, removed a discouragement to immigration, brought about the spread of the wage-system and increased the potential of the home market.

The coffee economy continued to be the major growth sector in the closing part of the nineteenth century. There was a shift towards São Paulo and neighbouring states, and a growth in São Paulo city as a financial and commercial, and also as a burgeoning industrial centre. On the other hand, large areas such as the north-east, showed little capacity for growth, while in others, cattle-raising and cocoa producing for export provided openings for investment and some employment.

The Amazon region also experienced a short-lived boom as a rubber producer following an increased world demand for this commodity. At its peak, rubber made up 20 per cent of the country's exports and temporarily attracted a large wage-labour force. After the First World War, Brazilian production wilted under the pressure from the new plantations in Asia. Throughout this period external economic relations were dominated by British merchant and financial houses. Loans were floated in the City of London, financing state spending; British capital financed railways and the rest of the infrastructure required by a primary-exporting country. British merchants controlled the import-export trade, which was carried in ships under the British flag, financed and insured in London. The informal British empire in Brazil did not extend into industry; investment here was modest and not particularly outstanding. At the same time, Britain did provide the model of a modern economy which many Brazilians wished their nation to emulate. British machinery, managers and technicians undoubtedly played a role in introducing modern industry despite the limited investment in this sector. British finance was indispensable in the primary export sector which was the motor of the whole economy; even so, it was not associated with direct control or decision-making. For all its financial dependence on Britain, Brazil remained an independent country with its own ruling class. Certainly they accepted their dependence on British investment and finance of trade. They could perhaps be described as junior partners, and Brazil as an informal or economic colony. When all that has been said, Brazilians owned the coffee plantations, then the main source of national wealth; as well as most of the other means of production with the exception of the transport system. For the Brazilian ruling class it was not a bad partnership.

MODERNIZATION

In any case, growing wealth, unequally distributed as it was, fostered urban growth and investment in public buildings and modern utilities. Nationalism found expression in building up the attributes of a modern state: armed forces, universities, schools, law courts, and hospitals could all be regarded as part of the process of modernization, which prepared the way for subsequent industrialization. Modernization began under the Empire (1822–89) and continued more vigorously under the federal Republic which replaced it. British domination of Brazil's finances continued while the City of London remained in the ascendant, that is to say until the First World War. To service its debt to London, Brazil depended upon the sale of its coffee, rubber, cocoa and other primary products. Its financial well-being hinged upon world trends in demand for these staples. Any fall in world market prices for these commodities meant a decline in income for the producers. It also made it more difficult to find the foreign exchange necessary to service the debt to Britain.

The coffee planters were in the front line here, and the economy as a whole was highly dependent upon coffee. It was a dangerous dependence, but the coffee-planters were powerful men in politics. Already, in 1906, the government agreed to buy up coffee surpluses in an attempt to keep up the market price and thus the income of the growers.

Until the First World War, industrial development was on a modest scale, but it was growing, particularly in food-processing and textiles. There had been sufficient growth in population and incomes to expand the home market for some goods with aid from tariffs in some cases. There was the beginning of the emergence of an entrepreneurial class investing in workshops, factories and mills. These initial, still hesitant steps on the road to industrialization were most visible in the São Paulo area. Capital and enterprise were attracted from the leading planter class, while the relative prosperity of the coffee-growing region widened the internal market for goods and services. Immigrant business men, often starting from small beginnings in trade (competing with the British in some cases), moved into industrial production. It was the familiar pattern of rootless newcomers doing better than the natives and seizing the opportunities presented by the development of market capitalism. Where they retained contact with their homelands (as in the case of some of the Italians for example), the newcomers turned this to their advantage. Immigrant businessmen had a sharp eye for new possibilities. While they came into conflict at some points with established industrialists from planter families, their common interests tended to predominate. These two streams contributed to the formation of a national industrial bourgeoisie which was to play an increasingly important role in the economic development of Brazil.

The First World War had contradictory effects on Brazil and there are disagreements among historians of the period as to their nature. On the one hand, Brazil's main suppliers were involved in the war and not able to supply the customary amounts of manufactured goods. Raw materials and intermediate goods soared in price or became virtually unobtainable. Apparently, then, there should have been new opportunities for industrial investment, in what was later to be called import-substitution, and Brazilian producers should have gained from the higher prices. Certainly there were some of these expected effects. Allied war demand generated increased production in some sectors. Local machine-shops tried to repair or replace machinery and equipment no longer obtainable

157

from abroad. In the main, however, there was no basic change in the structure of industry and any stimulus that the war may have given was short-lived. Thus it is necessary to be cautious when appraising the favourable consequences of the war.

With the restoration of peace, traditional sources of supply were reopened. American as well as European industry saw in Brazil a promising market and were able to sell many kinds of manufactured goods of a quality and at a price with which local industry could not compete. For some local firms the wartime boom was followed by a crisis.

Dating back to before the war, a debate was going on in economic and political circles over the tariff issue, especially as it related to manufactured goods. Some said that foreign imports should be checked to assist local production (the government had at its disposal what was known as the Law of Similars enabling it to impose duties on imports of goods similar to those which home industry could produce). Others saw the advantages of free trade and were content to see Brazil profiting, as it seemed, from its comparative advantage in the production of coffee and other staples. As long as coffee production remained profitable and the government continued to support coffee prices, the free trade argument seemed to prevail.

DEPRESSION

Industrial growth was slow in the 1920s, while imports rose. During the world depression of the 1930s the primary sector was hard hit, while industrial production continued its growth. However, it is doubtful whether this can be seen as a great advance along the road of import-substitution industrialization. True, new investment did take place in industry, some of it in the branch plants of American or European firms, mainly for assembly and processing, jumping over tariff walls. The home market remained narrow and circumscribed and, certainly for the type of product of these foreign firms, was confined to a relatively small number of higher-income recipients. As for the mass of the people, some were hit by the decline of the primary sector, and at the best their low incomes only permitted them to buy such items as cheap textiles whether home-produced or imported. Thus the industrial structure was bound to reflect the very unequal income distribution and the relative poverty of a large proportion of the population. Of more significance was the impact of the depression on the primary sector, hitherto the motor of the economy.

As the depression hit Brazil there was a catastrophic fall in coffee prices, a fall in internal purchasing power and a contraction of demand for manufactured imports. To deal with the plight of the coffee-growers, the government resorted to the drastic practice of buying up and burning surplus coffee, thus earning worldwide notoriety. In Brazil, industrial production fell off by 10 per cent between 1929 and 1931, but quickly recovered thereafter. Some accounts claim that industrial production rose by 60 per cent by the end of the decade. Lack of foreign exchange and the fact that home-produced articles became more competitive because of currency depreciation, assisted a transfer of consumer demand from imported to home-manufactured commodities. This tendency was accentuated during the Second World War as imports from belligerent countries were again sharply curtailed, especially those of manufactured and capital goods. Now the substitution of the Brazilian-made for imported manufactures, which took place initially as a spontaneous reaction to depression and war, became the basis for a new, and more conscious economic strategy: import-substitution industrialization (ISI).

As a primary producer Brazil gained during the Second World War from voracious Allied demand while imports were curtailed. As a result, export earnings built up at a faster rate than foreign exchange could be used to buy imports. Brazil accumulated currency reserves in the countries it was supplying which could not be used to buy goods for which there was a market at home. Export growth and economic expansion had meanwhile increased money incomes without a corresponding increase in output for the home market. Inflationary pressures resulted, driving up prices by 1944 to almost twice their 1939 level.

Meanwhile, Brazil's external relations had been quite substantially changed. The depression of the 1930s and the war of 1939–45 completed what the First World War had begun: the ending of British predominance and the opening of the way for the United States to take over. While the British stake in the economy had mainly been through trade and portfolio investment in state bonds and the infrastructure, the American interest was to include the establishment of branch plants which had a direct effect on the industrialization process. There were early signs of this between the wars, but it was not until the 1950s that it began to assume a massive scale.

To understand the depth of this change it is necessary to consider some of the main lines of development in the political economy of Brazil from the onset of the Depression. First there was the installation of the regime of President Vargas, of an authoritarian type, but with a nationalist and populist appeal. Rather than bringing any fundamental departure in economic policy, however, it sought to satisfy the demands of the coffee-producers and the commercial-industrial bourgeoisie which had become of increasing political weight. It satisfied the first, so far as it could (as already noted) by its coffee-support policy; the second it tried to placate by stimulating domestic production of industrial goods in an early, and still largely unconscious, application of the ISI strategy. It was only after the war, however, that this policy was adopted in a more coherent form. By then, under the pressure of nationalist, or anti-imperialist, sentiment there was a call for a policy which would reduce dependence upon the export of primary products. The prices of these products were subject to severe fluctuations, but those which Brazil supplied suffered from other disadvantages. They formed a declining proportion of world trade and there was little prospect of a big increase in earnings from them. Requiring little or no processing, they gave rise to only limited linkage effects for the Brazilian economy and could not be expected to promote staples-led growth along Canadian lines. It seemed, therefore, that continued excessive reliance upon the established staples would condemn Brazil to economic stagnation in the post-war period as well to as continued dependence upon foreign (now American) capital. This was not the complete picture; there had already been some preliminary steps along the road to industrialization, a class of industrial entrepreneurs was in favour of going further, and looked to the state for support. Likewise, there were strong reasons in the nationalist ideology which suggested the desirability of broadening the industrial base to give the nation the means to uphold its independence. This ideology had a broad appeal.

TOWARDS INDUSTRIALIZATION

Even without any clearly formulated ideology of economic growth or deductions from an analysis of Brazil's economic position, the experience of the war and the new world situation at the end of it, propelled the government into what was, in effect, an industrialization policy of a more positive character. Pragmatic at first, it increasingly took shape as a set of measures intended to endow the nation with a more diversified industrial base and a modernized infrastructure. Specific programmes along these lines were recommended by the Joint Brazil-United States Economic Commission in the early 1950s and then by the influential Economic Commission of Latin America (ECLA or CEPAL) set up under the auspices of the United Nations. The latter urged powerfully that industrialization was the way out of Brazil's problems and that it would substitute 'development' for 'dependency'. This became part of the ideology of a group of leading Latin American economists connected with this body. It was assumed optimistically that if the impetus for industrialization was given, with the state playing the active role, it would lead to a process of self-sustaining growth sufficient to overcome secular backwardness and bring about a rise in incomes and living standards. The ISI strategy was seen as the one best suited to Brazil's situation as a primary-producing country still largely dependent upon imported manufactures. As has been seen, the measures taken to deal with the depression and the trading problems created by the war had prepared the ground.

After the war, as economies began to be restored, the tide of imports into Brazil began to worry the government and from 1947, in line with past policies, it adopted a policy of selective import controls. The aim was to curtail the influx of consumer goods while still permitting the import of capital goods or raw materials required by domestic industry at low or no duty. Using the long-established Law of Similars it thus imposed tariffs chiefly on goods already made, or which could be made, inside the country. This policy of selective protection, or infant industries' tariffs, could thus be used to steer industry along the import-substitution path. At the same time, the existence of tariff walls on some manufactured goods which Brazil was not yet able to produce encouraged foreign (particularly American) firms to set up branch plants, at first mainly for assembly. Once they had embarked upon this investment, however, they might be prepared to go further until all, or almost all, the finished product was manufactured inside the country. The ISI strategy was expected to have beneficial results, but it also had others which were not so welcome.

RESULTS OF THE ISI STRATEGY

When the new industrialization policy began to take shape, in the early 1950s, Brazil was still an underdeveloped country. Despite the growth of industry and modern capitalist institutions in some parts of the country, vast regions were dominated by low-productivity agriculture. There was much rural unemployment and underemployment. Average per capita income was one of the lowest in the world. From the national point of view, huge disparities in levels of development and incomes posed many serious political as well as economic problems. Modern trade and financial activities as well as such organized and large-scale industries as existed, were concentrated in a few urban areas, principally in the south-centre region. Other areas, such as the north-east, centre of the sugar production which had prospered in distant colonial days, now stagnated at an extremely low level of average income. They had large populations but no resources or other advantages likely to attract industrial investment. Moreover, the mass of the people in agriculture, whether subsistence cultivators, casual labourers or estate workers, had little purchasing power. The main demand for industrial products came from the high income groups in the towns, from the growing 'middle classes' made up of state employees, small property owners and the business and professional people. Their disposable incomes put them much closer to their counterparts in the advanced countries in their lifestyle than to the rural masses. They were also the most susceptible to the 'demonstration effect'. That is to say, they were influenced by, and desired to emulate, the consumption standards and tastes of the high income countries. Many of these wants could only be met by imports. As the ISI strategy – if it can be distinguished by such a title – came into effect, it did so in response to market forces. It thus tended to encourage chiefly the production of consumer goods for those with higher incomes; it did little or nothing to raise the incomes of the mass of the people. The demand for this type of good could be met partly by local firms expanding and diversifying their production. As they did so, however, they found it necessary to import more advanced technology; so, instead of importing consumer goods, Brazil was importing the machinery to make them. Furthermore, at some point the actual or potential market in Brazil for particular commodities became large enough to attract foreign firms to set up assembly or production facilities behind the tariff wall. The tendency was, therefore, for production of certain items, such as consumer durables and other sophisticated products of high-income societies to increase, because they fitted in with the urban pattern of life of the middle and upper classes. At the same time, of course, there was a growth in the industrial labour force who also had to buy goods and services in the market, but with lower average incomes.

The contradictions of the ISI strategy arose out of the nature of the Brazilian economy. The nationalist, populist and military-style governments which have ruled modern Brazil have all upheld the principle of the private ownership of the means of production and the primacy of the market as a distributive mechanism. There has not been any question, therefore, of the nationalization of industry as a whole or of state intervention to correct the massive inequalities in the distribution of wealth and power which go back to colonial times. Brazil has accepted its dependence upon the world market dominated by a few capital-rich advanced countries. As the organ of the property-owners, the state has upheld and advanced their interests both against other classes in Brazilian society and in bargaining with foreign governments and business. In a country such as Brazil, the state could not avoid taking responsibility for those aspects of economic development which private capital, national or foreign, was unable or unwilling to finance and promote but which were nonetheless necessary for industrialization.

Thus there has been a history of state intervention in Brazil to supplement and correct market forces. For example, under the Law of Similars, tariffs were used to encourage investment in local industries as well as to raise revenue. As early as 1906 the state intervened in the coffee market in the interests of the big producers and it did so even more in the 1930s when it also imposed all-round tariff increases. The depression and the war pushed the state into deeper involvement with economic policy-making. In particular it assumed responsibility for financing and promoting some basic industries and additions to the infrastructure which were beyond the scope of private investment. It set up a development bank (BNDE) to assist private firms needing capital for expansion and promoted some joint ventures between the state and private firms. The Kubitschek regime launched the Programme of Targets in 1956, setting out production aims for achievement by both private and state enterprises. Brazil seemed to be adopting the kind of indicative planning which was fashionable at this time in a number of capitalist countries. Other special projects were put in hand, such as the initiation of a motor car industry, with private capital. A vast steel complex, Volta Redonda, had been launched during the war and it was followed in the early 1950s by the formation of several powerful state corporations, notably in the petroleum industry (Petrobras) and in electric power generation (Elektrobras).

These activities of the state in the ecomomic sphere had as their general outcome the promotion of capital accumulation (private and state) and the establishment of basic infrastructure without which industrialization could not have gone ahead. There was no need for a particular ideology or philosophy of state intervention, nor was the transition particularly dramatic. Objective conditions really compelled governments to take economic initiatives which would not have been acceptable before. There was no hostility to private capitalism as such in the state's measures, nor any intention to displace it (though at times it might have seemed to be so to some nervous foreign observers especially in the United States). State policy overall, operated more or less in harmony with the industrial bourgeoisie in Brazil and with the foreign multinational corporations which were to play a steadily increasing role in Brazil's industrialization. The range of state intervention and the new state bodies active in the economy brought a section of the bureaucracy onto the scene as an economic force. Linked with the upper and middle class, and with the armed forces – which came to play a dominant political role – they constituted a special interest group. Its members played an entrepreneurial role, not against, but in harmony with business, both national and international. However, it also had its own point of view and its own interests to defend.

The growing role of the state industry and public utilities had its corollary in the management of monetary and credit policy by the banks and the finance ministry. Once the objective of rapid growth under the ISI strategy had been adopted by the state, this meant, in practice, inflationary finance through state spending. Preventing inflation from getting out of hand without sacrificing other development objectives has been a besetting problem of Brazilian economic history for over three decades and no answer has been found. Inflation rates have soared to heights which seem fantastic by European standards, yet the economy has survived and grown. Perhaps inflation of this kind is inevitable in an underdeveloped country undergoing industrialization under the conditions of the capitalist market with state initiative.

Since the early 1950s, industrialization, although rapid, has taken place mainly in a series of forward surges followed by slowdowns. The reason for these fluctuations can be found partly in world market trends and partly in a self-generating cycle of reproduction and over-production. The first two major upswings can be traced to the initial ISI strategies, and took place in 1947–52 and 1956–61. Later growth surges, such as that of 1968–74 (the so-called 'Brazilian economic miracle'), have been strongly marked by the investment decisions of the multinational corporations, the new stage in ISI and the growth of manufacturing exports.

Although other Latin American countries adopted ISI strategies, which were recommended for many 'developing' countries in the 1950s, Brazil has been, in a sense, the model country. This was because of its size and power in Latin America, its varied resources (real or supposed), its large potential home market, its existing industrial base and its abundant supplies of labour. The strong nationalist bent of successive governments of the country, as well as the support and goodwill of the United States, facilitated the process. Industrial firms owned by Brazilians were ready to seize new profit-making opportunities, while a number of MNCs were already established in the country when the objective of rapid industrialization was adopted in the post-war period.

A closer look at the ISI strategy shows that it was bound to be imitative, in the sense that it aimed to replicate industries already flourishing elsewhere. However, it could not do so in the same way. For instance, since internal demand was limited, scale economies could not be realized to the same extent. What generally happened was that, having taken an existing foreign model, say of the motorcar industry, the basic plant and technology would be imported. In the early stages there would simply be assembly of imported components and parts. In time, some of these parts could be manufactured locally and a substantial amount of the bodywork and chassis could be produced in the main plants. Thus the imported component would decline.

As similar industries were set up they would create a demand for materials such as steel, rubber and aluminium and then for intermediate goods, machinery and machine-tools. As the market for these items grew, then capital would be attracted into producing them inside the country. In other words there would be a series of backward linkages which would extend the industrial base. At the same time, other linkages would appear. As more cars came on the road there would be a demand for petrol stations, servicing and repair facilities, motorways, urban traffic control systems, and so on. Workers employed in these activities, managers and other people receiving incomes, would create an increased demand for a wide range of goods and services. In theory, therefore, the economy could be launched into an all-round process of industrialization. The question was, however, how far, and how soon, such linkages would come into effect. Clearly, though some goods were now being produced that had formerly been imported, other goods would have to be imported to produce them. As industry became more complex, and as incomes rose, there would simply be a transfer to a different range of imports. Thus the net amount of substitution might be negligible, at least for some time.

Problems of this kind do not mean that the ISI strategy was faulty. In any case, in practice the picture in Brazil was a dynamic one: imports of some items fell off while others rose and the range of import-substitution did tend to become wider as it became more profitable to produce the items concerned inside the country, rather than importing them. This was discovered by the MNCs as well as by nationally-owned firms. In general, it was the newer product or the one incorporating the most advanced technology which would still have to be imported. Market forces, within the inherent limits of ISI, did tend to bring about, over time, a fairly balanced and broadly-based growth. However, if anything, Brazil's ties with the world market became stronger and more crucial as the operation proceeded.

A more significant criticism is that in Brazil the growth based on ISI was confined to some regions and in the main benefited only a minority of the population; in both cases those already relatively prosperous. Existing imbalances and disparities, instead of going away, became sharper. The structure of production brought about by ISI reflected the pre-existing distribution of purchasing power. Represented in the new industries were those which supplied the increasingly varied and growing volume of consumer goods, bought largely, if not exclusively, by the upper-income groups, as well as the intermediate and capital goods required for their producton. Some of the latter were, moreover, still imported. Only by opening up new job opportunities, directly or indirectly, did ISI provide an additional market for wage-goods (those consumed by workers). Only as the other varieties of goods were cheapened, or came onto the secondhand market (as in the case of cars and consumer durables), did the wage-earners and other low-income people gain any benefit.

As far as wages were concerned, these were probably higher, on average, in modern factories than in old-fashioned workshops or in ordinary labouring jobs. Under Brazilian political conditions, trade union bargaining has been impossible or greatly curtailed. It was in the interests of employers to hire no more workers than was necessary to maximize profits and to keep the average wage below productivity gains. If the benefits derived by workers from the ISI consisted mainly of a job, then more than 50 per cent of the population tied to the low-income agricultural sector remained as poor as before. During the period from the 1950s many hundreds of thousands moved into urban areas to escape rural poverty and to find work. Probably few found their way directly into factory employment; many remained unemployed, did casual work or were absorbed into the large low-wage, labour-intensive, tertiary sector (including much domestic service). With population growth continuing steadily throughout the period, per capita income grew less than national income or industrial output. An already biased income distribution tended to become more unequal, so that for a large part of the population the statistical rise in per capita income remained a meaningless figure.

In other words, the high rates of growth achieved by Brazilian industry at the height of the industrialization drive, putting it into the Japanese class, did not overcome the secular problems of underdevelopment. Large areas such as the north-east continued to stagnate, while rapid industrialization enhanced the advantages, and pulling power for new investment, of the existing growth-poles, notably the São Paulo area. It was here that the main new industries, whether nationally-owned or set up by the MNCs, were built up.

THE NEW REGIME

After the first surges of industrialization in the 1950s, the economy appeared to run out of steam and by 1961–62 it was in deep crisis. Balance of payments deficits had built up a large foreign debt, increasingly difficult to service. This indicated that ISI, thus far, instead of cutting down dependence on imports had actually increased it. Meanwhile, the MNCs had been moving in and foreign ownership and control of the modern manufacturing sector was increasing. Government expenditure constantly outstripped tax revenues by a large margin and fuelled an inflationary spiral which, in 1961, threatened to get out of control. As an engine of growth, import-substitution seemed to be running out of steam owing mainly to the limitations of the home market. In fact, inflation and the slowing down of growth were closely connected, but control of the former, however desirable, seemed likely only to bring ISI growth to a dead stop. In 1963 there was negligible economic growth while prices rose by what was then a record 81 per cent. A general slowdown then set in which was to last until 1967. Meanwhile a major political crisis erupted, for there was an army take-over in April 1964, which introduced a more repressive style of rule and also set economic policy on a new course.

The new regime's diagnosis of the crisis and of the problems facing the country did not differ fundamentally from previous diagnoses. For years official bodies and outside agencies had had their say about the Brazilian economy and on some points there was a measure of consensus about the main problems: hyper-inflation, sectoral and regional disparities, lack of employment opportunites, rural poverty and balance of payments deficits. Social unrest and even the direction of the previous government convinced the ruling class that there was a danger of revolution. There was no doubt about the nature of the new regime: it had to uphold the status quo by all means.

The regime brought about a revision of economic policy away from national-populism, towards an approach which placed more emphasis on market forces and encouraged the inflow of foreign capital. Authoritarian government was no novelty for Brazil, but whereas previous regimes had left some scope for party politics, parliamentary discussion and trade union bargaining, a general clamp-down was now imposed on such activities, even if some of them survived. The shaping of economic policy was placed in the hands of 'experts', known critics of the previous government's methods, and advocates of a stabilization programme designed to control inflation, bring down wage costs and restore profitability to industry. This programme was regarded as a pre-requisite for further growth. There was a much stronger emphasis now on market forces rather than on state intervention, and little sympathy for social goals. The main objective was to create a favourable environment for continued capital accumulation, including foreign investment and the attraction to Brazil of more branches of the MNCs. The initial response to the new policy was a slowing down in growth which lasted until 1967.

During the period following the military coup the ground was prepared for profitable investment in the future. Real wages were held down or reduced. Government spending was cut while additional credit was made available to industry and also to the market-orientated section of agriculture. The aim was to increase production and productivity by raising profit expectations of businessmen, landowners and farmers. The rate of inflation was slowly brought down from 91.9 per cent annual average in 1964, year of the coup, to 56 per cent in the following year; not until

1970 did it come down to under 20 per cent despite the declared intention of the new policy-makers to bring it down to 10 per cent in 1966.

After declining in the mid-1960s industrial growth rates rose again between 1968 and 1974 in what was sometimes described as the Brazilian 'economic miracle'. This can be seen partly as the deferred result of the new policies adopted under the military regime, but it also has to be remembered that international conditions were favourable. The oil crisis of 1974 was an important factor in ending this phase of growth. In any case, the 'miracle' was associated with the influx of foreign capital and the further proliferation of branch plants of the MNCs, attracted by high profit rates and the political stability offered by military rule. Although the production of these and already existing firms was directed partly towards the upper end of the home market, a new factor came on the scene: Brazil's exports of manufactured goods became increasingly significant. It also has to be underlined that the dictatorial methods employed by the military regime kept down wages, so that productivity gains were reaped mainly by business.

After 1964, the model of industrialization underwent a change. This was not so much a sharp break with the previous ISI strategy as a modification of it, even an inevitable outcome of the path already chosen. What happened was that continued industrialization became increasingly dependent on foreign capital and technology. Instead of breaking the ties of 'dependency', as the advocates of ISI had hoped, continued growth became increasingly linked to investment by foreign firms and to overseas demand.

Reviewing the process as a whole there were three participants in the industrialization process: the state, the national capitalists and the MNCs. Initially, by its investments in infrastructure and basic industries requiring heavy outlays of capital, the state had acted as trail-blazer and continued to play a supportive role. Its initiatives had opened the way for profitable investment and more rapid accumulation in the private sector. Nationally-owned industry had taken what advantage it could of the possibilities offered by the ISI strategy, but continued industrialization required recourse to foreign firms which had the capital and the technology to establish more advanced industries. The activities of the state and the build-up of industry owned by Brazilian firms, had only cleared the way for the massive incursion of foreign-owned firms whose prospects for profitable investment depended upon a certain level of industrialization having been reached in the host country. The branch plants of these firms were producing sophisticated products aimed mainly at the high-income market in Brazil. Local firms lacked the capital and know-how to push into these fields, in some of which the MNCs had been established for a long time. Instead of permanent conflict and destructive competition, a triple partnership of state, local capital and the MNCs was consummated, at least informally. ISI had indeed prepared the way for expansion and capital accumulation, but instead of being the basis for national independence, as its advocates had hoped, it became the vehicle for the penetration of foreign capital on an unprecedented scale. Its justification lay in the fact that it made possible rapid growth and the so-called 'miracle' but the dependence of the Brazilian economy, in a new form, was as unmistakable as ever.

The MNCs set up their branch plants in Brazil because it seemed good business to do so. Wages were being kept down and the military regime offered security. There was a large and growing market in Brazil and the country was a useful export platform to attack markets which could not be reached directly from the main plants in the USA or Europe. Another factor was that the MNCs had found that the market in their original homes was reaching saturation point, labour costs were rising and additional investment might not give an average rate of return. On the other hand they possessed valuable assets in know-how, brand names and management skills. They also had the finance, while growth could be provided for out of retained profits or by raising capital in the host country.

For reasons already referred to, Brazil was looked on with favour. As an apparently stable country, controlled by the military, the largest country in Latin America and sharing a common frontier with a number of other countries, it seemed the obvious candidate to back up US policy in Latin America, in what some called a 'sub-imperialist' role. Anything which strengthened Brazil economically was therefore held in favour in Washington.

More specifically, compensatory tariffs and other factors made it difficult if not impossible for the products of the MNCs to reach the Brazilian market from outside. Better, therefore, to leap over the tariff walls, get closer to the market and tap the reserves of low-wage local labour under a government not squeamish about suppressing trade unions or left-wing political parties. Indeed, after 1964, the government did everything it could, through favourable laws, to encourage foreign firms and to enable their profits to be repatriated. The urban, middle-class market in Brazil was not very different from that in the advanced countries. It was eager for cars, consumer durables and all those internationally-renowned brands with which its members had become familiar through travel, advertising and films. It was at this market that the MNCs aimed, and it was from the same source that, as time went on, they were even able to raise capital for further expansion. The state accepted that a substantial part of the economy would be foreign-owned and was happy to see jobs created and incomes, which it could tap for taxation, increasing. To be sure, there were some local interests which might be harmed, or which were jealous of big, powerful and foreign rivals, but in the main, the MNCs were complementary to, rather than competitive with, local industrial enterprise. On the whole, then, the triple partnership could function harmoniously.

THE CURRENT INDUSTRIAL SCENE

An investigation of the current industrial scene as it emerged during the upsurges of the 1960s and 1970s, shows that foreign direct investment has become concentrated in a small number of advanced industries; motor vehicles, rubber, machinery, electrical goods and the more sophisticated consumer goods. The state sector covers public utilities, petroleum, over 60 per cent of mining and about one-third of the metallurgical industry. National private enterprises predominate in most of the rest of industry. The amount of direct competition between the three sectors remains small while interconnections are of considerable importance. Where foreign capital is strategically placed, say in the new, large motor vehicle industry, its investment and current operations open up markets for local firms in the supply of parts and components on a subcontracting basis. Overall, the foreign ownershop of fixed assets works out at about 15 per cent, which may not sound excessive. However, in a country like Brazil that 15 per cent comprises the most modern plants in the advanced sectors of the economy. Nevertheless friction between local capital and the MNCs has been less than might have been expected; both look to the government to provide the conditions for the safe and rapid accumulation of capital; and the concept of the triple partnership seems to cover the case adequately. All in all, foreign MNCs have made a substantial contribution to Brazilian industrialization; what can be questioned is whether the type of industrialization they have promoted is what

Brazil needs. The long-standing problems of underdevelopment from which much of the country suffers remain unresolved.

So far then, under the original version of ISI, and the modified version with exports playing a larger role, industrialization has been no panacea. There are still forbidding problems of mass poverty in the rural areas, and unemployment and squalid housing in the urban slums and shanty-towns. The entry of the MNCs could do little to overcome such problems. Once the local market showed signs of slackening they moved into exports.

During the 1970s, manufactured exports became of increasing importance in the Brazilian balance of payments whether coming from the branch plants of the MNCs or from nationally-owned private firms. This emphasis can be seen as a result of the failure of the industrialization drive to create a mass home demand for modern industrial products. The distribution of income is extremely unequal, perhaps one of the highest in the world. The share of the national income going to the top 10 per cent of income-receivers rose from 39.6 per cent in 1960 to 46.2 per cent in 1983. The output of modern consumer goods goes principally to a minority of about 20 per cent. Meanwhile millions are short of food or actually dying slowly from malnutrition.

Meanwhile, import-substitution has not come to an end, it has simply moved to new items as industrialization has proceeded. Since the Development Plan adopted in 1971, more emphasis has been laid upon the need to build up domestic production of capital goods and basic industrial inputs. One motive for this has been to relieve the pressure on the balance of payments and the need for foreign capital. In fact, the experience of industrializing countries shows that import-dependence tends to increase. There is increased need for export markets to make possible scale economies in industry and to earn foreign exchange; there is need for imports to make good local deficiencies and to take advantage of the international division of labour.

Like other non-petroleum producing 'developing' countries, Brazil was hard hit by the 1974 oil price rise. The economic 'miracle' by which the military regime had sought to legitimize itself, came to an end. There was a slowing down of growth, costs rose relatively to selling prices and profitability fell. In the mid-1970s, inflation rates also began to turn upwards (40 per cent in 1976). The balance of payments deficit tended to increase. Foreign borrowing of all types rose, much of it being necessary to service existing debts and to make it possible to find foreign exchange for the payment of dividends and interest to foreign private investors. Nevertheless, debts to foreign countries continued to mount, international bankers presumably retaining confidence in the potential of the Brazilian economy.

As long as Brazil continues to have one of the 'moderately repressive' regimes favoured by Washington, to play a key role in its Latin American policy and to pursue a 'liberal' policy of internationalization, it is likely to continue to enjoy the support of foreign bankers. Knowing this, as long as the generals or their conservative successors hold power they are likely to continue with their policy: a modified ISI strategy with enhanced scope for the MNCs. The model of an autonomous capitalist development was, for practical purposes, finally abandoned after the coup of 1964. It gave way to the uneasy and still changing triple partnership between state, national capital and MNCs already described. This model has made possible rapid industrial growth even in periods of international economic turbulence such as the 1970s. It has endowed the country with a more diversified and up-to-date industrial base. It has brought affluence to the more fortunate 20 per cent or so of the population comprising the upper and middle classes. Some of the prosperity may have percolated down to other classes, including the industrial workers. However, wages have been kept down by an authoritarian regime which curtails civil liberties and workers' rights. Despite repression, big strike struggles have taken place in recent years, and the regime has had to make some concessions and adopt a more liberal posture.

Many basic problems of the Brazilian economy and the society as a whole have not been tackled. Rapid and uncontrolled growth has brought new social costs. Large regions remain backward and little has been done to assist their modernization; there has been little or no improvement in the plight of the rural population. In the cities, in which a high proportion of the population now lives, there are immense contrasts of affluence and misery existing side by side.

Although Brazil is less dependent than it was once on coffee and one or two other staples these still make a substantial contribution to export earnings. Changes in world prices can thus have a considerable effect on the economy. 'Dependency' has not ended, but it has taken new forms: the massive indebtedness of the state to foreign banks and international financial institutions and the penetration of the advanced industrial sectors by foreign-owned MNCs. The ISI strategy has led to more rather than less involvement with the world market.

Brazil's manufactured exports, although they have been competitive in some well-publicized cases, especially in the markets of less-developed countries, are exposed to intensified competition in the difficult world economic situation of the 1980s. Brazil's position remains that of a subordinate capitalist country. While industrialization has been going on for some decades, it is still one-sided and incomplete. While it has made possible an extensive, diversified and rapid growth of production and national income, it has come up against a number of constraints and the social costs have been high. The deep poverty which is still the lot of a large part of the population is as anomalous as slavery was a century ago, and seems still more difficult to resolve.

It is difficult to argue that consumption had to be kept down while the productive apparatus was built up. The upper and middle classes have not been conspicuous by their frugality and the privations of the half or more of the population living in poverty have served no useful purpose. They are still in the same position as they were before: they produce little and can therefore buy little and there seems no way in which their labour can be mobilized for production. If policy continues along the same lines nothing more than a slow and almost imperceptible improvement can be expected in the lot of those who live in the backward, low-income agrarian regions. Workers, especially those in modern industry, have had a better deal; on the other hand, it is they who produce the surplus which makes possible continued investment in industry. The problem, for Brazilian capitalism, is to turn more low-productivity or unemployed peasants into productive workers.

If any industrialization is better than none and rapid growth is an indicator of 'success' the Brazilian model must score high marks. But, as suggested, there is more to it than that. The continued existence of mass poverty, the inherent 'dualism' of Brazilian society between the affluent and the poor, the regional disparities, the spectacle of a still largely agrarian country which has to import staple foods, the large and growing foreign stake in industry and endemic inflationary pressures, hardly add up to an acceptable model. Social contradictions have been suppressed rather than overcome under military rule. Attempts to control inflation have produced recession and redundancy in industry which now needs foreign markets to remain expansive.

Continued industrialization and more growth, along existing lines, even if possible in the future – which is not certain – do not seem likely either to improve mass living standards or to reduce regional and income disparities. In the future, therefore, if

Brazil is to move from its present uneasy, semi-industrialized state, not only a modification of policy but a wholly different model of industrialization may be necessary. It would have to give greater priority to raising living standards through agrarian reform, mass education and the spread of skills, investment in social overhead capital such as housing and the production of cheap, standardized factory-made goods for mass consumption. Neither free market forces, nor a military-technocratic government susceptible to the interests of the property-owning classes, is likely to bring about such a development programme.

The early 1980s saw the Brazilian economy suffering from the effects of recession in the advanced capitalist countries. A popular movement hostile to military rule, supported by the trade unions, resulted in the restoration of civil rule in 1984 when José Sarney became president. The generals withdrew from centre-stage although not from influence over the economy. The new regime was essentially conservative but with no magical remedy for Brazil's mounting problems. During the period of easy international credit, Brazil had borrowed heavily from commercial banks and from the IMF. The huge loans had largely been squandered on military hardware, prestige projects and public spending, leaving little in the way of productive assets capable of generating the additional exports necessary to service them. In 1986 the government declared a moratorium on its foreign debts. Growth could no longer be fuelled with foreign money. At the same time, the economy was wracked with high rates of inflation, resulting in several 'plans' designed to curtail wage and salary increases and control prices. Despite the ending of military rule (for how long no one can say because the army still has its representatives in the government), there has been no fundamental change in policy. Brazil continues to pursue a modified ISI strategy with enhanced scope for the MNCs. In fact, the export sector periodically shows signs of a dynamism absent from other parts of the economy. Meanwhile, Brazil continues to export quality food products while millions starve because they cannot afford to buy food whether home-grown or imported. There is no shortage of arable land which could be turned to producing poor people's food; but that would require a government able to grasp the nettle of agrarian reform. Anything which would raise the income of the mass of the people in the disadvantaged regions of the country would also expand the market for cheap manufactured goods.

CHAPTER 7
Nigerian industrialization: African variant

Of the Black African states, newly independent in the past quarter of a century, none has so far made much progress on the road to industrialization, but of their number Nigeria would seem to have the greatest potential. By far the largest, with more than 100 million people, it has varied resources, a relatively well-educated and adaptable labour force and a favourable geographical position. On the face of it there is a potentially large home market and the basis for the accumulation of capital and its investment in manufacturing industry.

Long exposure to the market and familiarity with monetary incentives in the colonial period had already brought into being a local entrepreneurial class. In many respects, therefore, Nigeria seems to have an advantage over many other developing countries – an advantage which has increased with the development of its vast petroleum resources. Nevertheless industrialization has been slow and limited in character; the Nigerian economy still remains essentially a primary-producing economy, dependent upon exports to the world market.

THE COLONIAL INHERITANCE

An examination of the colonial experience is a necessary prelude to an analysis of Nigerian development since independence in 1960. Like other areas of West Africa Nigeria suffered from the debilitating effects of the slave trade until well into the nineteenth century. This tied it into the world market and when the slave trade came to an end, European merchants sought other commodities for which a market could be found. Palm products were the main exports for some time; then, as Europe industrialized, there was a growing need for raw materials or foodstuffs which could be cultivated in the climate of West Africa. In practice this meant that merchants bought up crops grown by peasant producers in response to cash incentives, encouraging more to turn over to production for the market. Already in the course of the second half of the nineteenth century Nigeria's future as a primary-exporting country was being shaped by its relationship to the world market and the needs of the industrialized countries. Britain began to take over this part of Africa from the 1850s, with Lagos becoming a colony in 1861. In 1900 the territories opened up in the north by the Royal Niger Company were brought under British rule, becoming the Protectorate of Northern Nigeria in 1902. These various territories were amalgamated to form the colony of Nigeria in 1914. Thus Nigeria was an artificial creation of European diplomacy and expansionism. As a colony of the British Empire it was made up of three main ethnic groups and many smaller ones, and its subsequent development, until the 1950s, was determined by its colonial status. Government by the British took the form of indirect rule through traditional or newly-created chiefs appointed by, and accountable to, an expatriate bureaucracy with no roots in the country.

The British administrators' perception of the Nigerian economy came chiefly through its foreign trade, in which British merchant houses played a predominant role. Like other colonies, Nigeria's role was seen as that of a primary producer for the advanced manufacturing industry of the metropolis, from whom it could obtain such manufactured goods as its people could afford. British civil servants scarcely considered it their job to promote internal development by direct intervention; as in India they took comfort in the belief that they brought the blessings of law and order. They assumed that the natives would respond to monetary incentives and produce for sale what the British economy needed in the way of primary products. It was taken for granted that external trade would continue to be in the hands of Europeans with capital, who had contact with markets and superior entrepreneurial skills than the Nigerians. At the same time, to facilitate trade, a modern infrastructure had to be built up, with ports and harbour facilities to link the area with the world economy, and railways and roads radiating into the hinterland. Like other parts of West Africa,

177

Nigeria was not considered suitable for white settlement; instead it became British policy to uphold native ownership of the land so that the export commodities were produced by small peasant proprietors rather than on white-owned plantations as in East Africa. This arrangement suited the needs of the foreign trading companies as well. Nigerians played a subordinate role in assembling agricultural products and distributing manufactured imports. However, some of the more sophisticated internal trade and finance was in the hands of immigrants, most of whom came from the Levant.

Known mineral resources in Nigeria at the colonial stage were not sufficiently important to exercise a determining role in economic development. British policy was to grant mineral concessions exclusively to Europeans, assumed to possess the requisite amounts of capital and technological knowledge. In addition, during the First World War, some coal-mining was undertaken by the colonial state. However, primary production by the peasantry constituted the basis of the colonial economy, the keys being held by the foreign trading companies which dominated the export-import trade by virtue of their ownership of capital. The limited nature of known mineral deposits gave the peasantry some protection against forced labour and large-scale dispossession as happened in other parts of Africa. In the case of tin mining on the Jos plateau and the Uri coalfields, however, conditions were similar to those to be found in other parts of colonial Africa and the administration used a measure of compulsion when it thought fit. Overall, however, the land and its cultivation remained in the hands of the indigenous peasantry rather than in those of an alien planter class. As trade expanded, if only on a limited scale, some sections of the native population increased their income and began to enjoy a modest prosperity.

Under the colonial regime capitalist relations penetrated the internal economy, in so far as the peasants went over to the production of cash crops and responded to market opportunities. This was necessarily an uneven process, having one-sided and limited results arising from the manner in which Nigeria was inserted into the world market. The home market also began to grow as some Nigerians increased their money incomes and peasant-farmers needed to buy more inputs: manufactured imports tended to rise. The colonial administration welcomed this development but it never conceived of developing manufacturing industry in Nigeria. The only source from which capital for industry could come on a large enough scale, apart from the state itself, was the foreign trading companies. Until the early 1950s they displayed little or no interest in setting up plants in Nigeria. It was still more lucrative to import cheaper and better-made foreign manufactures than to finance the production of Nigerian substitutes. Consumers also probably preferred the former for a variety of reasons.

Nigerians were able to accumulate capital on a limited scale, whether in agriculture, petty trade or such new fields as road transport. Local entrepreneurs were not able to make the leap into industry, mainly because they lacked adequate capital, technical knowledge and management skills. In any case they would have to face the competition of imported products, the supply of which was controlled by the big companies in an open-market situation. Returns on capital were higher in other fields where the risks were smaller. Hence, under colonial rule, Nigerians could hardly hope to generate an industrialization drive after, say, the Indian model. Likewise, there was little scope for the growth of a wage-earning class outside such limited fields as government employment and the railways and docks. It should also be noted that for the most part, economic activity continued on 'traditional' lines, producing food and raw materials for the home market or articles for everyday consumption, made in small-scale artisan-type workshops. Since Nigeria is a large country with a diversity of physical features and resources, inhabited by peoples of varied ethnic composition and different historically-constituted cultural patterns it is not surprising that, with the growing influence of the market, regional differences should persist and widen. Some areas, especially those near the coast, or those specially suited for the production of cash crops in world demand, were able to take fuller advantage of new commercial opportunities than did others. During the inter-war period, improved methods of agriculture, propagated by the government's Agricultural Department, were taken up more readily in some areas, thus widening the gap with those less receptive to change. Sections of the peasantry were able to increase their cash incomes, buy more in the market and accumulate capital on a modest scale. The sons of these favoured strata began to acquire an education and to seek employment outside agriculture. The growing economic infrastructure of roads, railways, storage facilities and docks (centred mainly on Lagos at first) provided new opportunities. So too did the growth of the administration and the tertiary activities associated with urban growth. Although manufacturing industry was virtually absent (at least in a modern form) before, during, and after the Second World War, there was a proliferation of people, linked with the peasantry, who had some degree of economic independence as well as of wage or salary earners associated with trade and government.

The Nigerian economy represented a type of dependent, colonial capitalism dominated by the extra-territorial companies concerned principally with marketing the country's primary products. The preservation of the peasantry and the modest prosperity of its more favoured sections, together with other developments made possible the constitution of a national petty bourgeoisie within the framework of this export-orientated, colonial economy. Its members were responsive to monetary incentives as well as to the demonstration effect of the expatriate bureaucracy and the foreign businessmen who dominated the economic life of their country. This was, in part, it seems, a result of the superior education and managerial and technical skills of the new bourgeoisie. As mentioned, there was little scope for native capital in industry, but it did seek outlets in fields which promised to be profitable although not sought after by the foreign companies. The fields which held promise included local trade, building construction and the operation and repair of road vehicles. While the economy grew little during the 1930s depression, the world demand for Nigeria's main exports did not decline as severely as that for some primary products upon which other countries were dependent. The export trade was not monopolized by one or two commodities, but by a more varied range; moreover, the demand for Nigeria's newer export staples, groundnuts and cocoa, showed a continuous, long-term upward trend. Under these relatively favourable conditions there was less difficulty in paying for customary imports than in the case of other primary-producing countries, and thus less pressure for the establishment of import-substitution industries. In particular, industry remained unattractive to the big foreign companies.

At the same time, a large part of the population was becoming imbued with what might be called a 'capitalist outlook': it produced for the market, it was familiar with the monetary incentives, it wanted to consume more and many of the things it wanted to consume had to be imported. Both the major exports and most of the manufactured imports passed through the hands of the extra-territorial trading companies who garnered the lion's share of the proceeds of a situation which was clearly in their interests. Moreover there was a definite trickle-down effect, which was to the benefit of export producers and others concerned with the modern trading sector, giving them an interest in the existing state of things. Individual acquisitive desires, induced by market forces, grew up alongside the traditional values of African society and tended to predominate as the modern sector grew. Foreign observers were later to see in the further development of these trends, and particularly in the strengthening of the local entrepreneurial class, the best hope for economic growth in Nigeria. However, the relative prosperity of some sections of the population before and after the Second World War depended completely upon a favourable trend in the world prices of a small number of primary products outside Nigerian control. These sections, in turn, became addicted to consuming manufactured goods from foreign cultures and regarded them often as superior to, and more desirable than, traditional products or home-produced substitutes. Again, it is understandable that in this situation foreign firms were not enthusiastic supporters of industrialization.

Meanwhile, traditional society was being disrupted and social relations were being 're-arranged' in accordance with the needs of colonial capitalism. In short, foreign concerns made large profits, but did not use them for industrial investment; some Nigerians increased their money returns and accumulated capital on a more modest scale, but had little incentive to invest in manufacturing. There seemed to be no way in which the colonial administration would wish to alter a situation which offered so many advantages to the metropolis and to the extra-territorial companies in particular. Nigeria's role as a primary producer, and a fairly successful one, seemed to be in conformity with the 'law' of comparative advantage. The country was thus locked into a colonial situation which virtually excluded industrialization as a way of raising income levels or increasing economic self-reliance. Production relations were frozen into a shape determined by the way in which the Nigerian economy had been fitted into the world market under the control of foreign business interests. In these respects, of course, Nigeria was no different from other colonial underdeveloped countries; indeed, in this Black African country a particular type of colonialism assumed a classic form. There was no expatriate class of mine-owners, large farmers or plantation-owners to represent colonial exploitation in a tangible way: only the invisible threads which tied the peasant producers to the world market through the dominant position of the foreign trading companies.

THE GROWTH OF NATIONALISM

As nationalism began to take shape, the immediate goal of its spokesmen seemed to be to take over the administration from the expatriate civil servants whose superiority as a ruling bureaucracy was based upon educational qualifications, and not upon the ownership of property. Nevertheless, the political power which they wielded ensured the prerogatives and privileges of the European firms who effectively controlled the 'commanding heights' of the economy. The European business community, with its network of relationships with powerful firms at home, formed an exclusive group which Nigerians could not penetrate. The goals of its members were short term, concerned as they were with the profits of trading activities in a fluctuating market, and did not include the long-term development of Nigeria, least of all its industrialization. Likewise, the expatriate civil servants, although renowned for their personal integrity, enjoyed high salaries and an enviable standard of living as the fruits of office. They too had no conception of the state playing a positive role in the economy.

This form of colonial dependence, disseminating small benefits to part of the ruled population, was consolidated between the wars and reached its zenith in the 1940s when Nigerian production was geared to the war effort of the United Kingdom. The main medium for the economic organization of primary production was the four Marketing Boards set up to control the trade in each of the main export commodities. The Boards were granted the exclusive right to buy up and market these commodities; they determined the prices actually paid to the peasant-producers and sold them at world market prices. The difference between these two prices, in a world hungry for supplies, was considerable and gave the Boards disposal of large revenues. During the war these proceeds were invested in Britain, thus helping to finance the cost of the war at the expense of the Nigerian producers who had no say in the matter. Subsequently these revenues became a valuable prize and a source of finance for internal development, representing as they did the main surplus generated by the Nigerian economy and available for investment apart from the profits of the foreign trading companies. The main difference, of course, between these sources of funds derives from the fact that the Marketing Boards were government bodies.

During the early post-war years, when primary product prices remained strong, the accumulated reserves and current earnings of the four Marketing Boards reached a high level. The proportion of income withheld from the direct producers amounted to 42 per cent in the case of cotton, 40 per cent for groundnuts and 39 per cent for cocoa. In 1954 the Marketing Boards were reorganized in line with the division of the country into three regions; about the same time as primary-product prices began to show a declining tendency and the terms of trade turned against primary producers. These changes were significant since the regional boards played a role in the regional rivalries which began to plague Nigerian politics as the country approached independence. Moreover, with economic development now becoming a primary objective, a more conscious use was made of the Boards' surpluses for this purpose. Although part was used for research and development in connection with the production of the commodities controlled by the Boards, an increasing proportion of their funds was channelled into general purposes through loans and grants to the regional governments, for road-building, university expansion and other projects. Part found its way to the financing of private enterprise through the banking system or through loans and share purchases benefiting private concerns.

Until 1954 British colonial policy in Nigeria had remained basically unchanged. During the 1950s, however, the winds of change began to blow around the African continent. The growth of the nationalist movement in Nigeria and increasing international pressure to promote development (however conceived) in the colonies, compelled the administration to consider internal development more positively and to bring Nigerians into the process of making decisions. It became clear that independence could only be a matter of time while, in this changing situation, the national bourgeoisie became increasingly self-conscious and politically organized. In the Nigerian context the bourgeoisie had some specific features which help to account for its subsequent behaviour. Coming as it did from the ranks of the more prosperous peasantry, leading families and small business people, it constituted an articulate elite whose members' social status derived largely from the acquisition of Western education which was particularly highly prized as a ladder of social advancement in the face of the expatriate rulers and business community. Although nationalist in outlook, there were also strong regional and ethnic loyalties and rivalries. Politically the members of the national bourgeoisie were pragmatic and moderate and certainly not revolutionary. They generally retained a respect for British education and the British way of life as exemplified by the colonial civil servants and teachers. Desiring social improvement and economic advance, for which they saw political independence as a necessary first step, they tended to be suspicious of the powerful foreign corporations which held sway over the Nigerian economy, but they had no viable alternative in the short run to the continuance of the existing organization of trade and production.

Thus when independence was achieved Nigeria continued along the capitalist road. Although phrases about 'socialism' figured in political statements and speeches it was no more than populist rhetoric, an expressed concern for improving the welfare of the masses. It never took coherent shape as a serious programme for remodelling the economy or promoting industrialization under the aegis of the state. The members of the elite, as they took over the levers of power, especially after full independence was achieved in 1960, accepted the ethos of capitalism. Already privileged economically and in the possession of educational advantages, they accepted personal advancement and enrichment as valid goals, modelling their expectations very much upon the life-style of expatriate Europeans in colonial times. The way was thus open for cooperation and collusion between politicians and civil servants on the one hand and indigenous entrepreneurs, of whom there was no lack of aspirants, and foreign businessmen on the other. Peculation and corruption became endemic in the new state, intertwined with regional and ethnic rivalries and favouritism which were to plague the country, bringing instability and a tragic war within less than a decade.

Meanwhile, there was some quickening of the pace of economic change in Nigeria in the 1950s, attributable in part to the shift in government policy. By the 1954 Constitution, more power was given to the regions, and the reorganization of the Marketing Boards gave them command over substantial financial resources for development. As Nigerians took command of regional government they declared their intention to promote development and diversify the economy. However, there was no clearly determined strategy at either the national or the regional levels. Despite higher government outlays and the verbal adherence to development goals, the main reliance was upon encouraging private enterprise which meant, in practice, foreign capital. Although the nationalists were committed to Nigerianization (or indigenization as it was generally to be called) of the economy, as well as of the government, this desire was tempered by the belief that Nigerians would be unable to provide the capital, the entrepreneurial and managerial abilities or the technical skill to enable them to take the places held by foreigners in business. All that could be done until new economic cadres had been trained or arose spontaneously, was to encourage local businessmen wherever possible and to set up public corporations under national control where foreign capital was not forthcoming.

By the 1950s, under the influence of United Nations agencies and world economic and political opinion, it was becoming accepted that if developing countries like Nigeria were to raise their income levels and reduce their dependence upon primary production they would have to industrialize. How this was to take place remained an open question, but Nigeria already seemed set upon the capitalist road, which meant import-substitution industrialization with foreign capital playing a leading if not dominant role. After independence in 1960, as before, European business firms continued to play a crucial role in economic decision-making through their control of the export-import trade and their contacts with the advanced capitalist countries. Indeed, already in the 1950s the extra-territorial companies began to finance some import-substitution industrial projects in which they had formerly been uninterested. They adapted both to a changing climate and to the growth of new business opportunities presented by an expanding home market. The shifting of responsibility for industrialization to the regional governments also helped to speed up the setting up of new industrial plants. The industrial base was small to begin with and its expansion can be seen as a response to the overall growth of the nation's income for which exports of primary products were responsible. The internal market for some sorts of consumer goods such as textiles, apparel and processed food and drink was a growing one, large enough to warrant home production. In addition there was a growing demand for industrial materials such as cement. So far as these new industries required the application of advanced technology and large-scale production foreign capital took the lead. Independence made little difference to an already established trend, except perhaps to speed up the relative decline of British influence in Nigerian trade and investment.

From an admittedly narrow base, there was a 25-fold increase in the output of manufacturing plants employing more than ten persons between 1950 and 1964. Production in small-scale and artisan-type enterprises also probably rose quite rapidly. The industrial structure which was emerging was extremely diversified both in terms of scale and product; it reflected the fragmented nature of the market in a society of great diversity in which 'traditional' and advanced capitalist elements coexisted. Again, as would be expected, modern industrial plants were mainly concentrated in a few areas where supplies of labour and raw materials were available and where there was a local market. The modern sector was overwhelmingly dependent upon foreign capital and enterprise or government support. The import-substitution character of this first stage of industrialization was quite pronounced.

The foreign trading companies, including the largest of them, the United Africa Company, moved into the industrial sector on a growing scale from the mid-1950s, at the same time they took the lead in modernizing retail trade and distribution. In some measure they moved from importing goods to manufacturing them on the spot. Their objective was clearly not to speed up industrialization *per se* but rather to take advantage of the new investment opportunities provided by the growing home market and probably to forestall a loss of markets to other potential entrants, foreign or Nigerian, into the manufacturing field. At about the same time, a number of MNCs began to set up branch plants in Nigeria for the same reasons instead of sending finished goods. Some foreign or indigenous entrepreneurs also made investments in manufacturing industry. On the whole, however, the modern consumer and intermediate goods sectors remained under foreign control or influence, Nigerian capital being mainly confined to small-scale industry at this stage. The indigenization policy had very limited success leading to token holdings of shares by Nigerians or employment only in subordinate positions. Nigerian capital flowed into other outlets. Public enterprises run by Nigerians also performed indifferently so that, overall, local capital and entrepreneurs made little contribution to industrialization.

NATIONAL PLANNING

As would be expected, the state began to play an enhanced role in Nigerian development, especially after independence. As early as 1946, the colonial administration had initiated what was called the Ten Year Development and Welfare Programme. Although not properly speaking an economic plan it was the first sign of a shift towards development goals. Government initiative was still limited to the public sector and welfare schemes, anything directly connected with industrialization being regarded as within the province of private enterprise. With the approach of independence, industrialization was seen by the nationalist politicians as both necessary and desirable to strengthen the national economy and raise living standards. Foreign economists were called in to give advice; committed to free-market solutions adapted to the special conditions of countries like Nigeria they saw industrialization as coming through the extension of capitalist methods and the encouragement of entrepreneurial initiative. The object of 'planning' as they saw it, and as it was accepted by the new rulers of Nigeria after 1960, was not to extend the activities of the state but to keep them within fairly well-defined bounds so that market forces could operate more successfully. Planning could promote improvements in the infrastructure, provide education and public services and help train farmers and businessmen but not be a substitute for the private capitalist. This attitude was not more than an updated and more sophisticated version of the nightwatchman attitude of the state in colonial days. However, since the Nigerian elite could not itself project a viable alternative it accepted the broad lines of this advice, as shown in the First National Development Plan for the period 1962–68. This Plan, and its successors, was not designed to change the social order but rather to enable the existing system to function more efficiently. Fitting in with what market forces were shaping independently, the Plan saw industrialization as proceeding on import-substitution lines, or as being concerned with the processing of locally-produced materials designed mainly for export. As success was to be measured mainly in the rate of industrial growth, in the short run this was perhaps an obvious course to pursue.

While giving priority to industrialization the Development Plans accepted the need for an economy of a mixed type, with the state supplementing and supporting market capitalism, rather than superseding it. The industrial sphere marked out for it involved the construction of large-scale plants, such as an iron and steel works and an oil refinery, which private enterprise was unable or unwilling to finance, and the operation of a number of smaller concerns. For the rest, the state was to offer incentives to private capital with a battery of measures: heavy depreciation allowances and other tax exemptions, low tariff rates on imported machinery and raw materials, and various financial advantages. While the country was divided into three regions, the revenues of the now regional Marketing Boards became available for financing development projects whether in the public or private sectors. However, rivalry between the regions made coordination difficult and corruption on the part of higher civil servants, as well as of politicians, became a serious problem. Factors of this kind militated against the carrying out of a coherent long-term developmental programme, and made for waste and inefficiency. These were among the growing pains of a new country experimenting with a parliamentary form of government and still heavily marked by its colonial past. Meanwhile growing struggles over the spoils of office and bitter ethnic rivalries erupted into bloodshed and turmoil: the pogroms against the Igbos in areas where they were an immigrant group, the unsuccessful attempt at secession by the Eastern Region (Biafra) so costly in human lives, military coups and dictatorship until 1979, and again after 1984.

These unhelpful political conditions provide the background for Nigeria's mediocre economic performance in the 1960s and early 1970s. It was a performance which certainly fell short of expectations. The annual growth rate, while over 4 per cent per annum, was below that for developing countries as a whole. Growth continued to depend principally upon foreign demand for the main exports. Here Nigeria was comparatively fortunate even before oil revenues began to flow in on a large scale (from about 1970) since it had a steady source of income accruing mainly as revenues to the government and the Marketing Boards. The export-orientated nature of the economy enabled foreign capital to consolidate its position during this period. Meanwhile, the belief inside and outside the country that performance should have been better, focused attention on particular short-comings in government policy the quality of entrepreneurship, the lack of capital, or the influence of the MNCs. Often these were more in the nature of symptoms than of causes, and to be expected, given Nigeria's history and structure. In any case, the kind of 'planning' pursued failed to capture popular imagination. Adherence to a markedly capitalist road gave free rein to the pursuit of individual goals and opened the way for illicit dealings and corruption. There was a lack of inspiring leadership or of social or national aims; military dictatorship filled the vacuum.

THE GROWTH OF INDUSTRIALIZATION

Nevertheless, in a quantitative sense, industrialization was taking place. Industrial output grew at an annual average of 10.3 per cent between 1963–64 and 1973–74, while industry's contribution to GNP rose from 5.4 per cent to 7.8 per cent over the same period. Industry's share of national output thus remained modest. Per capita growth rates (difficult to calculate because of uncertainties about Nigeria's population size) were also disappointing. Consequently a large part of the population experienced little or no improvement in living standards, despite the apparent boom in some sectors and parts of the country, even after the oil boom got under way.

Characteristically, industrial growth took place mainly in the established branches of production, in the already industrializing areas and in line with existing structures. Foreign capital retained its dominant position in the modern sector of industry, indigenous capital being more prominent in the small-scale, artisan or traditional type industries. The main thrust of the industrialization taking place was still in the direction of import-substitution, encouraged by the development policies already outlined. Public investment was confined mainly to improving the infrastructure or was directed into large-scale, loss-making prestige projects. Innovative investments and new technical developments came mainly from foreign-owned businesses in the modern sector. The geographical distribution of industry confirmed what was perceived to be an unbalanced and excessive concentration in a few locations. Over half of total manufacturing production was carried on in Lagos state and over one-third in greater Lagos. Lesser concentrations were to be found in the towns of Kano, Kaduna, Port Harcourt and Ibadan. Meanwhile, the continued growth of the modern sector, including the oil industry, and the building up of the infrastructure, took place against the background of an economy which remained predominantly agrarian, made up of a majority of low-income peasant households. Previous historical development had incorporated the agrarian sector into the market economy, linking part of it to the world market.

At the same time, as in other countries at a similar stage in their development, industrialization in Nigeria tended to create a 'dual economy', though the two economies were by no means separate. While not exactly an enclave, the modern sector was, in a sense, an off-shoot of the more advanced economies and remained largely under foreign influence and control. Part was concerned with exporting primary products, thus emphasizing Nigeria's continued dependence on the world market, part was concerned with import-substitution. As in the case of other countries, however, import-substitution did not itself guarantee greater economic independence.

In Nigeria, as in other developing countries, such as India and Brazil, import-substitution industrialization was geared mainly to the consuming power of the higher income receivers. It provided commodities which supported the life-styles of the dominant post-independence elites: the individualistic, prosperous and ambitious 10 or 15 per cent of the population which had benefited most from Nigeria's foreign earnings and government policies of 'development'. The incomes of many of these people depended upon political bargaining power, influence in government circles, illicit dealings and even corruption of officials and politicians. For example, some top civil servants had business interests which they used their official positions to promote. Salaries in government employment, especially for the top layers, were kept consistently at a level which made possible a high standard of living. Nevertheless, the Nigerian ruling class did not own or control the main means of production, especially in the modern industrial sector, and remained a junior partner in its dealings with foreign trading companies and the MNCs.

INDIGENIZATION

It became clear during the 1960s that if market forces continued to go unchecked, the sphere of operation of all but a few local capitalists would be confined to small-scale industry and petty trade. Commitment to free enterprise led to results which conflicted with nationalist aims, leaving the main manufacturing industries and key businesses in foreign hands. Although from the beginning of Nigeria's existence as an independent state indigenization had been a proclaimed policy, in practice it had been slow-moving during the 1960s. More positive state action would be required to speed it up, considering that as late as 1971, 58 per cent of industry was still under foreign ownership. The following year the government issued the Nigerian Enterprise Promotion Decree, the first of a number of measures intended to redress the situation. Under this law some business activities were in the future reserved, wholly or partly, for Nigerians and aliens were to be prevented from setting up new firms (with the exception of some Africans of other states). Equity capital in foreign-owned firms was to be made available to Nigerian nationals with state help and they were to be granted a more important role in the making of decisions. In formulating the policy a compromise was sought between the desire for indigenization, and the recognition that industry was dependent upon foreign capital and personnel. At the same time the state acquired, under this policy, a majority shareholding in such key sectors as insurance, banking and the oil industry.

During the 1970s the indigenization policy ensured the tranfer of large blocks of shares in foreign-owned businesses to Nigerian citizens and institutions, and more Nigerians were appointed to management posts in industry. The more energetic pursuit of the policy by the military regime was hailed as a triumph for nationalism and earned it much popularity. However, practice fell somewhat short of intentions. Dependence could not be ended by decree and, within the context of a mixed economy, foreign capital displayed considerable ingenuity in adapting itself to the new conditions. There was a lack of trained and experienced Nigerians to fill managerial posts and, when appointed, they often performed a token role, real power still remaining with foreigners. Nigerian entrepreneurs or executives might simply be the front men for firms effectively controlled by foreign capital. As to participation in equity capital, only a fortunate few with cash reserves or the backing of bank loans were able to buy shares under the decrees. Overall, therefore, the policy tended to consolidate the wealth and privileges of the newly-emergent Nigerian capitalist class, while social inequalities tended to widen. Indigenization during the 1970s, despite its limitations, began to shift a larger measure of ownership, control and management of business into Nigerian hands. By itself it could not increase the flow of dynamic entrepreneurs or able administrators called for under the industrialization programme followed since the 1950s, nor could it reduce dependence upon MNCs. Foreign private investment still remained the driving force in the more advanced sectors of the economy and the regime could not displace it without a radical change in economic strategy. Moreover, with the oil price rises of the 1970s the economy was swept along in an upsurge of prosperity which made such a change unlikely in the short run.

In reviewing the Nigerian case, it can be said to be an example of a capitalist-type industrialization in a former colonial territory, dependent upon private foreign capital and taking the lines of import-substitution. The newly independent state after 1960 inherited a one-sided economic structure determined by its colonial dependence upon Britain and its role in the world market as a primary-producing country. Long exposure to market forces and the turning of part of the agrarian sector to production for the market opened the way for a capitalist-type development which continued after Nigeria became an independent state. The creation of an infrastructure designed to link cash-crop production to the world market, together with the spread of education, helped to expand market opportunities and the supply of people ready to take advantage of them. When independence came, it represented a peaceful transfer of power to an educated political elite, leaving intact the production relations and the dominance of foreign capital, characteristic of Nigeria's economic dependence.

When Nigeria joined the ranks of the independent 'developing countries' in 1960 it followed a policy which gave a determining role to market forces despite the building up of the public sector. Such a policy placed a wager on the emergence of dynamic indigenous entrepreneurs able eventually to take over economic leadership. To begin with, however, the national bourgeoisie was weaker and less mature than its counterpart in some other countries, such as India, though stronger and better able to take over the reins of power than in most other Black African states. Divisions on regional and ethnic lines constituted a serious handicap to the formulation and pursuit of strong national goals. Despite the desire of the elite to take over full economic management and control, it had to accept the dominance of external trade by foreign firms and dependence upon private foreign capital to begin industrialization. Import-substitution did not break the ties of dependence, requiring as it did larger imports of machinery and intermediate products as well as trained foreign personnel. While continuing to pursue the capitalist road, the government pressed the policy of indigenization, with mixed results.

Throughout this period Nigeria was fortunate in that its primary export staples were in relatively strong demand. Funds provided through the Marketing Boards, representing the surplus extracted from peasant producers, were thus available to finance development projects and provide a foreign exchange reserve to cushion against external shocks. Nigeria thus escaped some of the acute problems facing most 'developing countries' in the 1950s and 1960s, subsequently joining the fortunate ranks of the oil-producing countries. As the country's vast reserves of petroleum came on stream, and prices soared, Nigeria's economic fortunes took a turn for the better.

Oil revenues did not break Nigeria's ties of dependence to the world market; indeed they strengthened them. Prosperity, as far as it went, still depended upon exports, and extraction and marketing were wholly or partly in the hands of powerful MNCs. Moreover, in the euphoria generated by oil wealth ambitious long-term projects were put in hand which depended upon foreign financing and technical assistance. The new flow of income fuelled inflation, provoked shortages and placed enormous strain on over-worked public services and infrastructure. Financial blessings were unevenly spread, and existing social inequalities became still more blatant. Unemployment remained a pressing problem and over much of the country average per capita incomes remained no higher than in less fortunate African countries.

Despite the role of oil in the economy and the attempt at import-substitution industrialization, Nigeria is still a predominantly agrarian country. Agriculture remains the principal occupation of some three-quarters of the population. Nevertheless, extensive areas of cultivable land remain unused (some estimates put it as high as 90 per cent) while population continues to increase at the rate of 3 per cent per annum and food imports rise. There are several reasons for this state of affairs. Agriculture emphasizes cash crops for exports, while in the subsistence sector productivity is low and little has been done in the past to encourage the small peasant producer to improve methods of cultivation. Clearly in present-day Nigeria it is oil, not agriculture, which generates the surplus for capital investment in industry. In that respect the country is fortunate but if the economy is to be placed on a healthy long term footing greater resources will have to be channelled into agriculture. The Fourth Plan (for 1981–1985) allocated 13 per cent of investment resources to agriculture and there is belated talk of the need for a green revolution, with the object of making the country self-sufficient in foodstuffs within five years. Though the resources exist to make this possible, the will may be lacking. The tendency is for the younger men to leave the rural areas leaving behind the problem of how a low-productivity peasant agriculture can be modernized through market incentives and village life be made more attractive. The agrarian problem presents itself differently in Nigeria than in many other developing countries; its serious long-term nature was concealed by the oil revenues which enabled increasing imports to be paid for. Without an attack on rural poverty, underemployment and low productivity during the 1980s prospects for further industrialization could be jeopardized by the lack of a mass domestic market: poor peasants cannot buy industrial goods.

The ending of the oil boom left Nigeria with a debt problem and an ambitious plan for industrialization which could not be sustained. Despite its limited absolute scale, accounting for about 8 per cent of national product, the degree of industrialization remains impressive compared with that of other Black African countries. But since Nigeria is such a large country, with a variety of geographical and climatic regions, its economy has not been so excessively 'monocultural', in the sense of dependence upon a single staple, as many other developing countries in Africa or Latin America. The indigenization policy, despite its vicissitudes, suggests a desire on the part of Nigerians to be masters in their own house. Nigeria is far from being an industrial country and the aim of self-reliance has received a setback from the collapse of oil revenues. Either way it is difficult to avoid dependence upon foreign capital and technology. Industry has not been able to develop the large actual or potential home market and other advantages as much as might have been expected. The limitations of import-substitution industrialization in a country like Nigeria have become more manifest. The governing force in economic growth has still been the export trade as shown by the disastrous consequences of the fall in oil revenues. Subsequently, there has been a search for alternative sources of foreign earnings, complicated now by the existence of a large external debt. It is possible that in the coming decade oil prices will rise again, but it would be unwise to count upon such a *deus ex machina* to solve Nigeria's problems. Import-substitution industrialization has meant growing dependence upon intermediate goods and plant, while much local industry concentrates upon the production of high cost or inferior goods behind tariff walls, the consumers of which belong mainly to the upper-income brackets. The really mass market required for sustained industrialization still seems a long way off and the harnessing of the surplus for large-scale industrial investment, requiring wider powers for the public sector, has not been tackled. The attempt to switch some capacity to export-orientated industrialization has not been a great success and has chiefly consisted of processing locally-produced materials. It is clear, in any case that expansion in fields such as petro-chemicals and fertilizers will have to depend more upon government support than upon market forces. Nigeria has not been able to build up industries able to win a place in the world market after the model of some Asian countries.

Booming oil revenues in the late 1970s and early 1980s encouraged the federal government to embark upon ambitious projects financed by foreign borrowing. There was massive investment in the petro-chemical industry, a steel industry was established and many government-financed or joint-venture firms were set up. The aim was faster industrialization on import-substitution lines, moving into the production of intermediate goods such as steel and chemicals. Foreign firms were encouraged to set up assembly plants for cars, trucks and tractors on the assumption that the proportion of locally-made components would steadily increase. This policy made possible a rapid rate of growth but it was flawed in several respects. There was a shortage of trained and skilled labour, the new industries required heavy tariff protection, their products were expensive and of dubious quality and the product-mix reflected the skewed income-distribution, while dependence upon the MNCs was not reduced. Some of these problems might have been tackled had it not been for the slump in oil revenues. Nigeria was now confronted with interest payment on a swollen foreign debt coupled with a sharp fall in revenue. The problem was complicated still further by the slow-down in world economic growth in the early 1980s.

After a brief return to civilian rule which lasted from 1979 to 1984, the military again took control, in inauspicious circumstances. By 1987 oil revenues were little more than a quarter of what they had been in 1980. The gross domestic product per capita was down from 405 naire in 1977 (the peak year) to 240 naire in 1987. The government had to seek ways of re-scheduling the external debt while being encouraged by the World Bank and the International Monetary Fund to modify or abandon past policies towards industry in line with the current mode of liberalization. To deal with the crisis the Structural Adjustment Programme was introduced in September 1986 and the Fifth National Development Plan was shelved. The aim was to restore international confidence by dealing with price distortions and inflation, imposing austerity and channelling more resources into agriculture. Meanwhile, in contrast with the euphoria of the years of the oil boom, workers and many members of the middle class experienced a reduction in purchasing power which limited the demand for the products of local industry. It was clear that many of the projects earlier put in hand were no longer viable. Meanwhile, responding to outside pressures, the government announced a major privatization programme which involved the full or partial sell-off of most state-owned companies. The current was running strongly in favour of increasing the scope for free market forces.

It remains to be seen whether these policies, as they work themselves out, will give rise to a more balanced development or to further distortions. In the short run they have aggravated unemployment and rural poverty. The main aim has been to restore the credit-worthiness of the economy and avert a catastrophe. The collapse of the oil boom at least revealed that the industrialization which had been carried out had not been financed by the mobilization of internal reserves but by the sale of a wasting natural asset. The period of easy oil money saw the intensification of social differences and increased opportunities for peculation and personal enrichment. The building up of a large public sector within the existing social and political set-up had as its counterpart greater opportunities for favouritism, corruption and political interference in economic management, inefficiency and even greater dependence upon foreign credits. While on the face of it the oil boom had activated some measure of industrialization, the lessons from Nigerian experience may be more negative than positive. The easy borrowing of the 1970s and early 1980s was used not to promote balanced growth, including the modernization of agriculture and the traditional sectors, but to finance extravagant and grandiose projects, wasteful government expenditure and corruption. When it came to an end, Nigeria had nothing to fall back upon. The fall of the civilian government was greeted with popular enthusiasm, but its military successors, confronted with a crisis situation, soon embarked upon an austerity programme which sparked discontent. It remains to be seen whether the new regime's espousal of liberalization and privatization at the behest of the International Monetary Fund and the World Bank will solve Nigeria's problems.

The extent of industrialization and economic development so far has not basically changed the structure of the Nigerian economy or its relationship to the world market. It remains a raw material exporting country, though the main export is now oil which, despite the fall in price, earns over 90 per cent of the country's foreign exchange and provides over 70 per cent of the revenue of the federal government. Its dependence upon foreign capital has been emphasized by having to re-schedule its debts, short as well as long term, in order to be able to obtain further credits. It is no longer as attractive to foreign investors or to multinational corporations as it once was. The kind of industrialization which will be possible in the future will depend to a considerable extent upon external constraints. In the short run it is likely to depend upon a continued inflow of capital and technology, but industry is at present (1988) running well below capacity because of the shrinkage of the domestic market. Unfortunately much of Nigerian industry has acquired a bad name for inefficiency, high-cost production and poor quality. It is not likely, therefore, that the MNCs will see Nigeria as a likely export platform, even for other African markets. In fact, it may have to be admitted that much of previous industrialization was on the wrong track, that a forced march to modern industry is not possible along the lines being pursued in the 1970s. On the other hand, more attention will have to be paid to food production; population is increasing steadily and is now estimated to be 105 million. If incomes are to be raised (or even restored to their 1970s level) and living standards improved, the country's resources will have to be mobilized for some form of industrialization, not only to bring about authentic development, but to avert disaster.

CHAPTER 8
Industrialization in the 'developing' countries

In the closing decade of the twentieth century, the poverty and stagnation of much of the non-Western world is bound to be a major international political issue if only because the areas concerned are likely to become centres of disturbance and revolution. Nevertheless, forms of industrialization have been spreading to a variety of countries somewhat euphemistically described as 'developing' or 'newly-industrializing'. This development has been characterized by its extreme unevenness; while the manufactured products of some of these countries have been playing a major role in world trade, their income levels remain low and primary production remains their predominant economic activity. The extremely rapid growth in the output of a few countries such as Brazil, Mexico or South Korea has to be set against the stagnation or slow growth which prevails in many others.

What has been remarkable, however, is that there has been an increasing flow of manufactured goods into the markets of the older industrial countries from these 'newly-industrializing' countries. In the intensified trade competition which has been going on since the early 1970s this has caused some concern and a protectionist reaction threatens. On the other hand, there is a wide agreement that without some degree of industrialization there is no possibility of the poorer countries raising their income levels.

The situation is obviously a complex one. Much of the industrialization which has been taking place in the non-Western world has not been a response to an expanding internal market. It has differed in fundamental respects (except in the case of Brazil) from the models examined in earlier chapters, whether undertaken in accordance with market forces or some form of planning. Controlled or stimulated by the great MNCs, this kind of industrialization in the 'developing' countries has not been the start of rounded and self-reliant economic development and social improvement. It has only brought higher living standards for a fortunate minority and, in general, has made no inroads into the secular stagnation of still predominantly agrarian and underdeveloped, dependent, countries. To explain how this has come about it is necessary to make a brief excursion into the historical origins of present-day underdevelopment.

ORIGINS OF UNDERDEVELOPMENT

The industrialization first of Britain and then of the other advanced countries of Western Europe and North America in the nineteenth century would not have been possible without bringing into existence a world division of labour in which most other areas of the world were turned into sources of primary products. This was the case whether the countries concerned remained politically independent, became spheres of influence, or were turned into colonies. Their economies were shaped to the needs of the advanced industrial and consuming countries of the Western World. In that sense they remained underdeveloped as primary producers with little or no modern industry, low per capita incomes and little growth outside the primary-producing sector. Taking the world as a whole, manufacturing industry was concentrated in a few geographical zones, with only odd outposts scattered elsewhere. These industrial areas could call on the resources of the less developed and dependent areas for their supplies of raw materials and foodstuffs and in addition to this could export manufactured goods to them. The success of industrialization, once established, depended upon insertion into this pattern. At one time it seemed that Japan constituted the last great success story, but in recent decades other countries, especially in East Asia, have been trying to follow her example. On the other hand, as has been seen, neither India nor China were able to emulate Japan, a major reason for this being their political and economic dependence upon the Western imperialist countries.

The international division of labour which grew up as a result of European (and later American and Japanese) industrialization appeared to contemporaries in the nineteenth century to be part of the natural order of things. Some countries apparently were destined to be workshops of the world, others had to accept the lowlier role of hewers of wood and drawers of water. European latecomers, such as Germany, had, of course, rejected this implication of free trade doctrine, as far as their economies were concerned, and had adopted protectionist policies to assist the early stages of their industrial growth. Japan had pursued the same course in its own way. As a result, they joined the dominant group of powers in the world market. Most countries were unable to follow their example, though protective tariffs were included among the demands of nationalists in colonies such as India. As a consequence of their weakness they were incorporated into the world market in a dependent relationship, often being annexed politically by the imperialist powers or being incorporated informally into their economic empires. Investment by the capital-rich countries built up an infrastructure in those parts of the world which held out promise as sources of raw materials and foodstuffs and as markets for manufactured goods. As in the case of India or Brazil, such investment did little to promote industrial development but merely increased their dependence and one-sided economic relationship to the world market. In the now fashionable terminology, they formed the periphery, while the advanced metropolitan countries made up the core.

Classical economic theory provided powerful ideological support for this division of the world into manufacturing and primary-producing countries, through the elaboration of the law of comparative costs. According to this so-called law, all trading partners would benefit most if each concentrated on the production of those commodities for exchange in which it had a relative advantage. This doctrine was by nature static; it did not allow for development and technological change and overlooked the unevenness of development between countries and regions. Its practical application offered great advantages to the industrializing countries of the nineteenth century, providing them with a theoretical and moral justification for what they were doing on a world scale: opening up the resources of dependent countries on the most favourable terms, while their own economies were becoming highly specialized as industrial producers, taking advantage of scale economies and enjoying other benefits. At the same time, world trade was controlled by merchant and financial capital in the advanced countries; this enabled the prices of primary products to be kept down while manufactured goods could be sold on the most favourable terms.

The pattern of the world trade was made up principally of exchange between the advanced countries on the one hand, and between them and the primary producers on the other; the latter did little trade among themselves.

The result of the international specialization which grew up in the nineteenth century was, first of all, to make possible the plunder of natural resources in the dependent areas of the globe with little benefit in the shape of local development – a process which is still going on. Secondly, in other cases, it riveted the cultivation of one or two cash crops onto many parts of the world, taking advantage of local conditions, such as climate, soil and labour supply (which was, if necessary, brought in from outside). Existing economic and social structures were undermined or destroyed. Incomes became highly dependent upon fluctuations in world prices with devastating effects when they fell sharply, as during the world economic depression of the 1930s. Thirdly, since the productivity of labour is generally lower in primary production than in industry, there was only limited scope for raising incomes, which remained, on average, at a very low level. Fourthly, the production and export of staples, especially under colonial conditions, had only limited linkage effects on the rest of the economy and generally failed to initiate economic growth.

These conditions explain why the primary-producing countries remained or became underdeveloped as a result of being dragged into the capitalist world market. Generally speaking, the mass of the population remained poor and, in some cases, the destruction of traditional forms of economy might result in them becoming worse off. In the agrarian sector, landlordism, peonage, chronic debt and other forms of exploitation of the peasantry prevailed. There was little interest either on the part of foreign capital or of local capitalists, when they appeared, in establishing manufacturing industry. The needs of the richer classes would be met by imports and, although the home market remained constricted, it also tended to be dominated by cheap manufactures from the advanced countries (the Indian market for Lancashire cottons being a classic case).

In the latter part of the nineteenth century, however, some manufacturing industry did begin to appear in India and even in China; nevertheless, the handicaps to the building up of local industry were usually considerable in most parts of the colonial and semi-colonial world until the First World War, and in most places until much later. Perhaps surprisingly at first sight, despite the existence of cheap raw materials in some cases, and of supplies of labour power in others, capital did not readily flow into industry. For local capitalists, trade, and perhaps investment in land, usually offered greater profits. They were more likely to handle imported manufactured goods than to invest in production. Where they did seek to invest in industry, as in the Indian cotton manufacture, they had to meet with the difficulties imposed by the colonial rulers, notably in refusing to impose a tariff on imported goods. Where industrialization did begin it took the form of import substitution, as in the case of Brazil. As for foreign capital, it rarely went into manufacturing industry in the colonial or dependent countries. Reluctance to compete with home-based industry may have been a deterrent; but the main reason must have been that other outlets for capital offered greater expectations of profit, mainly in the primary-producing sector or in related activities such as railways and shipping.

Continued technological change in the advanced industrial countries in the twentieth century brought further economies of scale and raised labour productivity. The new science-based industries in particular needed the support of a whole complex of facilities which did not exist at all, or only partially, in the underdeveloped countries and which were the product of a long historical process. Essentially this meant the existence of capitalist relations of production: profit-seeking firms (entrepreneurs), available capital, technological skill, a varied labour supply with the necessary range of skills, and a society long adapted to the needs of industrial capitalism, geared to the pursuit of material success. Some countries, or at least regions of them, were moving along this road, but it was a very uneven and quite protracted process. Moreover, it tended to be obstructed by the interests tied up with primary production and, perhaps, by the colonial rulers. While in the eighteenth and nineteenth centuries the industrializing countries had gained from their trading and other relations with the underdeveloped countries in the international division of labour, now the new industrializers were generally in an unfavourable position. They still depended a good deal upon the sale of primary products, their internal markets were limited, they lacked capital for industrial investment, as well as potential entrepreneurs, skilled labour and an adequate infrastructure.

At the same time, many parts of the world were being brought into contact with modern economic institutions and business practices as a result of their participation in the international division of labour. There were mines, plantations, banks, production of cash crops, organized markets, merchant houses, railways, modern ports and even some industrial enclaves (as in Bombay, Calcutta and the Chinese treaty ports) and thus a certain spread of capitalist relations. Pre-existing forms of economy were being undermined, especially by the commercialization of agriculture, the establishment of private property in land, and the recruitment of wage-labour for work in mines, plantations and, on a limited scale, in industry. In some cases (India and China again) there was the growth of a local capitalist class, some in a *compradore* relationship with foreign interest, others beginning to strike out on their own. There were signs, therefore, that some parts of the underdeveloped world, even before the First World War, were entering a 'pre-industrial' stage and would move more or less automatically on to industrialization.

MODERN DISADVANTAGES

Such a conclusion would, however, be mistaken. The position of these countries in relation to the world market still remained fundamentally different from that of the advanced countries on the eve of their industrialization. When the latter began to industrialize they were already the most advanced countries economically, they were already dominant commercially over the rest of the world. Their industrialization took place as the response of the owners of productive capital to market forces under especially favourable conditions. They led the way in applying new technologies and forms of organization to increase the productivity of labour in some of the more significant fields (e.g. spinning and weaving of textiles, and production of metals and machinery) in a revolutionary way. It was this which enabled them to grow, expand and dominate the world market – a market brought into being in a specific form which satisfied the imperative needs of growing industry both for raw materials and for markets. By the time that the underdeveloped countries, or rather their governments or businessmen, began to contemplate industrialization, their position in relation to the world market was about as unfavourable as that of the present-day advanced countries had been favourable when their industrialization began.

Underdevelopment has thus been an historical process generated through the relationship of the dependent countries to the world market, dominated by the earlier industrialized imperialist countries. This relationship was an unequal and one-sided one. Only those parts of the economies of the underdeveloped countries which supplied primary products to the world market had been activated by capital investment. Even where a local capitalist class had come into existence and was seeking to invest in manufacturing industry, this usually took the form of import-substitution and was, in any case, unable to initiate a process of industrialization comparable with that of the advanced countries. India again is a good example, and one in which, by the late nineteenth century, a nationalist movement had arisen with industrialization as one of its aims.

The reason why industrialization had made little headway in the underdeveloped countries before the Second World War can be briefly explained as follows: they were unable to make the necessary changes in social relations, to accumulate capital on a sufficient scale, form a disciplined industrial proletariat, command a large enough market at home and abroad, or to build an adequate infrastructure. A slow development of industry where possible made little difference. In most fields of industry, particularly the newer ones, all the advantages seemed to be held by the leader countries. They had a considerable technological advance, they produced on a large scale, and possessed management and marketing skills. Entry to many industries necessary for the establishment of an industrial base, such as steel, could only take place on the basis of relatively large investments and associated risks that local capital was unable to undertake. To establish modern plants, even in light industries, capable of making use of scale economies, necessitated dependence upon a large market and thus meant breaking into the world market. Japan had successfully done this, but at a time when technology was less complex and when factories could be established with smaller outlays than was the case later in the twentieth century. It had become more difficult for countries to follow the Japanese path. Successful industrialization would probably have to find some other route.

DEVELOPMENTS AFTER THE FIRST WORLD WAR

As a result of the dislocation of the world economy brought about by the First World War, some new factors entered the scene. The cutting off of exports from the industrial countries engaged in the conflict as well as the needs of war, encouraged manufacturing in the less-developed countries. This took the form partly of import-substitution, and partly of production for the war effort. More local capital was attracted into manufacturing in India, Brazil and other Latin American countries, for example. The nationalist movements gained ground in the colonial and semi-colonial countries and usually had industrialization among their aims, even if the term itself was not yet used. The Bolshevik Revolution of 1917 broke up the unity of the world market and later, through the Five-Year Plans, offered an alternative model for the industrialization of underdeveloped countries to that of the advanced capitalist countries. Conditions for the primary-producing countries remained difficult through the 1920s and deteriorated dramatically with the collapse of prices after 1930. The terms of trade worsened since the prices of manufactured goods fell less, making their import more expensive in terms of local products. There was, therefore, a greater incentive to set up local industries on the basis of import-substitution, which launched a number of countries, such as Brazil, into a partial industrialization. Tariff walls were erected to encourage such industrialization which became linked with nationalism. The import-substitution industries were not necessarily low-cost, and the plant and equipment for them had largely to be imported, thus the degree of economic independence they permitted was limited. Moreover, where new industries were implanted they tended to remain enclaves of modernity in a general sea of backwardness, showing few indications that they could become the instruments for a more general structural transformation. Instead they tended to reinforce economic dualism.

DEVELOPMENTS AFTER THE SECOND WORLD WAR

These trends were decisively reinforced by the Second World War and its worldwide consequences, a more significant turning point than either the First World War or the depression of the 1930s. The tendency towards import-substitution was even more marked, as was the harnessing of many countries to the war effort of the Allies or, in Asia, to that of the Japanese. Nationalist movements assumed an irrepressible character in one country after another and the defeat of Western countries by Japan in 1942–43 speeded up the process immeasurably. After the war, the old colonial empires were broken up and many new states came into existence in their place. During the war, and subsequently, people all over the world were brought into direct contact with the products of American technology and a new life-style. Labour employed on American bases was paid hitherto undreamed of wages and demand was created for such commodities as cigarettes, chewing gum, Coca-cola, toothpaste and canned or processed foods. Aspirations for other material attributes of the American way of life were also stimulated. After the war, US policy set about breaking up the old protectionist trading and currency blocs (imperial preferences, the sterling area and the franc zone) and the colonial empires of the European powers, with a worldwide open-door policy. This could only mean the more or less rapid demise of the old empires, formal and informal, and the hegemony of the dollar, backed up by the power of US industry which was said to account for no less than two-thirds of world industrial production in the mid-1940s.

Simultaneously with the rise of the American super-power, the forces of revolution gained ground, especially in Asia where United States policy suffered some serious setbacks. In 1949 the nationalist regime in China was swept away and the Communists came to power led by Mao Tse-tung with a policy of planned industrialization. The following year saw the outbreak of the Korean War which helped raise the price of raw materials. The onset of the Cold War in Europe introduced a wholly new dimension into international economic as well as political relations. As a result of the new division of the world, vast amounts of American military and economic aid were pumped into countries threatened by 'communism' or regarded as bastions against it. This favoured a number of newly-independent regimes, able to promote plans for more rapid economic development. The promotion of economic development (often loosely regarded as synonymous with industrialization) became the task of agencies of the newly-founded United Nations and of such organizations as the World Bank.

There was now a coincidence of purpose between the emerging nationalist elites, based upon the nascent bourgeoisie, such as it was, in the countries already independent or achieving independence after 1945, and the aims of the US and its allies. These countries – former colonies and semi-colonies – were promoted to the status of 'developing' nations. Their economies had to be strengthened to prevent them from falling into the Soviet or Chinese orbit which, it was believed, would close them to Western business. While the new rulers often carried on an anti-imperialist rhetoric and even spoke of socialist aims (the Congress Party in India, for example) they generally welcomed or sought foreign, mostly American, economic aid and were ready to see foreign capitalist enterprises extend their investment activity in their territories.

Meanwhile, a whole new field of study under the general title of 'development economics' came into existence, focusing on the problems of stimulating growth in the new 'developing' countries, with the assumption that this would help them overcome the results of underdevelopment and lead to a rise in living standards for the mass of the people. While the general consensus of Western studies was that industrialization should be promoted to bring this about, it was also assumed that, as far as possible, it should be done through market forces. The main prerequisite, therefore, was to assist in the creation of an environment favourable to the operations of private entrepreneurs, which ensured the prerogatives of private property and offered the freest possible field for the investment of private capital. It had to be recognized that in conditions of relative backwardness the state would have a positive role to play (this accorded with the growing influence of Keynesian economics) not only in creating this environment, but also in assisting with the creation of necessary infrastructure, and in making its own rule proof against internal ('communist') subversion or external attack. Economically, however, the principal role of the state was to promote the operation of market forces. In the post-war years military aid flowed where the dangers seemed greatest, for example, to South Korea, South Vietnam and Taiwan. Economic aid was also dispensed somewhat unequally and private foreign capital naturally followed lines of expected profitable returns.

As a result of all these linked changes in the international environment, new possibilities were created for the industrialization of the less-developed countries of the world. The Soviet Union also supported such a goal, hoping to win over the new national bourgeois governments. Gradually and unevenly, industries were established in various countries which had hitherto been mainly, or entirely, primary-producers. Whether or not the building of factories and their employment of an increasing number of people can properly be described as 'industrialization', is perhaps a debatable point. Leaving aside the question of whether it is justified in particular cases, this industrialization took a number of different, though not mutually exclusive, forms.

One very general one, examined in the case of Brazil, is import-substitution industrialization, where factories are built to turn out commodities formerly imported. Industrial development along these lines requires an adequate home market making possible profitable production, usually behind tariff walls. The aim of the import-substitution strategy was to open the way for a more diversified industrial structure, a varied assortment of interconnected sectors reducing dependence upon foreign capital. The outcome so far in Brazil and other Latin American countries has been different: dependence has not been reduced and continued industrialization has led to further foreign investment and industrial production for export.

A major objection to import-substitution is that it reflected market demand, itself determined by an unequal distribution of income. In the case of a number of countries as different as Brazil, India and Nigeria, industrialization has so far benefited mainly, if not exclusively, the top 10–15 per cent of income-receivers.

As it continues, import-substitution industrialization requires an increased importation of machinery and intermediate goods, suggesting further import-substitution in sectors of industry for which the country may not be well suited. One way of continuing import-substitution is thus behind tariff walls, which may encourage the setting up of inefficient or unviable industries. The alternative is to embark upon a new strategy, using the manufacturing base already created to produce for export. Export-oriented industrialization has been the path pursued with results generally deemed favourable, notably by the 'newly industrializing countries' of Asia, especially the famous 'gang of four', South Korea, Taiwan, Singapore and Hong Kong.

INDUSTRIALIZATION OF SMALLER COUNTRIES IN ASIA

Underdeveloped countries examined in earlier chapters, China, India and Brazil, have the advantage of being large in size and population and possessing varied (though not always very abundant) natural resources. At least they have, potentially, a large home market capable of sustaining a diversity of industries, including some supplying capital goods. Where 'self-reliance' has been pursued it has included such a goal. In the international race for industrialization these countries have not been star performers for reasons which have been examined. The pride of place for rapid and continuous growth has been held by the smaller Asian countries just referred to. While there are major differences between them – Singapore and Hong Kong are city states with small populations, South Korea is part of a divided country and Taiwan is a densely populated island – they have crucial features in common. The main distinguishing feature is that they successfully adopted the strategy of export-oriented industrialization based upon labour-intensive manufacturing. This does not mean that production for the home market has been insignificant. Indeed, their early industrialization was geared to import-substitution. Taiwan (with 20 million people) and South Korea (with about twice as many) have a fairly important home market, though one which could be satisfied by small-scale, traditional industries after the style of Japan at a corresponding stage of development.

A brief examination of these two countries may suggest to what extent their experience may have lessons for the smaller industrializing countries. Both were part of the Japanese colonial empire, grandiloquently described as the Greater East Asian Co-prosperity Sphere. Taiwan was annexed from China in 1895 and Korea was taken over in 1910. Under Japanese rule these countries were regarded as appendages to serve the interests of the dominant economy and thus mainly as primary producers. By the 1930s, however, partly to meet military needs, some industries were set up to take advantage of cheap and abundant labour. During Japanese occupation, capitalist relations were introduced and there was some scope for native capital in petty trade and industry. Especially in Korea, the nucleus of a national bourgeoisie was created. Labour conditions were harsh, Japanese rule was repressive and millions of Koreans emigrated to Manchuria and Japan in search of work. While part of the old feudal landowning class survived, much land in Korea was taken over by Japanese. In Taiwan a number of old landowning families collaborated with the Japanese and invested in industrial undertakings. Most capital goods as well as many manufactured consumer goods came from Japan. After the defeat of Japan in 1945 the government of South Korea was set up under American auspices, while the Communists took power in the North. The two states fought a civil war, 1950–53, with China supporting the North and the United States the South. It ended inconclusively and Korea remains divided. When Nationalist China took over Taiwan its agents plundered and wrecked the economy. After the defeat of the Kuomintang (KMT = Nationalist) forces in China in 1949, the government of General Chiang Kai-shek, accompanied by sections of the army and civilian supporters numbering up to 2 million people, took refuge on the island claiming to be the authentic government of China, with the goal of liberating mainland China from Communist rule. In the meantime they took over control of Taiwan.

The Chinese Revolution and the Korean War led to a revision of American strategy in which South Korea and Taiwan, as bastions against communism, played a key role. Their modern economies, as well as the form of state, resulted from the Cold War in Asia. Without it they could well have remained predominantly agrarian countries with some light industry, little more than economic backwaters. As it was they were thrust into the front line. Their armies were built up and equipped with American assistance; large amounts of economic aid were supplied together with agricultural products under Public Law 480. American advisers played an important counselling role in determining economic policy.

The American aim was to establish stable regimes in Taiwan and South Korea together with a revival of Japan. In both countries agrarian reforms took place which were fundamental to the economic changes which followed. In Taiwan the KMT appeared to have learned the lesson of their defeat in mainland China – their inability to carry out land reform and win over the peasantry owing to the links between the officer corps and the landowning class. In Taiwan they put into practice the radical policy of Sun Yat-Sen – revered founder of the KMT – of land to the tiller. An upper limit was set to landowning and a land system based upon small peasant proprietors was established. Likewise, in South Korea, a similar land reform was carried out in the 1950s which eliminated the landlord class.

During the 1950s the Korean economy was kept afloat with American aid. Industrial revival mainly took the form of import-substitution while there were various opportunities for traders and contractors to accumulate capital, some of which could find an outlet in manufacturing. US advisers pressed for economic changes which would strengthen the economy and reduce dependence upon aid, the amount of which was diminished. The Korean government first turned to more import-substitution to reduce the need for foreign exchange. Export promotion was mainly applied to primary products rather than manufactured goods. By the mid-1960s manufactures were already forming about half of exports and the government gave increasing incentive to often reluctant businessmen to use Korea's cheap labour to build up the export trade.

Although giving play to free-wheeling capitalism, the KMT regime in Taiwan conserves specific features from its origins as a military-bureaucratic apparatus imposed on a territory in which it had no social roots. It was not linked to a conservative landowning class. It did not have to contend with already entrenched foreign capital in the shape of MNCs or even with a local capitalist class of any importance. In order to build a viable economy of the type acceptable to its American mentors, the regime had to create an environment favourable to the appearence of a capitalist class while having to substitute for it in the meantime. There is still a substantial state sector similar to the bureaucratic capitalism of the old regime in China. By the 1960s the country could be opened up to the MNCs, especially in the new sectors like electronics, while the local business class had grown in size and self-confidence and become more distinctly Taiwanese.

Meanwhile, in the interests of cooperation with the People's Republic, Washington ended its recognition of the Republic of China on Taiwan. The legitimacy of the regime ceased to be connected with a future return to the mainland and was derived instead from its ability to manage the economy, raising incomes while keeping it internationally competitive. With almost half of its GNP attributable to exports and 60 per cent of those going to North America, Western Europe and Japan, Taiwan, like the other 'newly-industrializing countries', is in an exposed position. Its level of economic activity is bound up with the continued ability and wilingness of high-income countries to buy its exports.

From the mid-1960s the growth in the incomes of consumers in the advanced countries offered a large and growing market for imported manufactured goods made by labour-intensive methods in low-wage countries. Almost by accident, Korean policy-makers stumbled upon the opportunities this opened up to earn foreign exchange and substitute for the highly abnormal dependence upon US aid. A similar realization came to the government of Taiwan. Both countries were able to follow in the footsteps of Japan and pursue the path of export-oriented industrialization with great success. Moreover, once the process had begun, foreign corporations could be attracted by cheap labour and other facilities to set up their branch plants. Besides the appearence of locally-bred entrepreneurs able to take advantage of the new opportunities, American and Japanese firms began to see the value of Taiwan and South Korea as export platforms to supply the world market. American manufacturers did so to meet Japanese competition, the Japanese to regain their market shares. Taiwan and South Korea encouraged the MNCs to set up branch plants or enter into joint ventures. Government policies were significant in both cases in guiding investment into new channels, such as consumer electronics in the late 1960s. Both countries gained a further economic boost from the Vietnam War. Neither state was closely bound to a conservative landlord class or even to the indigenous industrial bourgeoisie; they used this relative autonomy to intervene effectively in the economy and shape industrial policy. They maintained a repressive stance both towards political dissent and to labour organizations. Thus, although the state operated through market forces, favoured capital accumulation and the pursuit of profit, its role in economic management was clearly apparent. Especially in Korea, local capitalists played the leading role, but it was made possible by US policy in furnishing the aid, support and advice in the initiation and the early stages of industrialization. Generous quantities of American aid smoothed the path of the Korean and Taiwanese economies in the troubled 1950s and early 1960s; once on the road to industrialization this aid could be dispensed with. In fact, the policy succeeded too well. Together with Hong Kong and Singapore, Taiwan and South Korea constantly increased their share of world trade in manufactures, more than doubling it between 1970 and 1986. The surpluses built up with other countries, notably the United States, have now become a source of imbalance in international trade. Like Japan, South Korea and, especially, Taiwan have been reluctant to open up their home market to foreign imports. Meanwhile the surpluses earned by these countries can be used to invest in other countries or held as a reserve fund against possible hard times. These countries are vulnerable to recession in their markets in the advanced countries, to a protectionist back-lash and to the rise of competition from other industrializing countries with lower wage costs.

To look more closely at the case of South Korea, it has an authoritarian form of government favourable to private capital and a market economy, but it has not hesitated to intervene to guide the economy along a predetermined course. While taking advantage of relatively cheap labour to expand production in the labour-intensive industries with the aim of penetrating foreign markets, the government has the ambition of making South Korea an advanced industrial country in the future. Like the Japanese government in the 1950s, it is not ready to accept the present comparative advantage in labour-intensive production as fixed. Looking ahead it aims to create a comparative advantage in the future in more advanced and capital-intensive industries which will endow the country with a stronger and more diversified industrial base. Various types of state favours and pressures have been used to direct capital into establishing modern steel plants, new shipyards, machinery and machine-tool production, electronics (a labour-intensive industry but of an advanced kind) and a motor car industry. Foreign as well as local capital has been encouraged to enter these fields by means of tariff protection, financial privileges, tax concessions, assistance with research and provision of factory space on industrial estates built with public funds. At the same time, government officials, playing an entrepreneurial role, use their influence with businessmen to encourage scale economies, the adoption of the latest production techniques and the drive for exports. The firms which receive the most government favours are those striving to increase their share of export markets; those producing mainly for the domestic market or not increasing their exports get little encouragement. The drive for export-orientated growth is a central part of the strategy. The impetus comes directly from the government and benefits the most enterprising, technologically-advanced and profit-seeking firms.

How far this strategy can succeed remains to be seen. In a sense it is based on the assumption that there is room for another Japan-type economy in Asia. It depends upon a government which favours business profits and helps keep wages low by authoritarian forms of rule. It assumes that Korean manufactures will be able to displace the Japanese in some lines of production and that there will be a continued growth in the market for an increasing volume of exports. The economy is thus vulnerable to any slowing down in world trade, to competition from other industrializing countries and to protectionist measures elsewhere (the Korean market is highly protected). Wages are already higher than in Taiwan and Hong Kong which may prove to be a liability in the future. Meanwhile, the enormous investment already undertaken has resulted in overcapacity in the face of the slowing down of foreign demand. Like Japan, Korea is sensitive to price increases for oil and other imported raw materials. Without continued rapid growth, especially in exports, the economy could be in serious trouble.

INFLUENCE OF THE MNCs

Export-orientated industry in the 'developing' countries has attracted considerable investment by the MNCs mostly with their headquarters in the United States though including some from Europe and Japan. Attracted mainly by the availability of

Table Industrialization indicators, 1976: non-Western industrialized countries

This is an orthodox classification of countries according to their degree of industrialization measured by value added in manufacturing and GNP. Countries classified as A have achieved some degree of industrialization by this measure. Countries classified as B can be regarded as 'newly-industrializing'; those classified as C have begun to industrialize, while those classified as D have made little or no headway.

Country	Population (millions)	GNP per capita (US dollars)	GNP per capita growth 1960-75 (percent)	Value added in manufacturing				
				Total (millions of US dollars)	Per capita (US dollars)	Growth 1960-76, in constant prices (percent)	Percentage of GDP	Percentage of value added in commodity production
ASIA								
Hong Kong (A)	4.46	2,110	6.5	2,541	570	11.6	28.0	77.8
Singapore (A)	2.28	2,700	7.6	1,459	640	14.1	24.4	66.8
Taiwan (A)	16.30	1,070	6.3	6,320	387	18.0	36.6	63.8
China (People's Rep. of) (B)	835.80	410	5.2	139,684	167	6.9	40.7	51.6
India (B)	620.40	150	1.3	11,966	19	4.4	16.3	23.1
Korea (Dem. Rep.) (B)	16.25	470	3.8	n.a.	n.a.	n.a.	n.a.	n.a.
Korea (Rep. of) (B)	35.97	670	7.1	5,692	158	18.8	26.6	42.8
Afghanistan (C)	14.00	160	-0.2	74	5	4.5	3.6	5.8
Bangladesh (C)	80.40	110	-0.6	319	4	2.6	6.0	8.7
Burma (C)	30.82	120	0.7	350	11	3.2	8.9	15.4
Cambodia (C)	n.a.	n.a.	n.a.	n.a.	n.a.	n.a.	n.a.	n.a.
Indonesia (C)	135.91	240	2.4	4,413	33	7.6	10.1	16.0

Malaysia (C)	12.65	860	4.0	1,866	148	12.0	19.6	32.7
Mongolia (C)	1.49	860	1.0	n.a.	n.a.	n.a.	n.a.	n.a.
Pakistan (C)	71.30	170	3.3	1,894	27	6.9	15.8	28.0
Philippines (C)	43.29	410	2.5	4,370	101	7.0	24.4	39.0
Sri Lanka (C)	13.81	200	2.0	324	24	5.0	14.5	25.0
Thailand (C)	42.96	380	4.6	2,917	68	10.8	18.3	33.4
Viet Nam (C)	47.60	n.a.	n.a.	n.a	n.a.	n.a.	n.a.	n.a.
Bhutan (C)	1.20	70	n.a.	n.a.	n.a.	n.a.	n.a.	n.a.
Laos (C)	3.25	90	n.a.	n.a.	n.a.	n.a.	n.a.	n.a.
Nepal (C)	12.85	120	0.5	157	12	n.a.	4.5	14.0
MIDDLE EAST AND NORTH AFRICA								
Jordan (B)	2.79	610	1.3	271	97	7.7	22.9	65.2
Lebanon (B)	3.06	1,070	n.a.	398	134	6.1	14.6	45.7
Algeria (C)	16.23	990	1.8	2,027	125	9.1	13.0	20.4
Iran (C)	34.30	1,930	8.1	6,979	204	13.5	10.2	15.1
Iraq (C)	11.48	1,390	3.3	1,076	94	7.3	6.7	44.3
Kuwait (C)	1.06	15,480	-2.9	n.a.	n.a.	n.a.	n.a.	n.a.
Morocco (C)	17.20	540	1.9	1,021	59	4.8	12.4	23.7
Saudi Arabia (C)	8.30	4,010	6.6	n.a.	n.a.	n.a.	n.a.	n.a.
Syria (C)	7.65	780	2.2	825	108	5.7	13.5	25.6
Tunisia (C)	5.73	840	4.1	431	75	9.8	10.8	21.5
Yemen Arab Republic (C)	6.04	250	n.a.	23	4	n.a.	23.9	4.5
Oman (D)	0.77	2,680	10.1	9	11	n.a.	0.4	0.5
United Arab Emirates (D)	0.69	13,990	13.7	n.a.	n.a.	n.a.	n.a.	n.a.
Yemen (People's Dem. Rep.)	1.49	860	7.6	11	73	8.2	7.4	23.7
AFRICA SOUTH OF SAHARA								
Zimbabwe (B)	6.53	550	2.4	851	135	n.a.	24.8	44.2

Country								
Cameroon (C)	7.07	290	3.0	324	46	8.0	13.5	25.9
Central African Empire (C)	1.83	230	0.4	89	49	5.8	22.9	31.1
Congo (People's Rep.) (C)	1.36	520	2.9	93	68	8.7	13.0	46.3
Ghana (C)	10.14	580	-0.2	1,973	195	3.0	24.8	33.5
Angola (D)	5.47	330	3.6	168	31	7.6	5.3	9.4
Benin (D)	3.20	130	-0.3	51	16	6.0	10.1	19.1
Botswana (D)	0.68	410	6.0	16	23	5.5	5.4	13.6
Burundi (D)	3.81	120	2.7	26	7	12.7	10.1	13.1
Chad (D)	4.12	120	-1.1	45	11	2.3	9.6	14.6
Ethiopia (D)	28.68	100	2.0	275	10	7.6	10.3	15.8
Equatorial Guinea (D)	0.32	330	-0.9	n.a.	n.a.	8.5	n.a.	n.a.
Gabon (D)	0.54	2,590	5.0	105	194	n.a.	7.4	14.9
Guinea (D)	5.69	150	0.2	n.a.	n.a.	17.8	n.a.	n.a.
Lesotho (D)	1.24	170	4.6	2	2	17.8	2.4	5.4
Liberia (D)	1.60	450	1.8	36	22	12.2	5.3	7.6
Mozambique (D)	9.46	170	2.0	314	34	8.5	12.0	20.1
Niger (D)	4.73	160	-1.3	99	23	12.5	16.4	25.8
Reunion (D)	0.50	1,920	3.9	n.a.	n.a.	n.a.	n.a.	n.a.
Rwanda (D)	4.21	110	0.5	29	7	7.0	10.0	13.5
Sierra Leone (D)	3.05	200	1.5	30	10	2.3	5.6	13.8
Somalia (D)	3.25	110	-0.3	25	8	16.8	8.3	20.9
Sudan (D)	15.88	290	0.1	397	26	1.9	9.7	17.0
Tanzania (D)	15.123	180	3.0	244	16	8.5	10.3	17.0
Togo (D)	2.28	260	4.4	63	28	6.7	10.6	30.0
Uganda (D)	11.94	240	1.0	176	15	1.9	6.7	10.7
Zaire (D)	25.39	140	1.6	210	9	8.0	10.0	21.5
LATIN AMERICA								
Argentina (A)	25.72	1,550	3.1	16,240	631	5.9	34.3	61.4

Country								
Brazil (A)	109.96	1,440	4.3	33,351	266	12.0	28.8	62.0
Chile (A)	10.45	1,050	1.3	2,383	228	2.8	21.6	51.7
Mexico (A)	62.02	1,090	3.2	20,537	331	8.2	26.1	58.9
Barbados (B)	0.24	1,550	5.3	39	144	3.2	11.3	35.3
Bolivia (B)	5.79	390	2.5	265	46	5.1	10.7	18.1
Colombia (B)	24.23	630	2.7	3,429	142	6.9	22.7	40.5
Costa Rica (B)	2.01	1,040	3.4	298	152	10.0	17.8	38.2
Cuba (B)	9.46	860	−0.6	n.a.	n.a.	n.a.	n.a.	n.a.
Dominican Republic (B)	4.84	780	3.4	757	161	7.8	21.0	39.1
Ecuador (B)	7.32	640	3.4	798	110	7.8	16.1	33.8
El Salvador (B)	4.13	490	1.8	349	85	7.1	16.0	33.7
Guatemala (B)	6.48	630	2.4	609	94	7.2	15.5	35.1
Guyana (B)	0.78	540	1.5	50	64	3.6	12.1	20.6
Honduras (B)	2.98	390	1.5	188	63	5.3	17.2	30.2
Jamaica (B)	2.08	1,070	3.6	593	285	4.4	19.5	40.8
Nicaragua (B)	2.33	750	2.4	393	169	8.8	21.3	41.8
Panama (B)	1.72	1,310	4.1	266	165	8.4	14.5	34.9
Paraguay (B)	2.63	640	2.0	272	104	5.6	16.0	28.2
Peru (B)	15.83	800	2.7	2,234	141	7.0	18.6	38.9
Trinidad and Tobago (B)	1.09	2,240	2.5	360	330	8.1	14.1	21.7
Uruguay (B)	2.80	1,390	0.5	792	283	1.7	24.8	53.0
Venezuela (B)	12.36	2,570	2.2	5,363	434	6.2	17.3	32.1
Haiti (C)	4.67	200	−0.4	150	33	2.0	17.1	27.4
Surinam (C)	n.a.	n.a.	n.a.	33	90	−3.6	7.1	13.5

Source: World Bank, *World Tables, 1976* Johns Hopkins University Press: (Baltimore, 1976), April 1979 data base. The tables are based on World Bank figures given in John Cody *et al.* (eds) *Policies for Industrial Progress in Developing Countries* (Oxford U.P. 1981) to which reference should be made for a full explanation of the sources. The countries have been regrouped under regional headings to bring out the limited amount of industrialization actually to be found in Africa and Latin America in particular and the great unevenness of development within continents.

cheap labour, they have set up branch plants in these countries, sometimes for the assembly of parts and components, sometimes for the manufacture of a complete product. In some cases manufacturing facilities have been closed down in the country of origin and expanded in low-wage countries. The explosive growth of the electronics industry requiring a large amount of labour-intensive assembly work has been particularly notable, but a wide range of other goods is also manufactured under the auspices of the MNCs. The low cost of transport, including air freight, has made possible global operations by manufacturing concerns on a scale which would have been inconceivable a few years ago.

Local capital has joined in this type of export-orientated industrialization either independently or in association with the MNCs. In any case, it is generally dependent upon firms in the advanced countries for technology; this is evident from the setting up of joint projects. Since the 1960s some types of industrial production have been almost entirely transferred to the periphery of 'newly-industrializing' countries. It has been claimed that a new international division of labour has taken shape and that a continuous process of industrial relocation can be expected. The attraction of investment in these countries is derived almost exclusively from the fact that they have almost inexhaustible supplies of cheap labour power, the use of which helps to keep up the overall rate of profit of the MNCs.

Whether controlled by the MNCs, or by local firms, or by some kind of joint operation between them, this export-orientated industrialization has served to underline the dependence of the 'newly-industrializing' countries on the world market, as well as upon imported capital and technology. What it has done, and this is its positive side, is to make possible more rapid rates of growth, a shift of resources into more productive sectors, raising overall income and creating more jobs. These are the aspects which are stressed by such bodies as the World Bank. It is an assessment of the process almost exclusively in quantitative and economic terms regardless of its social content. A closer look at the statistics themselves (see Tables) shows that the main participants in the industrializing trend have been a relatively small group of countries. There have been Latin American countries, of which Brazil is the leading example, and there have been the Asian countries such as South Korea, as well as Taiwan (the base of nationalist China), and the city-states of Singapore, Hong Kong and Macau without an agrarian hinterland (the last two being what is left of the old treaty-port system in

China). South Korean and Taiwan both received large amounts of American military and economic aid in the 1950s. Singapore and Hong Kong both enjoy a special role in international trade and finance which arises from their geographical situation. Most of these countries have one-party or military regimes and, while they may be protective of foreign capital, they generally prevent trade union bargaining and strikes.

Although there are differences in the strategies of industrialization pursued by these countries, they have as a common feature an emphasis on exports and hospitality towards foreign capital and the MNCs. The limitations of this approach have already been discussed with reference to Brazil and South Korea. It obviously has a different significance for city-states than for larger countries, with a substantial agrarian sector. In the case of the city-states and the free-trade zones set up in some larger countries, wages and incomes are generated but the main markets are found elsewhere. Their main attraction is simply that they have an abundant supply of relatively cheap labour-power. Countries which have a substantial agrarian sector are in a different position. Often it is underemployment in agriculture which ensures a continuous supply of cheap labour for industry. But this also restricts the expansion of the home market, in the absence of radical agrarian reform. Industrial production, being for export, does not assist change and growth in agricultural production. Instead of an agricultural revolution preceding and accompanying industrialization, as in the case of Britain, in these countries no real organic relationship is established with agrarian change. Although the export industries create some new jobs, other livelihoods may be destroyed; some regions expand, others may stagnate. Indeed, factory areas may assume an enclave character, as off-shoots of a more advanced economy in an otherwise underdeveloped country.

Much export-orientated industrialization has been sponsored by the MNCs in partnership with the government bureaucracy or local capitalists. In other cases the MNCs have played a role in import-substitution industrialization, aimed mainly at the higher-income market (as in Brazil). In Mexico there has been a growth of assembly plants along the frontier with the United States having that market in view. Whether the plants are located in Asia or Latin America the strategic decisions are taken in the headquarters of the operating corporations who bring in the necessary capital, technology and management skills. This can be seen as a new stage in the internationalization of capital, with manufacturing branches located to maximize profits and make possible the most rapid accumulation of capital. Its strategic aim is not industrialization as such and there is no necessary commitment to the economic development of the host country. In some cases processes may be used which, because they cause pollution, would not be permitted in more advanced countries.

Export-orientated industries in the 'new-industrializing' countries look for their markets mainly in the older industrial countries, thus creating a new challenge and new contradictions. On the one hand, the commodities exported are generally cheaper than those produced inside the markets they are entering, thus offering a gain to consumers. On the other hand, the competition of these imported products has already forced the contraction or elimination of industries in the advanced countries. The MNCs thus tend to relocate their factories away from the older industrial countries where costs are higher to the 'newly-industrializing countries' where they are lower, mainly because of low wages. For example, a South Korean worker – among the best paid of Asian workers – earns in a month what the American or German worker earns in a week or ten days – and produces as much.

Even where MNCs are not involved, factory industries in 'newly-industrializing countries' will have to export in order to realize scale economies. That means, in most cases, an attempt to penetrate the markets of the advanced countries where they compete with local industry. In the latter, some industries have already declined or ceased to exist owing to foreign competition. In a period of recession especially, there is a growing demand for protective duties or 'import controls'. In certain cases, such as the German footware industry, there has been a shift of capital investment to the 'newly-industrializing countries' and that is another trend which is likely to continue. Coming after the devastating effect of Japanese competition on some industries, a continuing flood of imports threatens to accelerate 'de-industrialization' in the older industrial centres, unless capital can be rapidly deployed into new fields, a process which is taking place all too slowly.

NEWLY-INDUSTRIALIZING COUNTRIES AND THE WORLD MARKET

There is some dispute about the extent to which industrialization, in the sense of the growth of manufacturing output, has actually taken place in the developing countries. In fact it has been a very uneven process between countries and also within their frontiers. On a world scale there is no doubt that the older industrial countries still maintain their dominant position. They are still the main source of technology and capital goods, without which industrialization elsewhere cannot begin. They are the homes of the giant MNCs whose policies determine how much industrialization can take place in many of the 'newly-industrializing countries' through their control of finance and technology. Most of the latter, if they are drawn into the world market, remain principally exporters of primary products, and income derived from these, unequally distributed though it is, provides the principal market for the purchase of manufactured goods.

In general, therefore, industrialization in the underdeveloped countries assumes a different form from that in present-day advanced countries. Quantitative measures of growth by themselves can be misleading without an appraisal of the total consequences of the introduction of factory industry. In many cases it may simply feed on the backward sectors of the economy and aggravate the problems of poverty and stagnation, leaving large areas of the country and many sections of the population seriously disadvantaged. Part of the output of manufactured goods may be exported, or consumed only by a minority of higher income receivers at home. Successful industrialization in the more highly-populated countries with a large agrarian sector must be accompanied by a structural transformation which enables problems of rural poverty to be overcome and makes possible balanced growth in the society as a whole.

While the quantitative change should not be underestimated. It does not necessarily indicate that a genuine industrialization process has begun. The Asian examples of rapid growth may be defined as peripheral industrialization, based as they are very much upon exports. The Latin American examples have been similar, with the MNCs playing a leading role as part of the 'new international division of labour'. The African countries have witnessed relatively little industrialization. The fragmentation of the continent by colonialism still has its effect in the many separate states, most of them too small to support major industries. Many of the industries which have grown up in the past two or three decades are high cost and produce mainly for the new ruling elite and the better-off minority. There has been no basic change in the relation of these countries to the world market; as primary producers with an export-orientated bias, their dependence on the extra-territorial companies and advanced countries is as great as in colonial days. Efforts to industrialize carried out by most African states on import-substitution lines have created new ties of dependence, this time for capital, technology, and technical and managerial know-how. In the main the new ruling elites support and benefit from the maintenance of capitalist relations of production and the continued dependence of their states upon the world market dominated by the advanced countries.

EGYPT

Actual cases show that it is extremely difficult for any under-developed country to carry industrialization beyond certain limits, because of dependence upon the world market. Attempts at industrialization in Egypt go back to the reign of Mohammed Ali in the early nineteenth century. He initiated a state programme, designed to strengthen the economy of his country, not unlike that of Peter the Great in Russia a century before. There was some success in founding new industries with imported machinery, notably in cotton textiles and food-processing. The effort was, perhaps, doomed to failure, depending as it did upon the drive of one man and continued support by the state of a still backward country. The Anglo-Turkish Treaty of 1838 insisted upon the ending of state monopolies, and Egyptian industries, already running into problems, subsequently collapsed. For the rest of the nineteenth century, Egypt became a primary-exporting, predominantly agricultural country. Heavy indebtedness resulted in the British occupation of 1882 which lasted until 1956.

During this period industrialization came to be identified with the drive for national independence. It was supported by some of the wealthy landowners and merchants who recognized the danger of undue dependence upon cotton-growing. Some import-substitution industries were established and, as in other underdeveloped countries, this trend was assisted by the two world wars and the slump in export prices during the 1930s. By the 1950s some industries had been built up, but they produced mainly for the wealthy minority; the mass of the people, employed in agriculture, could buy little. On a per capita basis, Egypt was one of the poorest countries in the world. With the death rates falling from the 1940s onwards, the country was faced with a population explosion, a virtual doubling, between the mid-1930s and the mid-1960s, to over thirty million. At least this meant a large potential labour-force and a home market, if only incomes in the agricultural sector could be raised.

Although the state had assumed some responsibility for economic development in fields such as irrigation and transport, free market forces held sway until 1939. It was not until after the taking of power by the Free Officers in 1952, and particularly after the Suez War of 1956 and the sequestration of enemy property, that the state actively began to promote industrialization. By 1957 the state was in control of the main channels of industrial investment. In 1961 banking and insurance, most organized industry and large firms in other sectors, including foreign trade, were nationalized. State control reached its high point in the period up to 1973, during which Egypt depended upon Soviet military and economic support. The breaking of these ties saw a turn to an 'open-door' policy designed to attract foreign, especially American and Arab oil-state, capital.

In 1960 the first Five-Year Plan was adopted and in the following years the state pumped large amounts of capital into industry and other types of public investment. However, although there was some redistribution of land from large to small owners by the land reforms of 1952, the distribution of property remained unequal. State employment, the professions, land ownership, trade and small-scale production provided relatively high incomes for the ruling elite and bourgeoisie. The continued poverty of the masses limited the size of the internal market and confined it to certain types of product.

Despite rapid growth of output in some periods and a shift towards a more diversified industrial base, Egypt remains basically underdeveloped, still in the stage of import-substitution and dependent upon primary-product exports, especially cotton (about 45 per cent of total merchandise exports). Difficulties in generating sufficient capital for investment necessary to continue industrialization has increased dependence upon foreign sources. Resources have also been diverted into military purposes by the wars with Israel and permanent tension in the region. Industrialization so far has not absorbed the country's surplus manpower or made possible an appreciable improvement in the living conditions of the masses.

Unlike some 'newly-industrializing countries' Egypt has not been very successful as an exporter of manufactured goods. There has been some export of textiles, replacing raw cotton, but industry

223

generally has not been export-orientated. Egypt has not attracted manufacturing plants of the MNCs on any scale despite the 'open door' policy pursued since 1973, and the supplies of cheap labour. This may reflect lack of confidence in the regime or, more likely, in the stability of the region as a whole in the light of the Arab-Israeli conflict and the assassination in 1981 of President Sadat.

THE WORLD ECONOMIC CRISIS

The change in the world economic situation which set in during the 1970s has created an environment generally less favourable to newly-industrializing countries. The four-fold increase in oil prices in 1973 (as OPEC realigned them with world manufacturing prices boosted by inflation) and the variously caused but interconnected economic crises of the advanced countries, aggravated their difficulties. While the oil price rise benefited the oil producers it was a blow to the oil-importing developing countries. Other primary producers have not been so successful in making cartel-type agreements to improve their terms of trade. As for the major oil-exporting countries, with a few exceptions such as Venezuela, Nigeria and Algeria, they are sparsely populated and merely came into possession of huge quantities of dollars for which there were no outlets at home and which had thus to be invested (or 'recycled') in the world's financial centres. The more densely populated countries have, it is true, been able to use the increased income to finance development projects. In the case of Iran, the excesses of the Shah's regime and Islamic opposition to 'modernization', sparked off a revolution resulting in a sharp fall in petroleum production in that country. This resulted in a further large increase in prices. The consequences for the non-oil producers was an unwelcome increase in import bills for essential supplies of fuel, fertilizers and other petroleum-based products, leading to balance of payments deficits and increased indebtedness.

While the oil shocks of 1974 and 1979 hit the oil-importing countries and greatly increased the revenues of the producers, other consequences followed. Re-cycling oil money enabled the commercial banks to lend more bountifully to 'developing' countries including those oil-producers, like Nigeria, who spent ahead of receipts. The early 1980s saw the collapse of oil prices and the end of the lending spree together with another recession in the advanced countries which hit 'newly-industrializing countries', especially the weaker of them. Inflation has driven up the price of manufactured imports such as machinery and machine-tools, while primary-product prices have generally not risen so much. At the same time, the demand for some of their exports has stagnated and markets have become more competitive, sometimes with sharp price fluctuations. Many 'developing countries' have thus found it increasingly difficult to pay for their imports and to service past debts. Since foreign banks and international consortia are heavily involved in lending to these countries, there is growing fear of defaults which could undermine the whole edifice of international finance.

On the industrial front, as a result of the crisis, investment, production and productivity have all tended to slow down in the industrially-advanced countries, though unevenly and in varying degrees. This has meant intensified competition for markets tending to grow more slowly in real terms than before, and has helped to focus attention on the challenge of exports from the 'newly-industrializing countries'. The inflow of competitively priced manufactured goods such as textiles, clothing, footware, cutlery and electronic products, results in the undercutting of home industries, and tends to aggravate the consequences of the recession. However, a protectionist reaction on the part of the richer countries can only make it more difficult for others to pursue their industrialization, especially where it has been export-orientated.

SUCCESS OF INDUSTRIALIZATION?

It is too early to say whether industrialization in the less-developed countries has been 'successful'. In quantitative terms many of these countries have been industrializing, some of them at a rapid rate, since the 1950s. Many different strategies have been pursued with little or no international coordination. Except in the case of centrally-planned economies, such as China, which consciously pursues policies of 'self-reliance', industrialization has meant greater rather than less dependence upon the world market. The export-orientated countries obviously must have not only a foreign market, but a growing one, if their economies are to flourish. Even countries committed to import-substitution find that they require increasing amounts of foreign capital and technology and probably an export market as well if growth is to continue. Most 'developing countries' (except those with so few resources that they seem condemned to stagnate) still export primary products and are sensitive to world market fluctuations. Moreover, where profits have been seen in industrial investment making use of cheap labour power and other advantages, the MNCs have moved in and tied the host countries into a 'new' international division of labour as dependent partners. Countries aiming at economic independence have not been able to avoid the need, in some degree, for foreign aid and credits. Even China has actively sought closer links with the capitalist world economy to make possible faster industrialization. In the generally less expansionist international environment since the 1970s, many governments have been looking for increased foreign aid, which they mostly believe has been on an inadequate scale.

Much of the ostensibly most 'successful' industrialization in the 'developing countries' has consisted largely of the establishment of a branch-plant economy, coupled with heavy government indebtedness not balanced by the creation of productive (i.e. income-producing) assets. Brazil is a rapidly industrializing country but most of its newly-built factories are foreign-owned and the state has heavy external debts. Despite having a large and impoverished agrarian population it imports foodstuffs, exports manufactures for which there is no internal market and still depends upon coffee sales for export earnings. As with countries in a similar position, the outflow of dividends and interest on existing foreign investment exceeds the inflow of new capital. Whether this type of industrialization can be accounted a success or not – and it has, admittedly, raised living standards for many Brazilians – it is distinctly different from that which took place in Europe, North America and Japan. The view that industrial capitalism would provide a firm basis for democratic institutions after the fashion of Britain and the United States has not been borne out in the 'newly-industrializing countries'. US policy in Latin America, as well as in East Asia, has supported 'mildly repressive regimes' when the alternative seemed to be a move to the left. Likewise, the theory that industrialization in South Africa would undermine the basis for apartheid seems also to have been falsified. The upheavals which have accompanied industrialization do not have the same results everywhere. Economic difficulties helped to bring about the end of direct military rule in Brazil but led to its restoration in Nigeria. Indebted countries and others wishing for aid are told by outside bodies like the World Bank to impose austerity programmes and liberalize their economic policies.

Whether giving more scope to the forces of the free market will contribute to political stability or bring social peace is problematic. It is safe to say that such countries will need strong security forces. Even countries which have been relatively tranquil in the past have shown a capacity for political upheaval, including South Korea and even Taiwan.

It is perhaps significant that the new urban middle class, which has been such a feature of countries otherwise as different as Brazil and Nigeria, is now having difficulty in maintaining its real income in the face of inflation and cuts in government spending. This may presage a shrinkage of demand for home-produced as well as imported manufactured goods and could be a de-stabilizing factor.

SOCIAL CONSEQUENCES

Meanwhile, the social consequences of industrialization in the 'developing countries' have not been dissimilar to those of the early industrial revolution in Britain. Long hours, low wages, poor working conditions, unemployment, urban overcrowding and slum housing have all been the rule. Despite statistics showing rising per capita GNP, this does not necessarily mean any perceptible improvement in the living standards of the great majority or any gain in welfare. Overall there has been a widening of income inequalities and increased social tensions with the main benefits going to a privileged minority. Moreover, in many 'developing countries' squeeze, graft and corruption of various kinds are rife; illicit activities, such as smuggling, bring rich rewards to those involved. In general, then, there has been widespread disappointment with the results of three decades of 'development'. Rapid rates of population growth consequent upon improvements in medical knowledge and hygiene, which have brought down mortality rates, have eaten up much of the increased output. Rural overpopulation remains endemic in many parts of the world and the rate of increase of the labour force far exceeds the rate at which new jobs can be created. In countries such as India, Bangladesh and Pakistan, some Latin American countries and much of Africa, the scale and intensity of mass poverty remains formidable.

On the other hand, industrialization cannot be blamed for these conditions and may have done something to alleviate them. Generally speaking, in any attack on poverty in the 'developing countries' industrialization, though not necessarily along present lines, will surely be a major weapon. The problems of an overpopulated, backward agrarian sector will have to be tackled with much more vigour than has so far been the case outside China and similar countries. Export-orientated industrialization, more investment by the MNCs and foreign aid will never make any impression on these problems, and may, in the long run, aggravate them.

The problem is to raise the income of the agrarian sector by harnessing under-used labour, thus widening the market for industry, whether located in the countryside or in the towns. In many countries, such as India, a far-reaching agrarian reform, or revolution, would seem to be a prerequisite for the kind of industrialization programme able to realize the declared objectives of governments and planners. Powerful classes in the countries concerned are bound to resist any change along these lines and they will be backed up by all those interests in the metropolitan centres which benefit from the existing international division of labour and the type of industrialization so far promoted.

Some have argued that capitalist development since the 1950s has brought benefits to the 'newly-industrializing countries'. That is true in the sense that any type of growth is better than stagnation and that the ending of colonial rule and the breaking up of archaic structures were steps forward. But these benefits are very relative and one-sided, as has already been shown. The old colonial forms have given way to new types of dependency. Industrialization has not really prepared the way for national economic independence, nor has it brought about, in most cases, structural transformation of the kind experienced in Europe, North America and Japan.

At the same time, an irreversible process has undoubtedly begun. New classes including an embryonic industrial proletariat have evolved. The demand for improvements in living standards and social welfare has been implanted, whether or not they have so far been enjoyed by more than a minority. This is a dynamic, indeed a revolutionary factor, operating in all the countries in which industrialization has taken place. The question of the developing countries has become crucial because millions of people are no longer willing to go on living indefinitely in wretchedness and hunger. They want to know who will deliver the goods and if present strategies and existing regimes fail, there will be a clamant demand for alternatives which will have international consequences.

CHAPTER 9
Conclusions

Although some comparative references between countries have been made in the course of these case studies, detailed comparisons will be left to the reader. However, some general guidelines can be suggested for further study.

The studies reveal a diversity of 'models' each of which has its unique characteristics reflecting the national and historical conditions of its own industrialization process. At the same time, the very fact that such a process can be conceptualized suggests that it has definable and repeatable components – as was pointed out in the first chapter. A review of the actual experiences of the countries selected confirms this assumption. Even from a superficial point of view it can be said that they produce the same artifacts, become more alike, at least in externals. The same impression can be confirmed from a quantitative point of view: output per head and income rise. Successful industrializers begin to close the gap with the leader countries; some late-comers have outstripped the early starters.

Only Britain, and to some extent the more advanced parts of north-west Europe, can be said to have generated industrial capitalism and the institutions and technology which go with it, as an autonomous development from the pre-industrial mode of production. In the case of Britain this was 'feudalism'. The countries studied in this book may, if left to themselves, have followed the same path in their own time. As it was, because of the priority of Europe, they received capitalism and modern industrial technology as an import.

COMPARATIVE MODELS

Of the examples studied, Japan stands out as being the most 'successful' of the non-Western countries in assimilating and adapting the Western development model, firstly, on a limited scale under Meiji, secondly, on a more spectacular scale after the Second World War. Not only did Japan establish a dominant position in the Orient, but it now ranks number three in world industrial power and is still growing. While profiting from specially favourable international conditions, in ways which remain a matter for investigation and controversy, Japanese society appears to have been especially receptive to modern technology. Some see in Japan's impressive rise the alternative form of capitalism for the twenty-first century. However, whatever it is specifically Japanese which has contributed to this outstanding success, it does not seem to be exportable; not, at any rate, to the advanced Western countries. The closest emulators are to be found in Asia, notably in South Korea and Taiwan.

Unique in a different sense was the experience of the Soviet Union. While able to build upon what Tsarism had already accomplished, in the shape of modern industry and infrastructure, the post-1917 regime broke with capitalism, nationalized industry, collectivized agriculture, and embarked, from about 1928 onwards, on a breakneck drive for industrialization on a scale never before witnessed. Accompanied by incredible barbarities and unnecessary human suffering, the crude type of planning imposed under Stalin transformed a relatively backward country into a modern industrial giant. Nonetheless, successive Five-Year Plans have not enabled the Soviet Union to catch up with the West. Its formerly unprecedented rates of growth have been exceeded by other, capitalist, countries, and it is now back to a more sober tempo of 4 or 5 per cent per annum. Besides, the Soviet economy is itself going through a structural crisis as the attempt is made to transform the more basic forms of growth to the production of an assortment of goods more in line with consumer needs.

The gap between the Soviet Union and North America and Western Europe is still appreciable, and the differences between the two social systems remains as sharp as ever despite what the 'convergence' theorists have suggested. The crisis of the Soviet Union is qualitatively different; it does not arise from pressure on the rate of profit, nor is it revealed in over-production or unemployment. The problem in the Soviet Union is under-production and the scarcity, or more strictly the maldistribution, of labour.

China, though never a colony, was drawn into contact with Western capitalism in a dependent relationship. It thus failed to take the same road as Japan and the extent of industrialization was relatively modest before the Chinese Communist Party took power in 1949. Modern industry was largely concentrated in the treaty ports and Manchuria, being partly import-substitution in nature, and partly export-orientated. It made little impact on the lives and living conditions of the huge rural mass. When a new phase of industrialization began under Communist leadership, the existing industrial base was thus much narrower than it was in Russia after 1917. While the supporters of Mao had reservations about the Soviet model, in the circumstances of the 1950s, where China faced a hostile capitalist world, it had to depend upon Soviet aid which took the form mainly of assistance in building up a heavy industry. A similarly centralized planning system was also adopted. Under Mao's influence, following the break with the Soviet Union, a new strategy was followed with agriculture carried on by huge communes and some decentralization of industrial production so that it could more directly serve rural needs. There followed a series of massive upheavals and the eventual reversal of Mao's course by his successors. They are now pursuing a more conventional industrialization programme, still much influenced in practice by the Soviet model and based on the adoption of Western technology and even the experience of Japan.

Japan's example undoubtedly influenced Indian nationalists whose case against British rule included the charge that it held back industrialization. Independent India embarked upon an ambitious industrialization programme influenced by the British as well as the Soviet model with serious handicaps as well as some advantages. The latter included some modern factory industry, mainly in textiles, a national entrepreneurial class and an industrial labour force. Despite the declared aim of 'a socialistic pattern of society' the ruling National Congress in fact chose a capitalist road. State planning was mainly confined to heavy industry and utilities, leaving the rest of the economy in private hands. There was no fundamental agrarian reform and social promises (to abolish poverty, for example) have not been translated into practice. Massive poverty and a low average per capita income still dog India, despite three decades of 'planning'. There has not been a structural transformation; a great mass of rural labour remains underemployed, and the capital flowing into industries serving mass demand has been inadequate simply because the internal market has been too small for profitability. On the other hand, there has been no shortage of investment in industries serving the top 10 or 15 per cent of income-receivers.

Indian economic performance has improved since colonial days but it must do more than tick over and serve the needs of the relatively affluent, if a disaster is to be averted.

Brazil is perhaps the least known of the models examined in this book. Sharing many of the problems of other Latin American countries, such as a backward agrarian sector and inflation, it has been the most successful in industrialization. In some ways it has been the Japan of Latin America in quantitative terms. The policy and approach to industrialization has, however, been fundamentally different. While Japan's industry has remained under national control and dependence upon foreign capital has been kept to a minimum, Brazil inherited a colonial legacy of economic dependence. Much of the industrial investment has been controlled by foreign MNCs, while the state has depended heavily upon external borrowing. While there is a local entrepreneurial class, it has had to lean heavily upon the state and enter into partnership with foreign capital. Brazil is a classic case of import-substitution industrialization and demonstrates its limitations. In fact the stranglehold of dependence has not been broken. Much of the output of the modern sector of industry is consumed by the better-off urban middle and upper classes. Mass poverty remains endemic, especially in the more backward agrarian regions such as the north-west. The limitation of the internal market has directed much of the capacity of the more modern industry towards the foreign market. Despite quantitative successes, Brazil can hardly be regarded as a satisfactory model for other newly-industrializing countries.

Post-colonial Africa has not been able to shake off the legacy of the past and enter a new economic era. It contains some of the poorest countries in the world and, in some, starvation and famine are ever-present realities. Where gains have been made they are small, insecure and dependent upon foreign aid. Nigeria is the most populated African country; in some ways, also, it has been the most favoured country in Black Africa, most recently as an oil-producer. The attempts at industrialization in that country, where only about 8 per cent of GNP comes from industry, deserve study and appraisal. After the sanguine expectation of prosperity held out at the end of the 1970s, Nigeria has suffered serious setbacks which critics would say are of its own making. A question mark hangs over future prospects for industrialization in that country.

The countries examined in these case studies were large in population and economic terms, as well as, in most cases, size. Size is, potentially, an economic advantage, but this advantage will only be realized if industrialization is successful. Small countries are not necessarily disadvantaged and most 'successful' newly-industrializing countries are small or medium-sized. The examples which are usually cited include Korea, Taiwan, Hong Kong and Singapore. These countries have succeeded in achieving spectacular rates of growth. They have done so largely by attracting foreign capital and branch plants, with much of the output of the modern industrial sector going into exports. In addition to this, they have depended upon export-orientated growth, thus tying their economies to the markets of the richer, consuming countries.

The kind of problems which have arisen have already been discussed. Industrialization has been based upon abundant supplies of relatively cheap labour and a docile population without trade union or political rights, kept in check by one-party or military regimes. If the less-developed countries are to industrialize, and if they do not they cannot develop, the smaller ones at least will have to export. The penetration of the market in the advanced countries by low-priced imports could perhaps be tolerated in a period of boom, but is causing increasing problems in a period of world recession.

It is not certain that recourse to export-orientated industrialization will even be an option for many countries on the periphery of world capitalism. This is due partly to their disadvantages of smallness, lack of resources, weakness of the entrepreneurial class, insufficient capital, and dependence upon primary production. In other words a whole complex impeding growth which it is difficult to break up. Partly it arises from outside influences. The pressure from the companies which control foreign trade and primary production may be one factor. Multinational corporations may be interested in setting up production facilities for any number of reasons. The state may be unable to launch more than limited industrialization, largely because of failure to get a place in the export field or to attract enough foreign capital; Egypt is a prime example of this.

The experience of industrialization is so different between countries that approaches which have paid off in one case may be of no relevance in others. To whatever school of thought they belong, therefore, economists are chary in generalizing about industrialization strategies. It is difficult to see how the experience of capitalist Japan could have much application, say, to the Soviet Union or other planned economies. Even between Brazil and India

233

there are so many differences that it is doubtful whether one country can supply any useful lessons to the other.

The planned economies have aimed at establishing a self-reliant, balanced economy with both capital goods and consumer goods industries. India has attempted something along the same lines with its own Five-Year Plans, with a heavy industry sector mainly under state control but with a consumer goods sector mainly under the control of private capital. The results have been disappointing, but that may be due partly to other difficulties which have not been overcome, notably rural poverty and under-employment.

Small countries have to make a choice; where they are influenced by private, profit-seeking firms it is likely that they will opt for import-substitution or export-orientated industrialization based on the production of consumer goods. This will give rise to, or intensify, dependence upon foreign capital and technology as well as on export markets. It means that they will have to fit into the 'new' international division of labour in what will probably be a dependent relationship with an increasing role for the MNCs. Success, in the sense of rapid growth, may mean that other goals of 'newly-developing' nations may have to be forgone. Building a more balanced economy will require state direction and is not likely to be favoured either by foreign capital or by such institutions as the World Bank.

The measurement of industrialization in quantitative terms is crude, especially in the 'developing countries'. There may be rapid growth in per capita income or in industrial production without real development. Thus the majority may be left poor, hungry and illiterate or, at best, lagging behind as far as living standards are concerned. The rural sector may remain stagnant while social inequalities widen. It may be a long time before the benefits of industrialization trickle down to the disadvantaged masses.

Other goals may be preferable to rapid growth, such as: greater national economic independence, a more equitable distribution of income, a higher level of employment or the overcoming of rural poverty. Selection of such goals cannot take place through the market-place but requires state direction, at least in determining the priorities. Certainly the Soviet Union and China, while pursuing growth, have seen it as necessary for different objectives from those pursued in the capitalist countries. Paradoxically, the consumer has often not been so fortunate as in some other 'successful' capitalist industrializations. Comparison here becomes difficult, if not impossible. Various attempts have been made to compare

India and China, for example, but these have been handicapped by inadequate factual and statistical information for the latter.

Of course, there is a danger that the advocacy of industrialization contains a Euro-centred bias. It suggests that the non-Western countries should follow in the footsteps of the advanced capitalist countries, adopting the same life-style and the same pattern of consumption. In a sense industrialization does, as usually understood, involve some measure of modernization along Western, or European, lines. Thanks to the 'demonstration effect', the ruling class, and a large section of the population of most 'developing countries' have accepted this implicitly, and without qualms.

Alternative strategies are conceivable to the advanced countries and those who emulate them. The Chinese, in Mao's time, claimed to have found one such strategy, and this gained some sympathy in the West. Since Mao's death, however, his successors have returned to a more orthodox course and seem anxious to learn from Western models. The Maoists used to say that the people 'wanted revolution', whereas in fact they wanted much more: an improved supply of food and consumer goods which the Chinese revolution appeared all too slow in providing. If there is an alternative way of industrializing, it cannot subsist on psychological benefits alone; it will have to yield tangible advantages for the rural as well as the urban population.

No alternative strategy can be laid down *a priori* as a general pattern or as the correct road for any particular country, centrally-planned or market-governed. It is necessary to take into account all the specific features of a given country, beginning with its resource endowment, the existing factors of production and its relationship to the world market (an important constraint in any case). The goal would then have to be decided, trading off growth *per se* against other desired objectives. How could these be determined? In the situation of a 'developing country' the market mechanism would seem to be an inappropriate instrument for making such decisions, responsive as it is in the first place to the pull of those with the greatest purchasing power. If market forces are allowed to determine the course of a country, then the social situation which results is simply a by-product of those forces. The situation in India or in Brazil is eloquent testimony as to what the results are likely to be, with, or without, growth.

However, it is not easy to frame an alternative which does not concentrate power at the centre, leading to people being given what the rulers think they should have, and not what they want. Another dilemma is that the people may not want what the rulers think is good for them. The problem is to enable democratic choices to be expressed in the policy while embodying a movement towards pre-conceived objectives. The Soviet model is not of much help and the Chinese model of only limited validity because of the special conditions in which it was worked out. The answer will probably have to be found in some compromise between central planning and decentralized industrial development which gives greater powers to the producers themselves and has a more direct relationship with agriculture.

There remains the external constraint, the international division of labour. At present this works unequally between nations, creating dependence and fortifying underdevelopment of the primary-producing countries. Ideally, world industrialization would be coupled with a fundamental change in these relationships, ending imperialist domination of the less-developed countries by the advanced countries. The pursuit of self-sufficient development is, in any case, vain; only a genuinely new international division of labour based upon cooperation and some degree of planning offers a real alternative.

Bibliography

The main reason for having a bibliography at the end of a book of this kind is to help the reader, probably a novice in the field, to find his way through a mass of literature. Interest in the subject of industrialization has, in general, intensified in recent years and this, with the broad geographical coverage of this book, means that there is an enormous number of relevant works and that number is constantly being increased. This bibliography must therefore be selective.

The previous books, (mentioned in the Preface) *Industrialization in Nineteenth Century Europe* and *Historical Patterns of Industrialization*, contain book lists which should be consulted. Although some titles have been repeated, it does not seem necessary to repeat those which refer to the older industrialized countries. The reader's attention is called, however, to a new study of European industrialization which stresses its regional character and diffusion from one region to another; it is *Peaceful Conquest* by Sidney Pollard (Oxford U.P. 1981). By way of contrast, see the interpretative account in Clive Trebilcock's *The Industrialization of the European Powers* (Longman 1982). Of interest as an explicit comparative study with a provocative new thesis is Patrick O'Brien and Caglar Keyder, *Economic Growth in Britain and France* (Allen and Unwin 1978).

The two main standbys on Japanese economic history are G. C. Allen, *A Short Economic History of Modern Japan* (4th edn Macmillan 1981) and W. W. Lockwood, *The Economic Development of Japan* (expanded edn, Princeton U.P. 1968). There are short introductions by Yoshihara Kusio, *Japanese Economic Development: a short introduction* (Oxford U.P. Tokyo 1979) and M. Takahashi,

Modern Japanese Economy since the Meiji Restoration (University of Tokyo 1967).

There has been a cascade of literature on Japan's expanding economy directed at the general public as well as the student, for example Herman Kahn's *The Emerging Japanese Superstate* (Deutsch 1970; also in Pelican but out of print) and Ezra Feval Vogel, *Japan as Number One; Lessons for America* (Harvard 1979).

A massive study of Japan's present-day economy by a team of American economists is that of Hugo Patrick and Henry Rosovsky (eds) *Asia's New Giant*: *How the Japanese Economy Works* (Brookings 1976); which is somewhat biased against the view that the state played a crucial role. Jon Halliday's *A Political History of Japanese Capitalism* (Pantheon 1975) is a useful corrective to the anodyne treatment of some Western scholars. See also, on Japan's past, John Dover (ed.) *Origin of the Modern Japanese State*: *Selected Writings of E. H. Norman* (Pantheon 1975). Also useful, is Andrea Boltho *Japan*: *an Economic Survey, 1953–73* (Oxford U.P. 1975). On the cultural and sociological side see C. Nakane, *Japanese Society* (Pelican 1970).

There is a massive library of books on Soviet economic development, a rich field for controversy. For a reasonably well-balanced survey, the obvious choice is Alex Nove's *An Economic History of the USSR* (Allen Lane 1969 and later Pelican editions); see also his *The Soviet Economic System* (Allen and Unwin 1977). An American textbook, among several, is Paul R. Gregory and Robert C. Stuart, *Soviet Economy*: *Structure and Performance* (Harper 1974) and an older translation from the French, Philippe J. Bernard, *Planning in the Soviet Union* (Pergamon Press 1966).

For the controversy in the 1920s, see Alexander Erlich, The *Soviet Industrialization Debate* (Harvard 1960) and E. A. Preobrazhensky, *The Crisis in Soviet Industrialization* (Macmillan 1980; translated and edited Don A. Filtzer). Developments in that decade have been dealt with in relevant volumes of E. H. Carr's *A History of Soviet Russia* (Macmillan and Pelican editions) and continued by R. W. Davies in the series now appearing with the overall title *The Industrialization of Soviet Russia*; so far Vol. 1, *The Socialist Offensive* and Vol. 2 *The Soviet Collective Farm* (Macmillan 1980) have appeared. The detail is immense, thus making it a reference book for students.

See also George R. Fiewal, *The Soviet Quest for Economic Efficiency* (Praegar 1967) and Moshe Levin, *Political Undercurrents in Soviet Economic Debates*, (Pluto 1975).

For the view of Soviet economists see T. Khachaturov, *The*

Economy of the Soviet Union Today (Progress, Moscow 1977) and *The Soviet Planned Economy* (Progress, Moscow 1974).

The best introduction to Indian economic development is still Andrew Maddison, *Class Structure and Economic Growth: India and Pakistan Since the Moghuls*. On industrialization under British rule the fullest study is Rajat K. Roy, *Industrialization in India, 1914–1947*, (Oxford U.P., Delhi 1979) which stresses profitability as the main factor determining its extent. For British economic policy as a whole see B. R. Tomlinson, *The Political Economy of the Raj* (Macmillan 1979) and Clive J. Dewey, 'The Government of India's 'New Economic Policy'', in K. M. Chaudhuri and C. J. Dewey (eds), *Economy and Society* (Oxford U.P. 1979).

Various views of the planning experience are to be found in J. N. Bhaghati and Padim Desai, *India: Planning for Industrialization*, Prem S. Jha, *India: a Political Economy of Stagnation* (Oxford, Bombay 1980) and Francine Frankel, *India's Political Economy, 1947–1977* (Princeton, 1978).

On China there are a large number of books by American scholars, surprisingly sympathetic on the whole considering the ascerbic treatment often given to Soviet economic planning. The best introduction is probably the books by Alexander Eckstein, which overlap: *China's Economic Development* (University of Michigan, 1975) and *China's Economic Revolution* (Cambridge U.P. 1977). For the 1950s and 1960s Jan S. Pribla's *The Political Economy of Communist China* (International Textbook 1970) is very full. The best study of the Maoist period is perhaps by Stephen Andors: *China's Industrial Revolution* (Martin Robertson 1977). The relevance of Chinese experience to other developing countries is discussed by American specialists in Robert F. Dernberger (ed.), *China's Development Experience in Comparative Perspective* (Harvard 1980).

The special features of China's past can be studied in Dwight H. Perkins (ed.), *China's Modern Economy in Historical Perspective* (Stanford 1975), Mark Elvin, *The Pattern of the Chinese Past* (Eyre-Methuen 1973) and Albert Feuerwerker, *China's Early Industrialization* (Harvard 1958).

There is little of note from official sources, although there was a good deal of writing by foreign supporters of the Cultural Revolution.

For the reasons why China's modern economic development differed from that of Japan, note the analysis by Frances W. Moulder, *Japan, China and the Modern World Economy* (Cambridge U.P. 1977).

The earlier history of Brazil is covered in Laura Randall, *Latin American Comparative Economic History* (Vol. 3.) *Brazil* (Institute of Latin American Studies 1977) and Celso Furtado, *The Economic Growth of Brazil* (Univ. of California 1963). For the British stake, see R. Graham, *Britain and the Onset of Modernization in Brazil* (Cambridge U.P. 1968). For the leading industrial region, Warren Dean's *The Industrialization of Sao Paulo* (Univ. of Texas 1969) is very enlightening. The views of a leading 'dependency' theorist, Theotonio dos Santos, on Brazil are to be found in Ch. 4 in Ronald H. Chilcote, and J. C. Edelstein (eds) *Latin America: the struggle with dependency and beyond* (Schenkman 1974).

More 'orthodox' treatments can be found in books by American specialists such as Werner Baer, *Industrialization and Economic Development in Brazil* (Irwin 1965) and Donald E. Syvrud, *Foundations of Brazilian Economic Growth* (Hoover Institute 1972). The interpretation here has been greatly influenced by Peter Evans, *Dependent Development* (Princeton 1979). On inflation see the chapter on Brazil by John Wells in Rosemary Thorp and Laura Whitehead (eds), *Inflation and Stabilization in Latin America* (Macmillan 1979).

For a general introduction to the industrialization of Nigeria, see Gavin Williams (ed.), *Nigeria: Economy and Society* (Rex Collins, London 1976) especially the editor's own contribution, 'Nigeria: a Political Economy'. Another Marxist approach is to be found in the chapter by Barbara Callaway in *The Political Economy of Africa*, Richard Harris (ed.), (Schenkman, Cambridge, Mass. 1975). The earlier stages of industrialization are covered in detail by Peter Kilby in *Industrialization in an Open Economy: 1945–1966* (Cambridge U.P. 1969). The same period is seen in the perspective of a Nigerian scholar in Ojetunji Aboyade's *Foundations of an African Economy* (Praeger, New York and London 1966). There is a German view in Manfred Berger, *Industrialization Policies in Nigeria* (Weltforum Verlag, Munich 1975). A thought-provoking study by an American scholar is Sayre P. Scharz, *Nigerian Capitalism* (Univ. of Cal. Berkeley, 1977) which considers alternatives to the present course. Theodore J. Biersteker attempts to estimate the effect of the MNCs in *Distortion or Development: Contending Perspectives on the Multinational Corporation* (MIT 1978). For indigenization see *Indigenization of African Economies*, Adebayo Adedeji (ed.), (Hutchinson 1981), Chapter 7 by Emeka Ezeife.

The writing on industrialization in 'developing countries' is abundant and diverse. Here is a brief selection. From the World Bank, John Cody, *et al.* (eds) *Policies for Industrial Progress in*

Developing Countries (Oxford U.P. 1981). A very different view is expressed in Paul Baran, *The Political Economy of Growth* (Monthly Review Press 1962, and Pelican), the writings of Andre Gunder Frank, for example, *On Capitalist Underdevelopment* (Oxford U.P., Bombay 1975) express a similar, neo-Marxist view. This has been heavily criticized by another self-styled Marxist, Bill Warren in *Imperialism: Pioneer of Capitalism* (New Left Books 1980); a reply in James Petras, *Critical Perspectives on Imperialism and Social Class in the Third World* (Monthly Review Press 1978), Chapter 4.

Earlier works include Albert Hirschmann, *The Strategy of Economic Development* (Yale U.P. 1958) and Harvey Liebenstein, *Economic Backwardness and Economic Growth* (Wiley 1963).

On 'developing countries' today see the Brandt Report, *North-South : a Programme for Survival* (Pan 1980) and a critique by Teresa Hayter, *The Creation of World Poverty* (Pluto Press 1981). See also, Gyorgy Cukor, *Strategies for Industrialization in Developing Countries* (Hurst 1971) translated from the Hungarian, and a Soviet view, V. I. Tyagunenko (ed.), *Industrialization of Developing Countries* (Progress, Moscow 1973).

Supplementary Bibliography (Second Edition)

The study of industrialization, past, present and future, in varied geographical settings, from different angles and with varied theoretical tools, continues to attract increasing attention from scholars. Bordering on and interpenetrating with other processes, such as economic growth, development, urbanization and associated problems, it generates a vast amount of literature from the newspaper report to the learned paper. It is impossible to keep track of this mounting volume of material; in any case, this bibliography confines itself to books (in English), while much of the most useful work is in journal articles (and can be picked up from the bibliographies of the specialised works cited).

This is not a book about the present-day 'third world' only; indeed, it eschews use of this term, though it will be found in many of the sources used. In fact a bibliography of industrialization is bound to include many books and articles which are concerned mainly with 'economic growth' or 'development'. This supplementary bibliography includes some of these and is deliberately selective. It includes those books which have come the author's way and help to bring the study up-to-date.

COUNTRY STUDIES

Japan's continued drive for economic pre-eminence is a permanent subject for concern and discussion. The latest trends can only be gleaned from the press — for example, the *sogo–soshas* (trading companies) have recently begun to diversify into industrial investment, theme parks and leisure centres. A useful recent book is *Japan: Facing Economic Maturity* by J. Lincoln (Brookings Institution 1988); see also C. McMillan, *The Japanese Industrial System* (Walter de Gruyter 1984). An excellent short introduction to the economic history of the country is W. J. McPherson, *The Economic Development of Japan, 1868–1941* (Macmillan 1987).

Glasnost and *perestroika* have already generated a considerable literature. The present state of the Soviet Union is surveyed, for example, by E. A. Hewett in *Reforming the Soviet Economy* (Brookings Institution 1988) and M. I. Goldman in *Gorbachev's Challenge* (W. W. Norton 1987). A contribution to the historical argument is R. Bideleux's *Communism and Development* (Methuen 1985).

On India, see especially I. J. Ahluwalia, *Industrial Growth in India: Stagnation since the mid–Sixties*, (Oxford U.P. Delhi 1985) and V. N. Balasubramanyam, *The Economy of India* (Wiedenfeld and Nicolson 1984).

The great changes in China since the death of Mao Tse–tung have attracted a good deal of attention. V. D. Lippit provides a balanced view in *The Economic Development of China* (Sharpe 1987). See also, H. Harding, *China's Second Revolution* (Brookings Institution 1987), Carl Riskin's *China's Political Economy* (Oxford U.P. 1987), *China: Asia's New Economic Giant* by D. H. Perkins (Univ. of Washington 1986) and, by M. Chossudovsky, *Towards Capitalist Restoration ?* (St Martin's Press 1987).

From Beijing comes the compendious *China's Socialist Economy: and Outline History* edited by Liu Suinian and Wu Qungan (Beijing Review 1986).

The newly industrializing Asian 'gang of four', alternately described as 'the hungry tigers' or 'the four young dragons', pursue their industrial advance, regarded with curiosity and some apprehension by the rest of the world. Since this book has only referred to the experience of South Korea and Taiwan, only works concerned with them will be mentioned. No work has achieved a wider public, as with several books about Japan. Most are directed at specialists, but they are a frequent subject of reports and articles in the press.

General books on the East Asian countries include F. C. Devo (ed.), *The Political Economy of the New Asian Nationalism* (Cornell U.P. 1987), *In Search of an Asian Development Model* (Transaction Books 1987) edited by P. L. Berger and Hsin–Huang Michael Hsiao; on these and other newly industrialising countries see N. Harris, *The*

End of the Third World (Pelican 1987) and the reportage by M. Smith *et al, Asia's New Industrial World* (Methuen 1985).

On Korea a good introduction is *Economic Growth and Structure in the Republic of Korea* by P. W. Kuznets (Yale U.P. 1977); see also *Government, Business and Entrepreneurship in Economic Development: the Korean Case* by L. P. Jones and Il Sa–Kong (Harvard U.P. 1980) and *Economic Development and Social Change in Korea*, Sung–Jo Park *et al*, editors (Campus Verlag 1980). More critical is C. Hamilton's *Capitalist Industrialization in Korea* (Westview 1985).

Studies of Taiwan available are also rather uncritical, see, for example, Yuan Li–wu, *Becoming an Industrial Nation* (Praeger 1985), S. P. S. Ho, *Economic Development of Taiwan 1860–1970* (Yale U.P. 1978) and T. Gold, *State and Society in the Taiwan Miracle* (Sharpe 1986).

Not very much new is available in book form concerning Brazil or Nigeria. For the former a recent historical study by S. Topic is useful, *The Political Economy of the Brazilian State, 1889–1930*; there is also a translation of a standard work by L. B. Pereira, *Development and Crisis in Brazil, 1930–1983* (Westview 1984). On the latter, note *Political Economy of Nigeria* edited by C. Ake (Longman 1985).

SOME GENERAL WORKS

For advanced studies there is the work by H. Chenery, S. Robinson and M. Syrquin, *Industrialization and Growth* (Oxford U.P. for the World Bank 1986) an imposing study. By way of contrast, E. L. Jones in *Growth Recurring* (Oxford 1988) puts all the emphasis on 'growth'.

In their *Theatres of Accumulation* (Methuen 1985), W. Armstrong and T. G. McGee consider the urban consequences of industrialization. There is another geographical perspective in S. Corbridge's *Capitalist World Development* (Macmillan 1986). Another aspect is taken up by G. Sen in *The Military Origins of Industrialization and International Trade Rivalry* (Pinter 1984). See also, G. Kitching, *Development and Underdevelopment in Historical Perspective* (Methuen 1982).

J. Toye considers the new emphasis on free market policies in the developing countries in *Dilemmas of Development* (Blackwell 1987). For some Marxist views see *Marxian Theory and the Third World* (Sage 1985) edited by D. Banerjee.

Index

245